D1447221

International Library of Psychology
Philosophy and Scientific Method

Five Types of Ethical Theory

Five Types of Ethical Theory

By
C. D. BROAD

LONDON
ROUTLEDGE & KEGAN PAUL
NEW YORK : HUMANITIES PRESS

First published 1930
by Routledge & Kegan Paul Ltd
Broadway House, 68-74 Carter Lane
London, EC4V 5EL

Second impression 1934
Third impression 1944
Fourth impression 1948
Fifth impression 1950
Sixth impression 1951
Seventh impression 1956
Eighth impression 1962
Ninth impression 1967
Tenth impression 1971

ISBN 0 7100 3080 0

Printed by offset in Great Britain
by Alden & Mowbray Ltd at the Alden Press, Oxford

TO
JACK DONALDSON

"Others apart sat on a hill retired
In thoughts more elevate, and reasoned high
Of providence, foreknowledge, will, and fate ;
Fixed fate, free will, foreknowledge absolute,
And found no end, in wandering mazes lost.
Of good and evil much they argued then,
Of happiness and final misery,
Passion and apathy, and glory and shame—
Vain wisdom all, and false philosophy !
Yet, with a pleasing sorcery, could charm
Pain for a while or anguish, and excite
Fallacious hope, or arm the obdured breast
With stubborn patience as with triple steel."

(MILTON, *Paradise Lost*, Bk. II.)

ANALYTICAL TABLE OF CONTENTS

CONTENTS

CHAPTER III : BUTLER

CONTENTS

CHAPTER VI : SIDGWICK

CONTENTS

xvii

CONTENTS

CHAPTER VII : CONCLUSION

CONTENTS

PREFACE

THE history of the present volume is as follows. The essay on Butler's ethics was first delivered as a public lecture at the University of Bristol, a city which seems hardly to realise how great a moralist and theologian it once had for its bishop. It was afterwards published in the *Hibbert Journal*, and I have to thank the Editor for kindly allowing me to republish it. The essays on the ethics of Spinoza, of Hume, and of Kant formed the *Donnellan Lectures* which I delivered in Trinity College, Dublin, towards the end of the summer term of 1929. I must take this opportunity of expressing my thanks to the Provost and his family, and to the Fellows, for the kindness which made my all too short stay in Dublin so pleasant. The essay on the ethics of Sidgwick, and the concluding outline of the main problems of ethics, were written specially to complete this book. Although it has never been part of my duties to lecture on moral philosophy in Cambridge, I have had to teach it privately to the undergraduates whose studies I direct. These two chapters contain the thoughts which have occurred to me on the subject while reading and criticising the essays done for me by candidates for Part I of the Moral Sciences Tripos.

I am inclined to agree with Kant's view that almost every one is interested in ethical questions, though the interest can be killed by a boring enough presentation of the subject. Partly for this reason, and partly because every one has the necessary materials at his disposal without previous technical training, ethical problems perhaps form the best introduction to the study of philosophy for most men. I hope that my book will be of some use to professional philosophers ; but I also hope that it may be found interesting by intelligent amateurs, and may lead some of them to pursue the subject further for themselves. I have not wittingly shirked any difficulty in order to make the book easy ; but I do not think it contains anything too hard for an intelligent amateur to understand provided he will give to it the amount of attention which any abstract discussion demands.

It is perhaps fair to warn the reader that my range of experience, both practical and emotional, is rather exceptionally narrow even for a don. Fellows of Colleges, in Cambridge at any rate, have few temptations to heroic virtue or spectacular vice ; and I could wish that the rest of mankind were as fortunately situated. Moreover, I find it difficult to excite myself very much over right and wrong in practice. I have, e.g., no clear idea of what people have in mind when they say that they labour under a sense of sin ; yet I do not doubt that, in some cases, this is a genuine experience, which seems vitally important to those who have it, and may really be of profound ethical and metaphysical significance. I recognise that these practical and emotional limitations may make me blind to certain important aspects of moral experience. Still, people who feel very strongly about any subject are liable to over-estimate its importance in the scheme of things. A healthy appetite for righteousness, kept in due control by good manners, is an excellent thing ; but to " hunger and thirst after " it is often merely a symptom of spiritual diabetes. And a white-heat of moral enthusiasm is not perhaps the most favourable condition in which to conduct the analysis of ethical concepts or the criticism of ethical theories. So, having thus given fair warning to my readers, I may at least claim the qualities of my defects.

I must end by thanking my friend, Mr A. A. Wynne Willson, for his kindness and care in reading the proofs. If it be true, as has been alleged, that he owes (under Providence) such knowledge as he has of the difference between Right and Wrong entirely to his Director of Studies, he has now more than repaid the debt.

C. D. BROAD.

TRINITY COLLEGE,
CAMBRIDGE,
August 1929.

FIVE TYPES OF ETHICAL THEORY

CHAPTER I

Introduction: Biographical Details

I PROPOSE in this book to expound and criticise five typical theories of ethics, viz., those of Spinoza, Butler, Hume, Kant, and Sidgwick. My choice of these five systems was largely determined by the following considerations. In the first place, they are extremely unlike each other, so that between them they give a very fair idea of the range of possible views on the subject, though they by no means exhaust all the alternatives. Secondly, all five authors are thinkers of the highest rank, so it is reasonable to suppose that the types of ethical theory which they favoured will be worth very serious consideration. Since their views differ fundamentally from each other, they cannot all be true in all respects, and it is of course unlikely that any of them contains the whole truth and nothing but the truth about ethics. But it seems likely that each of these great men will have seen some important aspect of the subject, and that the mistake of each will have been to emphasise this aspect to the exclusion of others which are equally relevant. It appears to me that the best preparation for original work on any philosophic problem is to study the solutions which have been proposed for it by men of genius whose views differ from each other as much as possible. The clash of their opinions may strike a light which will

1

enable us to avoid the mistakes into which they have fallen ; and by noticing the strong and weak points of each theory we may discover the direction in which further progress can be made.

I have treated the five moralists in their historical order, and I have not cumbered the discussion with biographical matter or textual criticism. The minute study of the works of great philosophers from the historical and philological point of view is an innocent and even praiseworthy occupation for learned men. But it is not philosophy ; and, to me at least, it is not interesting. My primary interest in this book is to find out what is true and what is false about ethics ; and the statements of our authors are important to me only in so far as they suggest possible answers to this question. I hope and believe that I have not misrepresented any of the moralists under discussion. I have always tried to put what seems to me to be their fundamental meaning in modern terms and as plausibly as possible. But I am well aware that, in many places, alternative views about what they may have meant can quite reasonably be held. This applies in the main to Spinoza, whose whole terminology and way of looking at things is extremely unfamiliar to us nowadays, and to Kant, who, as Lord Balfour happily says, contrived to be technical without being precise. Butler, Hume, and Sidgwick are admirably clear writers, and they belong to our own country and tradition ; so that there is seldom any doubt about their meaning.

For the sake of those readers whom it may concern I will give here very short biographical sketches of our five moralists. Spinoza belonged to a family of Portuguese Jews which had fled to Holland to escape persecution. He was born at Amsterdam on 24th November 1632. He studied at a rabbinical school, where he read the Old Testament, the Talmud, and various Hebrew commentators and philosophers, such as Ibn Ezra and Maimonides. At one time he also read a good deal of Cabalistic literature, but in the end it filled him with contempt. Spinoza was eighteen years old when Descartes died, and he learned Latin in order to be able to read Descartes' works. Though he differed profoundly from Descartes, and criticised him severely, he said that he had won all his own philosophical possessions from the study of Descartes.

By 1656 Spinoza had departed so far from orthodox Judaism that he was excommunicated by the Synagogue and solemnly cursed in the name of God and His holy Angels. Shortly afterwards a pious member of the congregation, remembering that divine Providence often condescends to act through secondary causes, tried to murder Spinoza in the street with a dagger. This was not the only narrow escape which Spinoza had from death by human violence. In 1673, when the French were invading Holland, Spinoza accepted an invitation to visit the French camp at Utrecht in order to discuss philosophy with Condé, their general, who was a Cartesian. The Dutch, like other nations in war-time, were seeing the " hidden hand " in the most unlikely places, and Spinoza was suspected to be a spy and was in great danger from a mob which demonstrated outside the house in which he lodged at the Hague. In this very ugly situation he displayed the most admirable courage and coolness, and succeeded in convincing the mob of his innocence and making it disperse.

After his encounter with the Zealot with the dagger Spinoza left Amsterdam and lived for a time at a house in the country belonging to the Collegiants, a sect of evangelical

Christians. In 1669 he moved into the Hague, where he lived with a painter called *van den Spijck* till 21st February 1677, when he died of consumption at the age of forty-four. He made his living by grinding and polishing lenses for optical instruments, and he seems to have been highly skilled at his craft. He corresponded with several people on philosophical and scientific subjects, and his letters are important as throwing light on obscure points in his philosophy. His most important work is the *Ethics*, in which he expounds his complete system in the form of definitions, axioms, postulates, and theorems, as in Euclid. This was not published until after his death.

Spinoza was offered the professorship of philosophy at Heidelberg on highly favourable terms by Karl Ludwig of the Palatinate, a very enlightened prince. He refused on the double ground that he would be certain sooner or later to get into trouble for religious unorthodoxy and that he did not want to have to interrupt his own work by formal teaching. It is to be feared that Spinoza would not have been enlightened enough to appreciate the beneficent system of the Ph.D. degree, introduced into English universities as a measure of post-war propaganda, whereby the time and energy of those who are qualified to do research are expended in supervising the work of those who never will be.

Joseph Butler was the son of a linen-draper who had been successful in business and had retired on a competency. He was born at Wantage on 18th May 1692, the youngest of a long family. His father intended him for the Presbyterian ministry and sent him to a dissenting academy, first at Gloucester and then at Tewkesbury. He stayed on for some time as an usher, and in 1713, whilst still there, he wrote anonymously to Samuel Clarke an acute criticism of certain points in the latter's Boyle Lectures on the *Being and Attributes of God*. The modesty of the younger man, and the courtesy of the older, do the utmost credit to both. A number of letters were exchanged, and in time Clarke came to know and admire Butler.

Soon Butler began to emerge from the slavery of Geneva into the reasonable liberty of Lambeth. He decided to become an Anglican clergyman, and, after some difficulty, persuaded his father to send him to Oriel College, Oxford. He took his B.A. degree in October 1718 at the age of twenty-six. Almost directly afterwards he was ordained priest and deacon at Salisbury. Through influential friends and his own merits he now started on a steady course of ecclesiastical preferment. He became preacher at the Rolls Chapel in London in 1719, Prebendary of Salisbury in 1721, Rector of Houghton-le-Skerne near Darlington in the following year, and Rector of the then extremely valuable living of Stanhope in Durham in 1725.

His *Sermons on Human Nature*, which are his most important contribution to ethics, were delivered at the Rolls Chapel, and were published in 1726 after he had resigned his preachership there. In 1736 appeared his other great work, the *Analogy*, which is perhaps the ablest and fairest argument for theism that exists. A short appendix to this is devoted to ethics.

In 1736 he became Prebendary of Rochester and Clerk of the Closet to Queen Caroline. The queen was a lady of very great intelligence both practical and theoretical, as anyone can see who gives himself the pleasure of reading Lord Hervey's *Memoirs*. She was keenly interested in metaphysics and theology, and she greatly appreciated

Butler's gifts. She died in the latter part of 1737, commending Butler to the attention of the Archbishop of Canterbury. Butler preached an eloquent sermon on " profiting by affliction " to the heart-broken widower, who had declared through his sobs to his dying wife that he would never marry again but would only keep mistresses. George II was deeply affected, and promised to " do something very good " for Butler.

After such happy auspices Butler was naturally a little disappointed when Walpole offered him only the See of Bristol, at that time one of the poorest of the English bishoprics. However, he bore his cross and entered on his duties in 1738. He remained at Bristol till 1750, collecting in the meanwhile such minor scraps of preferment as the Deanery of St Paul's in 1746 and the Clerkship of the Closet to the King in 1747. In the latter year he was offered and declined the Archbishopric of Canterbury. In 1750 his journeys through the wilderness terminated in the promised land of the Bishopric of Durham. This he did not live long to enjoy. His health broke down, and he retired first to Bristol and then to Bath, where he died in 1752. He is buried in the cathedral at Bristol, and the visitor may read a long and flowery inscription, put up in the nineteenth century, in which his achievements as a theologian are fittingly recorded.

Butler seems to have been a thoroughly unworldly man whom the world treated very well. He took no part in politics ; and, although he was no doubt fortunate in having certain influential friends, it is probably true that he owed his advancement mainly to his sheer merits as a moralist and a theologian. We all know how greatly Church and State have advanced in morality since the corrupt first half of the eighteenth century; and it is gratifying to think that a man like Butler would now be allowed to pursue his studies with singularly little risk of being exposed to the dangers and temptations of high office or lucrative preferment.

David Hume was born at Edinburgh on 26th April 1711. He was a younger son of a Scottish country gentleman, who, like most Scottish country gentlemen, was of good family and small means. At the age of twenty-three Hume went into a merchant's office at Bristol; but he found the life intolerable, and decided to live very economically in France, pursuing his studies on his own tiny income. He settled at La Flèche, where Descartes had been educated by the Jesuits. While there he wrote the first two volumes of his *Treatise on Human Nature*. He came home in 1737 to arrange for their publication, and they appeared in 1739. They failed to attract any attention, and Hume was bitterly disappointed. He continued, however, to work at the third volume, on Morals, which appeared in 1740. In 1741 he published a volume of *Essays Moral and Political*. This was more successful; it went into a second edition, and he added a second volume to it in 1742.

During this time Hume had been living on his elder brother's estate at Ninewells in Berwickshire, trying meanwhile to get some congenial and remunerative employment. Twice he tried and failed to be appointed to a university professorship. To vary the monotony of life he spent a year as tutor to a lunatic nobleman; he went with General St. Clair as secretary on one of those strange expeditions which English war-ministers were liable to send to the coast of France; and in 1748 he took part in a diplomatic mission to Vienna and Turin.

In 1748 he published a third volume of *Essays*, and also a condensed and simplified form of *Book I* of the *Treatise*, entitled *Philosophical Essays concerning Human Understanding*. In 1758 this reappeared under the title of *An Enquiry concerning Human Understanding*. His most important ethical work is the *Enquiry into the Principles of Morals*. This is founded on *Book III* of the *Treatise on Human Nature*. It was published in 1751, and Hume considered it to be " incomparably the best " of all his writings.

In 1752 the Faculty of Advocates in Edinburgh made Hume their librarian. The salary was vanishingly small ; but the position gave Hume the run of a fine library, and he started to write a *History of England*. He began with the House of Stuart. The repercussions of the events of that period were still being felt, and Hume's sympathy with Charles I and Strafford raised an almost universal outcry. In 1756 he published the second volume, which dealt with the period from the death of Charles I to the Revolution. This gave less offence to the Whigs, and its success helped on the sale of the peccant first volume. In 1759 appeared the volume which treated of the House of Tudor. It also caused great scandal ; but Hume worked steadily away at his *History* and completed it in two more volumes published in 1761.

Hume was now fairly well off, and had determined to settle down for the rest of his life in Scotland. But in 1763 a pressing invitation from the Earl of Hertford took him to Paris, where he became secretary to the English embassy. Hume had great social success in the society of Paris, and enjoyed his life there very much. In 1766 he returned to London with Rousseau, whom he had befriended, and who, it is scarcely necessary to add, afterwards quarrelled with him. In 1769 he finally returned to Edinburgh with a private income of £1000 a year.

Here he had expected to spend many happy years. But in 1775 he was stricken down with an internal complaint which he recognised to be mortal. He suffered little pain, and bore his steadily increasing weakness with wonderful cheerfulness. He died on 26th August 1776 in Edinburgh, causing the deepest offence to Dr Johnson by the happy and even jocular frame of mind in which he approached the great unknown. Shortly before his death he had written a brief autobiography, which was published in 1777 by his friend Adam Smith. In 1779 his nephew David published his uncle's *Dialogues on Natural Religion*, which, so far as the present writer can see, leave little further to be said on the subject. Hume wrote two essays, one on *Suicide*, and the other on *Immortality*, which were suppressed and remained unpublished for many years after his death. Both are masterly productions. To philosophers Hume is best known for his criticisms on the notion of Causation and on the logical foundations of Induction. It is unfortunate that the general public should know him mainly as the author of the one thoroughly silly production of his pen, viz., the notorious *Essay on Miracles*.

Immanuel Kant was born at Königsberg in East Prussia in 1724, thirteen years after Hume. He survived Hume by twenty-eight years. His father was a saddler, and his family is said to have been of Scottish origin on the father's side. Kant's parents belonged to the evangelical sect called *Pietists*, and his very rigoristic ethics bear witness to the stern moral principles which he absorbed in youth.

Kant is the first professional philosopher with whom we

have to deal in this book. He became professor of Logic and Metaphysics at Königsberg in 1770, and continued to hold this office till his death in 1804. He used also to lecture in the university on Anthropology and Physical Geography. His life was regular and uneventful to the last degree, but he was one of the most important and original thinkers of whom we have any record. He has, indeed, been described by Mr. Bertrand Russell as "a disaster"; but it seems a pity to apply to him an epithet which should obviously be reserved for Hegel. His most important works are his three *Critiques*, that of *Pure Reason*, that of *Practical Reason*, and that of *Judgment*. The first edition of the *Critique of Pure Reason* appeared in 1781, and the second considerably modified edition in 1787. This is probably the most important philosophical work which had appeared in Europe since Aristotle's *Metaphysics*. It is abominably obscure, but one feels that the obscurity is that of a man who has to deliver a very complicated and important message in a short time, and whose words and ideas stumble over each other.

The *Critique of Practical Reason* was published in 1788. It contains Kant's theory of ethics, and the metaphysical conclusions which he claimed to be able to prove from ethical premises after denying that they could be proved in any other way. The purely ethical part of it is stated more simply and briefly in the *Foundations of the Metaphysic of Morals*, which appeared in 1785. There is a second part of this work, which deals with the particular virtues and vices in terms of the general theory. This was not published until 1797.

The third *Critique*, that of *Judgment*, was published in 1790. It contains Kant's theory of the Beautiful and the

Sublime, and also an extraordinarily able and balanced, but terribly long-winded, discussion of the notions of mechanism, design, and teleology, their mutual relations, and their legitimacy as principles of explanation.

There is no important problem in any branch of philosophy which is not treated by Kant, and he never treated a problem without saying something illuminating and original about it. He was certainly wrong on many points of detail, and he may well be wrong in his fundamental principles; but, when all criticisms have been made, it seems to me that Kant's failures are more important than most men's successes.

He was keenly interested in philosophical theology, and there is a progressive widening in his treatment of this subject from the mainly negative dialectic of the *Critique of Pure Reason*, through the purely ethical argument of the *Critique of Practical Reason*, to the reconsideration of the argument from design in the widest sense which occupies so much of the *Critique of Judgment*. If any reader who is interested in this subject will study Butler's *Analogy*, Hume's *Dialogues on Natural Religion*, and the theological parts of Kant's three *Critiques*, he will learn all that the human mind is ever likely to be able to know about the matter, with just one grave omission. The omission is that he will find nothing about the claims of specifically religious and mystical experience to give information about this aspect of reality. It is, perhaps, worth while to add in this connexion that, just as Butler treated specifically Christian doctrines in the second part of the *Analogy*, so Kant treated them in a book called *Religion within the Bounds of Mere Reason*. This work, which was published in 1793, also throws light on certain points in Kant's ethical theory.

With Henry Sidgwick we come to comparatively recent times. He was born at Skipton in Yorkshire in 1838. His father, the Rev. William Sidgwick, was headmaster of Skipton Grammar School. Sidgwick went to Rugby in 1852, and came up to Trinity College, Cambridge, in October 1855. He had a brilliant undergraduate career as a classic, and became Fellow and Assistant Tutor of Trinity in 1859. He early developed an interest in philosophical and ethical subjects, and was noted among his undergraduate contemporaries for his acuteness of thought and clearness of expression. He was a member of the society called the *Apostles*, and he used to take part in philosophical discussions in a small society which met for that purpose at the house of John Grote, the Knightbridge Professor of Moral Philosophy in the University of Cambridge.

The Moral Sciences Tripos was founded in 1851, and Moral Science was admitted as a qualification for a degree in 1860. Sidgwick examined for this tripos in 1865 and 1866. In 1869, finding that his interests had become predominantly philosophical, he exchanged his classical lectureship at Trinity for one in Moral Science. In the same year, however, he began to have conscientious scruples about the religious declaration which it was then necessary for a fellow of a college to make. He accordingly resigned his fellowship, but was permitted by the College to retain his lectureship. Within a short time, the religious tests were abolished ; so Sidgwick, like Charles Honeyman, had the advantage of " being St. Laurence on a cold gridiron ". It is fair to say, however, that it would have made no difference to his action if the gridiron had been red-hot. In connexion with this incident he published a tract on *The Ethics of Subscription*, and the subject is also discussed very fully and fairly in his *Methods of Ethics*. It is interesting to remark that the Utilitarian Sidgwick took a more rigoristic view on this question than the Idealist Green.

In 1872, on the death of F. D. Maurice and the consequent vacancy in the Knightbridge Professorship, Sidgwick applied for the post. He was at this time unsuccessful; the electors considered that the soundly evangelical views of one of the other candidates more than atoned for any slight lack in philosophical distinction. The disappointment was only temporary, for in 1883, when the Professorship again fell vacant, Sidgwick was elected, and continued to hold the chair until his death in 1900.

In 1875 he had been appointed Prelector in Moral and Political Philosophy at Trinity; in 1881 an honorary fellow; and in 1885 he again became an ordinary fellow of the college. In the meanwhile he had married a sister of the present Earl of Balfour, who shared his two great interests apart from philosophy, viz., the higher education of women and the investigation of alleged supernormal psychical phenomena. Sidgwick and his wife must take a great share in the credit or discredit for founding and fostering Newnham College and for the present position of women in the University of Cambridge. Whether the object which they accomplished was a good or a bad one is a question on which equally intelligent and virtuous persons are likely to differ till the end of time; but no one can fail to admire the single-minded devotion with which they spent time, labour, and money to bring it about.

The foundation of the *Society for Psychical Research,* and the keeping of it in the straight and narrow path of science in face of dogmatic materialism and enthusiastic credulity, are achievements on which they can be congratulated without reserve. Sidgwick was president of the society from 1882 to 1885, and again from 1888 to 1893, whilst Mrs Sidgwick remains one of its most prominent and valued members. It would be difficult to imagine anyone better fitted by the perfect balance of his mind for research in this most difficult and irritating subject than Sidgwick.

Sidgwick's chief ethical works are his *Methods of Ethics* and his *Ethics of Green, Spencer, and Martineau.* He was at once critical and eclectic, and he tried to make a synthesis of a chastened Intuitionism with a chastened Utilitarianism. In the course of his work almost all the main problems of ethics are discussed with extreme acuteness, and that is why I have devoted a much longer essay to Sidgwick than to any of the other moralists whom I treat in this book. In the other essays exposition and criticism have been about equally mixed. But, in dealing with Sidgwick, I have let the argument carry me whither it would. In each section of the essay I start from some point in Sidgwick and I eventually return to it ; but I often wander very far afield and express my own thoughts, for what they are worth, in the meanwhile.

In conclusion I must say that I have confined myself as far as possible to the purely ethical views of the writers under consideration. In the case of Kant and Sidgwick their theology is so closely bound up with their ethics that I have had to say something about it. But in the other cases I have felt myself justified in letting sleeping Gods lie.

CHAPTER II

Spinoza

THOUGH Spinoza's main work is called *Ethics*, it is not a treatise on ethics in our sense of the word. Nor did Spinoza ever write any such treatise. His views on ethics, in the modern sense, have to be gathered from various passages scattered about his books and his letters. Nevertheless, the ultimate and explicit aim of his philosophical works was ethical. It was to discover in what human perfection consists, to explain the difficulties which prevent most men from reaching it, and to show the way which they must follow if they would overcome these difficulties. Before I begin to expound Spinoza's ethical theory I must state that I shall ignore everything in his system which depends on what he calls *Scientia Intuitiva* or the *Third Kind of Knowledge* ; *i.e.*, I shall ignore his doctrines of the Intellectual Love of God, of Human Blessedness, and of the Eternity of the Human Mind. Such an omission would be inexcusable if I were claiming to expound Spinoza's system as a whole, for they are among the hardest, the most interesting, and the most characteristic parts of it. But for the present purpose it is justified by the following facts. These doctrines, I am convinced, are the philosophic expression of certain religious and mystical experiences which Spinoza and many others have enjoyed and which seem supremely important to those who have had them. As such they belong to Spinoza's philosophy of religion rather than to his ethics in the ordinary sense. Spinoza himself recognises that he is passing into a different realm when he begins to expound them, for he introduces them with a remark which is extremely startling as coming from him. He says that he has now done with " all that concerns this present life ", and that henceforth he is going to discuss " the duration of the human mind without relation to the body ". That Spinoza was right in thinking that these experiences are of the utmost importance and that philosophy must deal seriously with them I have no doubt ; but I am equally sure that his theory of them is not consistent with the rest of his system. For these reasons I think I am justified in ignoring the doctrines in question.

I must begin by explaining Spinoza's view about the nature of man and his position in the universe. Each man is a finite part of the general order of Nature. He is a system of very great internal complexity having a characteristic kind of unity and balance. He is in constant interaction with other men and with the rest of Nature, and these interactions constantly tend to upset the balance in one direction or another. So long as the balance is approximately maintained he lives and remains in bodily and mental health. When it is temporarily upset to a marked extent he is ill or mad ; and when it is upset so far that it cannot be restored he dies. Now in man, as in every other natural unit, there is an inherent tendency to react to all changes in such a way as to maintain this characteristic unity and equilibrium. This inherent tendency in any finite natural unit Spinoza calls its *conatus*. The *conatus* of anything is the essence of that thing ; the particular way in which it behaves in any particular situation is just the expression of its *conatus* under the special circumstances of the moment. It is of interest to remark that, so far as organisms are concerned, modern physiology agrees entirely with this doctrine of Spinoza's, and that its researches have established it in much greater detail than Spinoza could have dreamed of.

Now a man, like everything else in Nature on Spinoza's view, is a thing with two fundamentally different but inseparably correlated aspects, a physical and a psychical. If we regard a man under his physical aspect and leave his psychical aspect out of account, we call him a human organism. If we regard him under his psychical aspect and leave his physical aspect out of account, we call him a human soul. Both these points of view are abstract and one-sided; everything which is a soul is also a body, and everything which is a body is also a soul. Suppose now that a change takes place in a man, through his interacting with some other part of Nature. This change, since it takes place in a thing which has two inseparably correlated aspects, will itself have these two aspects. Regarded on its purely physical side, it will be called a modification of the body; regarded on its purely psychical side, it will be called a modification of the soul. Every event which is a modification of my body is also a modification of my soul, and conversely.

We come now to a further specification of this doctrine which is highly characteristic of Spinoza. Suppose that a certain psycho-physical event $e_{\psi\phi}$ happens in a certain man. Regarded in its purely psychical aspect it counts as a psychical event e_{ψ} in his soul. Regarded in its purely physical aspect it counts as a physical event e_{ϕ} in his body. Now Spinoza's view is that e_{ψ} is what we call the act of sensing the change e_{ϕ} in the body, whilst e_{ϕ} is what we call the sensum which is the immediate object of the act e_ψ of the soul. Many philosophers would agree with Spinoza to the extent of holding that the act of sensing and the sensum are two distinct but inseparable aspects of a single event and are not two distinct events. But of course his doctrine goes further than this. He identifies the sensum, which is the *objective constituent* of a sensation, with the bodily change which is the necessary and sufficient *bodily condition* of the sensation. Very few philosophers have followed him in this. It is enough for me to say that there are great and glaring objections to this identification ; and, although I think that most of them could be avoided with a little ingenuity, I am sure that this could be done only at the cost of giving up Spinoza's doctrine that there is nothing positive in error, which is an essential part of his system.

Every idea in my mind then, whatever else it may be, is at least an act of direct acquaintance with a certain modification of my body. And every modification of my body, whatever else it may be, is at least the immediate object of a certain idea in my mind. This doctrine seems at first sight to be wantonly paradoxical, and one thinks at once of objections which seem perfectly conclusive. But Spinoza was quite well aware of these difficulties, and he strove with some success to meet them. We have now to consider two propositions which are of great importance in the further development of Spinoza's theory, and which do something to remove the appearance of paradox. (1) The ideas in my mind of most of the changes in my body, though they are acts of direct acquaintance with those changes, are highly confused. The reason, according to Spinoza, is this. When an event B is caused by an event A the former, taken

apart from the latter, is not a natural unit. The whole
AB is much more nearly a natural unit. Consequently the
psychical aspect of B, taken apart from that of A, is not a
natural unit. The psychical aspect of AB would be a
relatively clear idea, and any mind which had it would have
a relatively clear idea of the physical aspect of B. But a
mind which contained the psychical aspect of B without
that of A would have only a confused idea of the physical
aspect of B. The application of this general principle will
be most easily explained by an example. Suppose I eat
some cucumber and have a feeling of stomach-ache. To
feel stomach-ache is to be directly acquainted with a certain
physiological process in my stomach which is in fact caused
by a certain chemical process in the cucumber. But I am
not directly acquainted with this process in the cucumber,
because the cucumber is not a part of my body and therefore the psychical correlate of the process in it is not a
state of my mind. So my idea of the process in my stomach,
which constitutes my feeling of stomach-ache, is a fragmentary part of a complete idea, and its complement is not
in my mind but elsewhere. It is therefore an inadequate
and confused, though direct, acquaintance with this bodily
process. Now contrast this with the idea which a physiologist
might have of the process in my stomach. He would know
a great deal about its causes, and his idea of it would
therefore be fairly clear and adequate. But it would not
be direct *acquaintance with* the process, for he cannot *feel*
my stomach-ache; it would only be *knowledge about* the
process. The above example is typical of all those ideas
of my bodily modifications which we call " sensations " and
" feelings ". They are all ideas of effects cut loose from the
ideas of their causes, and therefore fragmentary, inadequate,

and confused. But they are all acts of direct acquaintance with their objects, whilst the clearer and more adequate ideas of science are not. I think it will be useful at this point to introduce two names which do not occur in Spinoza's writings. I propose to call my direct acquaintance with the process in my stomach, which, on Spinoza's view, constitutes my feeling of stomach-ache, an " intuitive idea ". And I propose to call the sort of idea of the process which another person might have a " discursive idea ".

(2) The second important point is this. Although my mind contains intuitive, but confused and inadequate, ideas of every change in my body, I am not aware of all these ideas. On Spinoza's view corresponding to every idea there is an intuitive idea of a higher order which has the former for its immediate object. But he holds—though I doubt whether he be consistent in doing so—that an idea may be in one mind whilst the intuitive idea of it may be, not in the same mind, but in some other. I am almost certain that he would hold that, in the case of the lower animals, their minds contain nothing but ideas of the first order, and that the ideas of these ideas are elsewhere in what he calls the " Attribute of Thought ". Everything, for Spinoza, is conscious, but not everything is self-conscious ; and the extent of a thing's self-consciousness may vary from time to time.

We are now in a position to understand, so far as is necessary for our present purpose, what Spinoza meant by the distinction which he draws between the *First* and the *Second Kinds of Knowledge*. The materials of the First Kind of Knowledge are those confused intuitive ideas of our own bodily modifications which we call " sensations " and " feelings ". And these ideas are interconnected only by associations, which depend on the order and the frequency with which other things have affected ourselves. In this way the ideas of objects which have no intrinsic relation to each other may be connected, whilst the ideas of objects which are intrinsically related to each other may be disjoined. Thus the First Kind of Knowledge is the level of mere sense-perception and imagery, and of uncritical beliefs founded on animal instinct, association, or hearsay. This is the only kind of knowledge which animals have. Men start as infants with nothing but this kind of knowledge, and every man continues to move at this level for long stretches throughout the whole of his life. But all men have some capacity for another kind of knowledge, and all men to some extent realise this capacity, though most of them do so to a lamentably slight degree. This Second Kind of Knowledge is rational insight. At this level one sees intrinsic connexions and disconnexions between objects, and one's ideas are connected and disjoined according to these intrinsic relations between their objects. The best example of the Second Kind of Knowledge is pure mathematics ; but we must remember that Spinoza, like most of his contemporaries, thought that physics, when properly understood, would be seen to have the same necessary character as pure mathematics. Spinoza is quite certain that the Second Kind of Knowledge presupposes the First Kind, whilst the First Kind might exist, and in animals presumably does exist, without leading on to the Second. His account of the transition is vague and radically unsatisfactory, and we need not waste time over it. The essential points for our purpose are these. There are two fundamentally different kinds of cognition :—the sensitive, instinctive, and associative, on the one hand, and the

rational, on the other ; both men and animals have the
first ; men have, and animals have not, the capacity to
rise from the first to the second ; men in this life start
with nothing but the first and the capacity to reach the
second from it ; and they all realise this capacity to various
degrees in the course of their lives. All this seems to me
to be plainly true, and to be unaffected by the facts that
Spinoza overestimated the range of rational cognition and
failed to give a satisfactory account of the details of the
process by which it is reached.

It has been necessary to give this outline of Spinoza's
theory of knowledge, because his theory of human perfection
and imperfection is so closely bound up with it. We are
now in a position to explain his doctrine of the will and the
emotions. It is based on the notion of *conatus*. Spinoza
calls the *conatus* of a human being *Appetitus*, which I propose
to translate by the phrase *Vital Impulse*. It has, of course,
two inseparably connected aspects. Viewed on its purely
physical side it is the tendency of the human organism to
maintain its characteristic form and balance in spite of and
by means of its interaction with its surroundings. I will
call Vital Impulse, when only its bodily aspect is considered,
Organic Self-maintenance. Spinoza does not give a special
name to it. The purely psychical aspect of Vital Impulse
is the tendency of the human mind to maintain its characteristic unity and purposes in spite of and by means of the
influences that are constantly affecting it. This aspect of
Vital Impulse Spinoza calls *Voluntas* ; I propose to call it
Mental Self-maintenance. A man's Vital Impulse then is
the fundamental thing in him ; and all his particular
behaviour, bodily and mental, is just an expression of the
reaction of this Vital Impulse to particular situations. In

accordance with Spinoza's general principle one's Mental Self-maintenance is the intuitive, but often very confused, idea of one's Organic Self-maintenance. Now, as we have seen, the idea of an idea may or may not be in the same mind as the original idea. My mind *must* contain an intuitive awareness of my Organic Self-maintenance, for this awareness is the psychical aspect of that Vital Impulse of which my Organic Self-maintenance is the physical aspect. But my mind need not contain an intuitive awareness of this awareness; *i.e.*, I need not be conscious of my own Vital Impulse, although my Vital Impulse is, in one aspect, a state of my consciousness. Spinoza gives a special name to Vital Impulse when the man whose *conatus* it is is also aware of it. He then calls it *Cupiditas*, which we might translate as *Volition*.

We can now tackle Spinoza's very peculiar theory of voluntary decision. Spinoza is, of course, a rigid determinist. He regards " freedom ", in the sense of indeterminism, as meaningless nonsense. The only sense in which the word " free " can intelligibly be used is in opposition to the word " constrained ". An action is free in this sense in so far as the cause of it is wholly contained in the nature and past history of the agent. It is constrained when some essential factor in its total cause lies outside the agent. It is clear that nothing can be a completely free agent in this sense except the Universe taken as a single collective whole. And we cannot ascribe free *will* to the Universe ; for will belongs, not to the Universe as a whole, but only to certain finite parts of it such as men.

So far Spinoza's doctrine is not very startling, and it would be accepted by a great many other philosophers. We come now to something more interesting. He holds that the ordinary analysis of choice and voluntary decision, which most determinists would accept, is radically mistaken. The usual view, even of determinists, is that we contemplate various possible alternatives ; that we are attracted by certain features in each and repelled by certain others ; and that finally the balance of attractiveness in one alternative determines our choice in its favour. According to Spinoza all this is wholly wrong. We do not desire things because the prospect of them attracts us, nor do we shun things because the prospect of them repels us. On the contrary the prospect of certain things attracts us because we already have an impulse towards them, and the prospect of other things repels us because we already have an impulse against them. We may or may not be aware of these impulses. If we are, they are called " volitions " and we are said to deliberate and to act voluntarily. If we are not, we are said to act blindly and impulsively. The presence or absence of consciousness of an impulse makes no difference whatever to the impulse or its consequences. The decision and the action are completely determined by the impulses, whether we be aware of them or not ; and the process of deliberating and deciding, if it be present, is a mere idle accompaniment which can only give a formal recognition to a *fait accompli*, as the King does when he gives his assent to an Act of Parliament. It is amusing to notice that this is precisely the theory which Mr. Bertrand Russell puts forward in his *Analysis of Mind* as a wonderful new discovery which we owe to the Psycho-analysts.

Spinoza's theory seems to me to be true in what it asserts and false in what it denies. It is true that the *mere* thought of an alternative neither attracts nor repels us. This is obvious from the fact that the thought of the same alternative will be accompanied by attraction in one person, by repulsion in another, and by neither in a third. It is evident from this that the attractiveness or repulsiveness of the alternatives which we contemplate depends upon certain relatively permanent factors in ourselves. These we may call " conative dispositions ". It is possible, of course, that there may be some conative dispositions common to all sane human beings. If so, some types of alternative will be attractive and others will be repulsive to all such beings whenever they happen to contemplate them. In such cases the essential part played by the conative disposition might easily be overlooked, and it might be thought that the *mere* contemplation of the alternative sufficed to stir desire for it or aversion from it. But this would be a mistake. Now it is of course true that one need not be aware of one's conative dispositions in order that they should make certain alternatives attractive and others repulsive to us. A disposition, *i.e.*, a more or less permanent tendency, is not the kind of thing of which one could be directly aware by introspection. We have to infer what our conative dispositions are by noticing what kind of things we do habitually desire and what kind of things we do habitually shun. If Spinoza wished to assert no more than that (*a*) the attractiveness and repulsiveness of alternatives depend on our conative dispositions, and (*b*) that, so far from being acquainted with our conative dispositions, we have to infer what they are from our desires and aversions, he was certainly right. But there can be no doubt that he did mean to assert something more, viz., that my awareness or unawareness of my own desires makes no difference to their consequences in the way of decision or action.

Now this doctrine has a certain ambiguity in it, which

I will point out. But, in whichever sense it is interpreted, there is no reason to think it true, and strong reason to think it false. (i) Spinoza might mean that any contemplated object attracts or repels us in consequence of certain characteristics which it *actually has*, whether we recognise their presence or not, and that it makes no difference whether we do or do not believe these characteristics to be present and to be the cause of the object's attractiveness or repulsiveness. This doctrine certainly cannot be true. In most cases of desire and deliberation none of the contemplated objects actually exist at present. You therefore cannot talk of the characteristics which they actually have, or suppose that these excite our conative dispositions as the presence of a magnet might stir a compass-needle. What affects our conative dispositions and calls forth desire or aversion *must* in all such cases, so far as I can see, be our *beliefs about* the characteristics which the various alternatives *would have* if they were actualised. (ii) Let us then pass to a more plausible interpretation. I may have a number of beliefs about the characteristics which a contemplated alternative would have if it were actualised. And I may be aware of some of these beliefs and unaware of others. Thus I may in fact believe that a certain alternative would have the characteristic c_1, and I may also believe that it would have the characteristic c_2, but I may be aware of the first belief and unaware of the second. Spinoza might mean that my desires and aversions are determined by the beliefs which I in fact have, and that my beliefs excite my conative dispositions in exactly the same way whether I happen to be aware of them or not. As regards this view there are two things to be said. (*a*) It is not *prima facie* particularly plausible. It is not obvious

that the simpler cause-factor " belief that so-and-so would
have a certain characteristic, unaccompanied by awareness
of that belief " must always have precisely the same effect
on our conative dispositions as the more complex cause-
factor consisting of this belief accompanied by awareness
of it. (b) In many cases it is plainly false. In so far as
I am unaware of some of my beliefs about the characteristics
which an alternative would have, I may be unaware of
some of the conative dispositions which the contemplation
of this alternative is exciting. Now some of these may be
such that I should strongly object to their being excited.
They might have led to disastrous consequences in the
past, or I might regard them as morally disreputable. If
I became aware of these beliefs, and thus of the conative
dispositions which were coming into play, I might decide
to act very differently. To take a fairly obvious example.
A person X of decent moral character may contemplate an
act of generosity to another person, Y. He may in fact
believe (a) that this will make Y happy, and (b) that it will
make it easier for him to seduce Y. Of these two beliefs
X may be aware of the first and unaware of the second.
Surely it is perfectly ridiculous to maintain that his decision
will always be precisely the same whether he remains in
ignorance of the second belief or becomes aware of it. When
he realises that a part of the cause of his desire to do this
act was a purely sensual conative tendency, which he may
regard as intrinsically disreputable or may know to have
led to disastrous consequences in his past life, he will be
provided with a motive against doing it which would not
have been present otherwise. Of course it is true that
mere awareness of one's own beliefs and conative tendencies
will no more modify one's actions than *mere* awareness of

anything else. But the point is that we have conative
tendencies of the second and higher orders as well as those
of the first order ; *i.e.*, we have conative tendencies which
lead to desires or aversions towards other conative tendencies.
And awareness of one's beliefs about a desired object may
lead to recognition of the conative tendencies to which it
is appealing ; this may excite conative dispositions of the
second order which would not otherwise have been excited ;
and this may make a profound difference to our final action
or decision. (iii) There is yet a third possible interpretation
of Spinoza's doctrine to be considered. I might contemplate
a certain alternative, and be aware of all my beliefs about
the characteristics which it would have if it were realised.
And I might desire it. But I might not be aware that I
was desiring it. I might fail to recognise that I was taking
up any conative or emotional attitude towards it, or I
might think that my attitude was one of aversion when it
was really one of desire. Spinoza may have meant to assert
that the result of desiring an alternative *without* recognising
that one was taking up this attitude towards it would be
precisely the same as the result of desiring it *and* recognising
that one was desiring it. This, again, does not seem to me
to have the least plausibility on the face of it. And it
seems not to be true. If I recognised that I was desiring
something which I think an unfitting object of desire, this
would be a motive for suppressing the desire or averting
my attention from this object. If I did not recognise that
I was desiring this object no such motive would operate
on me. And the presence or absence of this motive might
make a profound difference to my final decision.

I cannot think of any other interpretation of Spinoza's
doctrine beside the three which I have just discussed and

rejected. It therefore seems to me that the most characteristic part of Spinoza's theory of the will is a failure. And the fact that some of the exponents of the " New Psychology " have unwittingly plagiarised it does not, to my mind, materially reduce the probability that it is nonsense.

We will now deal with Spinoza's theory of the emotions. Whenever my body is acted upon by another body one of three things may happen. Its vitality may be increased, or diminished, or it may remain at the same level in spite of the interaction. In my mind there will be an intuitive but confused awareness of these changes or of this main-tenance of my bodily vitality. And this awareness is the mental aspect of those psycho-physical states which we call " emotions ". There are thus three primary emotions ; viz., pleasure, which is the consciousness of a transition to heightened vitality ; pain, which is the consciousness of a transition to lowered vitality ; and what Spinoza calls " desire ", which is the consciousness of the constancy of one's vitality throughout a change in the body. Spinoza distinguishes two kinds of pleasure and of pain. (1) The vitality of the body as a whole may be increased. The consciousness of this he calls *Hilaritas*, which we may translate as " Sense of Well-being ". (2) The vitality of a part may be increased without any increase of the total vitality, or even at the expense of it. The consciousness of this he calls *Titillatio*, which we may translate as " Localised Pleasure ". The two corresponding kinds of painful emotion he calls *Melancholia* and *Dolor* respectively. We might translate them as " Depression " and " Localised Pain ".

The above is Spinoza's general account of Emotion. He now draws a distinction, which is vitally important for his ethics, between *Passive* and *Active* Emotions. Passive emotions correspond to the confused and inadequate ideas of the First Kind of Knowledge. Active emotions are the affective correlates of clear rational knowledge. We are said to be " passive " in respect of any change that happens in us when part of the cause of this change is outside us. When the complete cause of a change in us is itself in us we are said to be " active " in respect of that change. Now at the level of the First Kind of Knowledge, as we have seen, our minds contain intuitive ideas of changes in our bodies and do not contain ideas of the causes of these changes. That is why the First Kind of Knowledge is confused and irrational. We now see that we are passive in Spinoza's sense at this level, and that the intellectual inadequacy and confusion are bound up with the passivity. The emotions which correspond to this intellectual level are thrust on us. We do not understand them or their causes, and, for that very reason, they tend to be inordinate and obsessive. Panic fears, overmastering loves and hates and jealousies, are the typical excesses of passive emotion. So long as we are at this level we may fairly be called slaves of passion, instinct, impulse, popular opinion, convention, and superstition. This state Spinoza calls " Human Bondage ".

Now the essence of the human mind, that which distinguishes it from animal minds, is the striving to understand, to think clearly, and to connect its ideas rationally. This, in human beings, is the psychical aspect of the Vital Impulse which is their *conatus*. Whenever a human mind passes from a state of greater to one of less mental confusion its vitality is increased, and this transition is felt as pleasure. Since this kind of pleasure depends on the mind's own characteristic activities it is called " Active Pleasure ". It is the sort of pleasure that we feel when we solve a problem for ourselves and replace muddle and confusion by order and rational arrangement. Active Desire would be the feeling that we have when we manage to keep our existing level of clearness in spite of distractions and difficulties. There is no active emotion corresponding to the passive emotion of pain. Of course the mind may pass from a level of greater clearness and insight to one of relative confusion, as it does when we are ill or tired. And this transition will be felt as painful. But it is a passive emotion, since the change is not due to the mind's own characteristic activities but to its falling under the dominion of other things. Certain active and certain passive emotions are called by the same names, and may lead to actions which are superficially alike. We might compare, *e.g.*, the case of a doctor and of an ordinary man in presence of a bad accident. The ordinary man may feel an emotion of sympathetic pain, and this may make him try to help the sufferer. But his actions will tend to be fussy and inefficient, and he may feel too sick to do anything even if he knows how to. The doctor feels very little of this sympathetic pain, but he has a clear idea of what is needed and an active emotion of helpfulness. Yet these two very different emotions would often be called by the same name of " sympathy " or " humanity ". Even the more amiable passive emotions are apt to degenerate into the state which Dickens illustrated in the character of Mrs Jellyby, who neglected her duties as a wife and a mother in order to promote the education of the natives of Borrio-boola-Gha.

According to Spinoza the active emotions fall under

two main heads, which he calls *Animositas* and *Generositas*. These are equivalent to Rational Self-love and Rational Benevolence. The state of predominantly clear knowledge and predominantly active emotion is called " Human Freedom " ; and the problem of practical ethics is to discover how men may pass from the state of Human Bondage, in which they are all born and in which most of them remain, to that of Human Freedom, which some few of them do reach. We must now consider Spinoza's teaching on this topic.

He certainly cannot be accused of underestimating the difficulties ; for he begins by insisting on the power of the passive emotions over human beings, and it seems almost overwhelming. In the first place, we are, and cannot cease to be, parts of the general order of Nature. Now the rest of Nature, taken together, is stronger than any one of us, and it is not specially designed for the benefit of any one of us. Consequently every man, by reason of his finitude, is always liable to passive emotions ; and, if external circumstances be specially unfavourable, it is always possible that he may be completely overcome and obsessed by some passive emotion : *e.g.*, the character of the wisest and best man is at the mercy of an accident to his brain and of infection by the germs of sleepy sickness. Secondly, an idea which is clear and adequate has not for that reason any special power to expel an idea which is confused and inadequate. The clear discursive idea of the sun as a vast sphere millions of miles away coexists with the confused intuitive idea of it as a small disc a little way above our heads. One emotion can be expelled only by another emotion, and the clearest and most exhaustive knowledge that certain emotions are irrational

in themselves and harmful in their consequences will not
have the faintest tendency to expel them unless it be itself
accompanied by some emotion which is stronger than they.
This is of course profoundly true.   If a person be obsessed
by jealousy the mere conviction that this emotion is
irrational and degrading will have no tendency to overcome
his jealousy unless the thought of himself as irrational and
degraded stirs an emotion of disgust in him.

The power of the mind over the passive emotions, such
as it is, arises from the following causes: (1) We can to
some extent form clear ideas of our own passive emotions,
and regard them and ourselves from the disinterested
scientific standpoint of the introspective psychologist.   In
so doing we largely dissociate these emotions from the
idea of such and such an external cause, and substitute
for them the emotion of scientific curiosity.   We thus cease
to be so much perturbed by excessive love and hate of
external things and people.   (2) In the long run emotions
towards ideal and impersonal objects which we clearly
understand are more permanent than emotions towards
particular things or persons which we know only confusedly
through the senses and remember by images which grow
vaguer and fainter with lapse of time.   *E.g.*, emotion at
the beauty of a mathematical theorem is no doubt far less
intense than the emotion of love or hate for a particular
person who is actually present.   But this person will change
or go away or die, and in his absence the image of him
will recur with decreasing frequency and distinctness, and
the emotion will fade away.   But the thought of the mathematical theorem can be reproduced with equal clearness at
will.   And so the less intense emotion gains in the long
run over the more intense one.   (3) Every event is really

due to an infinite network of contemporary cause-factors. And again it is the inevitable outcome of an infinite chain of successive total causes stretching back endlessly into the past. Now much of the obsessiveness of the emotions which we feel towards an event at the non-rational level is due to two illusions. We think that we can single out one particular thing or person as completely and solely responsible for the event. And we think that, although the event happened, it need not have done so. Now, when we clearly understand that nothing that happens could have fallen out otherwise, a great deal of the bitterness of many of our emotions tends to evaporate. And when we clearly understand that every event is the inevitable consequence of an endless chain of total causes, each of which is of infinite complexity, our emotion ceases to be concentrated on any one event or thing or person and is spread over all these infinitely numerous conditions. The result is that we no longer feel an intense and obsessive love or hate of any one thing or person when we view the world from the level of rational knowledge. *E.g.*, in the late war ignorant people could regard the Kaiser as its sole and sufficient cause, and could feel an intense and perturbing emotion of hatred for him. But this was impossible for anyone who was intelligent enough to know, and intellectually honest enough to bear in mind, that the war was the inevitable outcome of immensely complex causes, stretching back for centuries, and many of them quite impersonal. (4) In moments of calm a rational being can deliberately form certain habits of thought and certain associations and dissociations of ideas which will persist and will check passive emotions when they threaten him. All these four ways of replacing obsessive passive emotions by calm active emotions are plainly genuine and important ; and Spinoza shows here his usual profound psychological insight. The path from Human Bondage to Human Freedom is thus steep and slippery, but it does exist and it is not impassible. As Spinoza says in a famous passage : " If it were not very difficult why should so few have travelled it ? But all supremely excellent things are as difficult as they are rare."

We come now to a topic which is of the utmost importance in all ethical systems, viz., the relative positions which are to be assigned to egoistic and to altruistic emotions, desires, and actions. There are always two questions, one psychological and the other ethical ; and the answer to the first has a direct bearing on the answer to the second. Now Spinoza's psychology is fundamentally and explicitly egoistic. Every emotion, volition, and action of a man is an expression of the Vital Impulse, which is his essence. And this Vital Impulse, like every other *conatus*, is a striving for *self*-maintenance and *self*-preservation and for nothing else. All our primitive instincts are therefore instincts of self-preservation ; and, when we reach the rational level, we can only pursue deliberately and with clear insight the same end for which we formerly strove instinctively and blindly. Thus deliberate self-sacrifice is literally impossible ; and, since it is impossible, it can be neither right nor a duty. Now any such theory as this is at once faced with two objections. The first is that there seem to be non-egoistic emotions and actions at both the instinctive and the rational level. And the second is that we seem to regard self-sacrifice in certain cases as right and even as a duty. We must now see how Spinoza deals with these objections.

We will begin with the question of fact, and we will

consider it first at the instinctive level and then at the rational level. It seems to me that the apparent exceptions to Spinoza's theory which we find at the pre-rational level come under three main heads: (1) Certain emotions and actions which are concerned with the preservation of a species, viz., those which are involved in sexual intercourse and parenthood. The action of the male spider, who is generally eaten by his wife, and the action of the hen, who attracts the attention of a hawk to herself in order to divert it from her chickens, are certainly very odd expressions of an impulse towards nothing but self-preservation. (2) The general sentiment of sympathy towards another member of one's race or species, as such, when one sees him in pain or difficulty. That this is often overcome by other emotions and impulses is true enough. But it is equally certain that, when there is no special cause to inhibit it, it is evoked and may lead to actions which do not make for the preservation of the agent. (3) Certain kinds of emotion and action towards particular persons whom we already love or hate. If A either loves or hates B strongly enough he will often feel emotions and perform actions which are, and can be seen to be, most detrimental to his own welfare and even to his own survival. Acts done in a passion of jealousy or spite are obvious examples.

Spinoza does not explicitly deal with the first class of apparent exceptions, and I cannot see that any general principle which he uses in his treatment of the other two would provide a plausible explanation of them. I think that they make it certain that he has taken the notion of Vital Impulse too narrowly, and that this impulse certainly involves a primitive striving to propagate and preserve one's species in addition to the primitive striving to preserve

oneself. These two factors may conflict ; and, at the
pre-rational level, the former seems often to be stronger
than the latter. Spinoza does explicitly treat the other
two kinds of apparent exception, and we will now consider
his theory.

Spinoza's attempted explanation of the sympathetic
emotion which I feel when I contemplate any other human
being in a state of pleasure or pain is as follows. If A and
B be two bodies of similar nature, and a certain modification
of A determines a certain modification of B, then the latter
modification will resemble the former. This general principle will apply to the case of two human bodies. Suppose
now that a man A is having a certain emotion, and that
another man B is perceiving A's body at the time. A's body
will have a certain characteristic modification, which is the
physical correlate of the emotion which A is feeling. This
will cause a certain modification in B's body, which will
be the physical correlate of B's perception of A's body. By
the general principle just enunciated this modification in
B's body will resemble the modification in A's body which
causes it. It will therefore be correlated with an emotion
in B which is similar to the emotion which A is feeling.

I think it is quite certain that this explanation will not
work. In the first place, there is no reason to accept the
general principle or its particular application. If one human
body emits a shriek and a second human body be within
earshot it will be affected by the event in the former. But
it will not in general be so affected as to emit a shriek
itself. Secondly, even if the principle were true it would
not be sufficient. When A has a certain emotion the only
part of the physical correlate of this emotion which can
affect B's body is its external expression, *e.g.*, a shriek,

a smile, a frown, and so on. Now this is certainly not the whole, or even the principal part, of the physical correlate of A's emotion. So, even if it were to produce a similar modification in B's body, it would produce only a small and rather trivial part of the total physical correlate of the emotion. It is therefore quite possible that B would not feel an emotion like that which A is feeling and expressing at the time. Even if I could not see a fellow-man frown without frowning myself it would not in the least follow that my frown must be accompanied by an internal bodily state like that which accompanies the other man's frown. So Spinoza's explanation of the second class of apparent exceptions is a complete failure.

Spinoza's theory of the third class of apparent exceptions is as follows: To say that I "love" A means that the perceived or imagined presence of A gives me pleasure, and this is a sign that it heightens my vitality. To say that I "hate" A means that the perceived or imagined presence of A gives me pain, and this is a sign that it lowers my vitality. I shall naturally try to preserve and strengthen anything that heightens my vitality, and to destroy and weaken anything that lowers my vitality. For by so doing I am indirectly preserving and increasing my own vitality. Thus I shall tend to do actions which give pleasure to those whom I love and pain to those whom I hate. That such actions at the pre-rational level often overshoot the mark must presumably be ascribed to the state of intellectual confusion which is characteristic of this level. This explanation seems to me to be sound so far as it goes. But I doubt if it accounts for all the facts. Is not the presence of those whom we hate sometimes highly stimulating? Is it not a perfectly well-known fact that many people delight in hurting those whom they love ? And does not the whole theory over-intellectualise the mental processes of animals and of men at the level of impulse and passion ? I conclude on the whole that Spinoza has failed to answer the *prima facie* case against egoism as an adequate psychological theory of emotion and action at the pre-rational level.

We have now to consider the question at the level of rational knowledge, active emotion, and deliberate action. Here Spinoza's contention is that actions performed at this level which are commonly counted as altruistic are simply those which a clear-sighted egoist would see to be essential to his own ultimate interests. His theory is as follows. Self-preservation and the performance of the characteristic activities of the self are our only ultimate end. And all our other desires are subordinated to it ; for, as he says, " We cannot desire to be blessed, or to act rightly, or to live rightly, without desiring to live." At the rational level we pursue this end deliberately and wittingly, and we choose the right means to it ; whereas at the instinctive level we pursued it blindly and were often misled by association. Now the one essential activity of a human being is to think clearly and understand rationally. Everything that we do which does not consist in or involve the exercise of this activity can be done as well or better by animals. So the self which a human being who clearly understands his own nature will strive to preserve and develop is a self which thinks clearly and understands rationally. He will tolerate or further other activities in himself or in others only in so far as they are indifferent or helpful to this end. Now Spinoza maintains two very important propositions, one negative and the other positive. The negative contention is that men come into conflict with each other only in so far as they live at the pre-rational level. The goods which belong to that level are limited in amount, and the part of them which belongs to A cannot also belong to B. This is obvious as regards the pleasures which are derived from the exclusive possession of a bit of property, of a beloved person, and so on. But rational insight is a non-competitive good ; the possession of such knowledge of a certain subject by A does not prevent B from having just as clear and just as extensive knowledge of the same subject. And the same would apply to all those goods which depend on, though they do not reduce to, rational insight, *e.g.*, the admiring contemplation of beautiful objects. The positive contention is that rational insight, and the other goods which depend on it, cannot exist except in an ordered community of human beings, and that it cannot reach any high degree in one unless it reaches a high degree in all. A solitary hermit would have to spend so much time and energy in securing the bare necessities of life and defending himself against his foes that he would have hardly any left for cultivating the specifically human excellences. And no man could carry his own intellectual development far, even though he lived in a society which supplied him with defence and the necessities of life, unless he had the constant stimulus and co-operation of other men of intelligence and culture.

Thus the " Free Man ", as Spinoza calls him, would have positive egoistic grounds for wishing to live in a society of some kind rather than in solitude ; and he would have positive grounds for wishing the other members of this society to be Free Men, like himself, rather than ignorant slaves of superstition, instinct, and passion. And, since he is a clear-sighted rational being, he will know that omelettes cannot be made without breaking eggs. He will tolerate and desire, as a necessary means to the existence of an organised society and to the development of its members into Free Men, much that is *directly* indifferent or even detrimental to his own intellectual development. For he understands the properties of the materials with which he has to deal, and he knows that he is but sacrificing a smaller immediate gain for a greater ultimate return. And the process which he sets in motion is cumulative ; for, the nearer his society approaches to a society of Free Men, the fewer will be the grounds of possible conflict between its members, and the less often will he have to sacrifice a sprat to catch a mackerel. In this way, Spinoza would say, we can explain and justify all actions at the rational level which would commonly be counted as altruistic. And egoism remains the fundamental principle ; for, although the Free Man wills the perfection of other men as well as his own, he wills his own as an end, whilst he wills theirs, not as an end, but only as a necessary means to his own.

What are we to say of this doctrine of Spinoza's ? It is quite certain that there would be far less friction and mutual frustration in a society of rational egoists, each of whom cared for nothing but his own intellectual develop-ment and unhesitatingly took the most effective means to secure it, than there is among men who are partly ruled by the instincts, passions, and loyalties of the pre-rational level. And I think it very likely that many of the actions which it would be reasonable for a rational egoist to perform in a society of rational egoists would not differ much externally from those which are now praised as altruistic. This we must grant to Spinoza. But there remains much to be criticised in the theory.

(1) We must not assume that, because many types of action which are alleged to spring from non-egoistic motives *would* also be done by a rational egoist who understood his business, therefore these actions *do in fact* spring from egoistic motives. We have already seen that the Vital Impulse, even at the pre-rational level, must include factors beside the instinct of self-preservation, factors which may conflict with and sometimes overcome that instinct. So, even if Spinoza be right in holding that there is nothing new on the conative side at the rational level, and that we have here only the old Vital Impulse grown conscious of itself and of the necessary conditions of its own satisfaction, there would still be no ground to expect that egoism would be an adequate theory of deliberate action.

(2) The contention that " we cannot desire to act rightly, or to live rightly, without desiring to live " is no doubt true when the proper qualifications are made. But it then becomes trivial. For we must substitute for it the statement that I cannot desire to act rightly without desiring to live long enough to perform the right action which I am intending. Now this would be true even if the action which I judge to be right and intend to perform to-morrow is to sacrifice my life for my country in a forlorn hope or to science in a certainly lethal experiment. I should still desire to live till the charge is sounded or until the apparatus is ready and the observers are assembled. Consequently this principle cannot disprove the possibility of deliberate self-sacrifice. I think it is true that no rational being deliberately wills his own destruction as an end ; but it is quite clear to me that such a being may deliberately choose an alternative which he knows at the time will involve his destruction as a necessary condition of its fulfilment.

(3) The distinction between competitive and non-competitive goods is superficially striking, and it has a certain relative importance. But I believe that it is ultimately rather misleading. It is of course obvious enough that knowledge can be shared without being divided, in a sense in which property cannot ; and that it is capable of being indefinitely increased. But, although knowledge itself is not a competitive good, some of the necessary conditions for acquiring and exercising intellectual powers plainly are competitive. Philosophers and scientists and artists need as much food, clothing, shelter, and warmth as anyone else. And they need considerably more leisure, and a long and expensive training. Now the supply of all these things is limited. Unless some people mainly devote themselves to producing such things, and thereby forfeit their own chance of any great intellectual or artistic development, it is certain that scientists and philosophers will not have the leisure or the training or the freedom from practical worries which are essential to their intellectual development and activity. So, to be quite frank, I do not agree that a perfectly rational man, in Spinoza's sense, would want *all* men to be perfectly rational. He would indeed want to co-operate with a *great many* such men, and, *within this class*, he would want the members to be as highly developed in intellect as possible. But he would recognise that the very existence of a class of disinterestedly scientific or artistic persons depends on the labours of people like bed-makers, bricklayers, miners, etc., who cannot and must not make intellectual curiosity their main motive or develop their intellects too far. No doubt these humble and dutiful lives are amply rewarded by knowing that they are the soil from which spring such fine flowers of culture as our-

selves. But the fact remains that, so long as our intellects
are bound to animal organisms which have to be clothed,
fed, warmed, and housed, all talk of disinterested knowledge
and æsthetic appreciation or production as non-competitive
goods which all men might enjoy together to the highest
degree is, to put it plainly, moonshine.

We have now, I hope, gained a fairly clear idea of the
range of application of the words " good " and " bad " on
Spinoza's view. And this is one important part of the
total problem of ethics. But there is another part of that
problem to which we must now turn our attention. The
question is : " What is the *meaning* of ethical terms, like
' good ' and ' bad ', ' right ' and ' wrong ', ' ought ', etc. ?
Can they be analysed ; and, if so, what is the right analysis ?
And how are they related to each other ? "   On these
questions Spinoza has much less to say. But his views are
characteristic and important, though they are not stated or
defended in as much detail as would be desirable.

The first point to notice is that all implication of praise
or blame must be removed from ethical judgments, in so
far as this implies that a thing or person might have been
other than it is or might have done otherwise than it did.
Any such implication, on Spinoza's view, is simply a delusion
due to partial ignorance of the conditions. The judgment
that a thing or person or action is good or bad, when freed
from these delusive implications, must be as purely positive
as the statement that a thing is round or square. There is
one and only one sense in which the words " perfect " and
" imperfect " can properly and literally be used, and that
is " realising or falling short of the intentions of the
designer ". They can thus be applied properly only to the
artificial products of deliberate design, such as plates or

motor-cars. When men apply them to each other and to things in the outer world which are not the products of human design they are making a certain tacit assumption. They are thinking of God as a being like themselves who desires ends and uses means to secure these ends ; they are thinking of themselves as deliberately designed and produced by God, as plates and motors are designed and produced by men ; and they are thinking of the non-artificial part of the outer world as designed by God for the benefit of men. The whole of this tacit assumption, according to Spinoza, is philosophically absurd. And it is daily refuted by the experience that the rest of Nature is perfectly indifferent to man and his welfare. In face of such experiences men do not give up their false assumption, but sink still deeper into folly by talking of the " inscrutable wisdom " and the " mysterious purposes " of God when earthquakes, pestilences, and famines devastate humanity. This Spinoza calls " taking refuge in the asylum of ignorance ". We must therefore rigidly confine our use of the words " perfect " and " imperfect " to things that we know to be the products of deliberate human design.

What then are we to say about the meaning of the terms " good " and " bad ", " better " and " worse " ? Spinoza's view seems to be the following. If we take any species of beings there will be certain powers and activities which are common and peculiar to the members of it. Within a given species to say that one member is " better " than another simply means that it has the characteristic powers of the species to a greater degree and that it performs the characteristic functions of the species more efficiently. The fundamental ethical judgment is of the form " A exercises the characteristic functions of his species more efficiently than B, who belongs to the same species ", and this is what is meant by " A is better than B ". But it is not always convenient to express ethical judgments in this comparative form. It is often more convenient to put them in the form " A is a very good man " or " B is a fairly bad man ". We arrange members of a species in an order according to whether they perform the specific functions more or less efficiently. This series has neither in theory nor in practice a first or last term or an upper or lower limit. Thus the notion of a " perfectly good " or " perfectly bad " man would be meaningless. But we can form the notion of an average or typical member of the species, though it is of course a fiction to which nothing actual exactly answers. A member of a species will then be called " good " if it performs the specific functions with decidedly greater efficiency than the average member, and it will be called " bad " if it performs them with decidedly less efficiency than the average member. The notions of " good " and " bad " are thus doubly relative. In the first place, they mean " better or worse than the average ". And, secondly, the average is that of a certain species, and " better " or " worse " refer to the relative efficiency with which the characteristic functions of this species are performed. Still, there is a sense in which " good " is a positive term, whilst " bad " is a merely negative or privative term like " blind " or " short-sighted ". For the relation of worse to better within the species is simply the relation of less to more of the positive powers and activities which are characteristic of the species.

Is there any sense of " better " and " worse " in which they relate members of different species to each other ? E.g., would there be any sense in saying that the worst

man that we can imagine is " higher than " the best
mouse that we can imagine, or that human good is " to be
preferred to " canine or equine good when it conflicts with
them ? So far as I can understand, Spinoza's answer would
be as follows : When and only when the powers which are
characteristic of species A include all and more than all the
powers which are characteristic of species B we can say
that any member of A is " higher than " any member of B,
and there is an objective ground for preferring the good
of A to that of B if the two conflict. This relation holds
between men and all animals. For men have the power of
rational cognition, whilst animals have not. And, although
men are physically weaker and less skilful in many ways
than certain animals, yet by using their rational cognition
they can in the end accomplish everything that any animal
can accomplish and do it far more efficiently. Where this
kind of relation does not hold, as, *e.g.*, between dogs and
cats, there is no sense in talking of " better " and " worse ",
" higher " and " lower ". On the general principle of egoism,
which we have already discussed, any man will treat any
other individual, whether human or non-human, simply as
a means to his own intellectual development. But, in the
case of other human beings, the form which such treatment
takes will be enormously modified by the fact that the
companionship and co-operation of other rational beings are
vitally important to one's own intellectual welfare and
growth. In the case of animals there is no such modifying
influence ; and, although the Free Man will not treat them
with wanton cruelty, he will unhesitatingly use them for
food, clothing, haulage, and scientific experiments. Spinoza
would not have had the faintest sympathy with vegetarianism
or the agitation against vivisection ; and I am afraid that

he would have regarded the pleasure which most decent people get from the love and companionship of cats, dogs, or horses, as a form of passive emotion from which the Free Man would have freed himself.

A " virtue ", on Spinoza's view, is any active power or capacity which is part of the nature of a thing. The fundamental human virtue is to understand clearly, and all other human virtues are subordinate to this. It will be worth while to say something about Spinoza's views on certain alleged virtues and vices. The vice which he thinks most evil is hatred, for it is bad both directly and indirectly. In the first place, it is an extremely disturbing passive emotion which tends to make us hurt and destroy other human beings. Now, as we have seen, the Free Man will want to preserve other men and to make them rational enough to be his companions and colleagues. The Free Man, if he is hated, will not return hatred but will try to return love. For it is a plain psychological fact that to return hate for hate always increases the original hatred, whilst this may sometimes be overcome by love. This is of course true ; but it is a truth which goes so much against the grain that men will not act upon it even when it is promulgated by what they regard as divine authority and supported by daily empirical verification.

Spinoza has a low opinion of what Hume calls " the monkish virtues ", viz., deliberate asceticism, pity, humility, repentance, and shame. They are not strictly virtues, but passive emotions which spring from our weakness and not from clear rational insight. And they are bad in two respects. In the first place, they are all painful emotions, and therefore signs of diminished vitality in the man who feels them. Moreover, the actions to which they lead, being based on inadequate knowledge, are quite as likely to do harm to ourselves and others as to benefit them. The Free Man will aim directly at good, and, in so doing will incidentally avoid evil. He will not be constantly thinking about evil and trying to avoid it. And he will enjoy in moderation all those bodily and mental pleasures which are not hurtful to his intellectual development. Spinoza compares him to the healthy man who eats what he likes and incidentally avoids illness. The man who devotes himself to avoiding evil is like the valetudinarian who is always thinking of his own ailments and has to diet himself in order to keep alive. " The last thing that the Free Man thinks about," says Spinoza, " is death ; and his wisdom is a meditation, not of death, but of life."

Nevertheless, Spinoza allows a certain relative value to these " monkish virtues ". After all, most people are not Free Men, just as most people are not perfectly healthy. And it is only those who " know that sin is in vain " who can safely " whistle the Devil to make them sport ". If a man is to be swayed by passive emotions at all it is better for him to be moved by pity, humility, repentance, shame, etc., than by malice, hardness of heart, and insolence. We must then recognise, beside the ethics of Free Men living in the society of their equals, a kind of *Interimsethik* which governs the relations of those who are still in bondage. It is at this level, on Spinoza's view, that we find the State, as we know it, with its laws, customs, and institutions. Every man, whether he lives at the rational or the pre-rational level, has a natural right to preserve his own existence. And from this follow the natural rights of seeking what he judges to be to his own advantage, of avenging injuries to himself, of cherishing what he loves and injuring what he hates, and so on. At the rational level the exercise of these natural rights would lead, not to conflict, but to co-operation. But, when men have confused ideas and passive emotions, they make mistakes about their own real interests and about the proper means to secure them. They thus come into perpetual conflict with each other ; and the only way out of this is for all of them to forego some part of their natural rights and to refrain from actions which injure each other. But at this level they will not be able to see this fact steadily, nor will they be able to adjust their lives at all times to these limitations merely because it is reasonable to do so. At this level some men at all times and all men at some times will refrain from inflicting injury only in so far as they fear a greater injury for themselves. And the State is an institution, which arises at this partially rational level, with power to lay down rules of conduct, to define what are and what are not injuries, and to prevent injurious actions by punishment and the threat of punishment. There is no property, and there can be no justice or injustice, apart from a State and its laws. " Sin " is disobedience to the laws of one's State, and " merit " is obedience to them. And so, Spinoza says, " it is evident that justice and injustice, merit and sin, are extrinsic ideas, and not attributes which display the nature of mind."

The State, then, exists primarily, not for the Free Man, but for men who are partly rational and mainly at the level of confused ideas and passive emotions. But the Free Man will have to be a citizen of some State and to make the best of it. For, although he will often feel, as one often felt during the late war, that he is living in a lunatic asylum which is being conducted by the inmates, even the society of homicidal maniacs with occasional lucid intervals is incomparably better for one's intellectual health than the squalor and stagnation of the hermit's cave. The situation of the Free Man in a society of those who are still largely in bondage is of course a delicate and difficult one. He must not make the mistake of treating them as if they were free, or he will outrage their prejudices and incur persecution and perhaps death. On the other hand, he must not visibly make a difference between them and himself or adopt offensive airs of superiority. Spinoza had ample opportunities of practising this difficult art of combining the wisdom of the serpent with the harmlessness of the dove ; and all that we know of his life suggests that he acquired great skill in it. He always avoided giving provocation or seeking martyrdom ; yet, when the occasion arose, he displayed a calm heroic courage in face of a murderous patriotic mob. And he was equally successful in " the long littleness of life ". He shared the joys and sorrows of the simple people among whom he lived in a perfectly natural un-self-conscious way ; and he tolerated and respected in them beliefs and practices which would have been impossible for himself. In the meanwhile he earned his own living by his skill as a practical optician, and was a burden to no one. He thus accomplished one of the hardest of all tasks, viz., to be a prophet without being a prig and to be a saint without being a sponger.

There remains one other point of general ethical interest to be mentioned before we leave Spinoza and pass to Butler. This is the position of pleasure and pain in Spinoza's ethical system. He is not a Hedonist, in the strict sense. States of mind and actions are not good *because* they are pleasant or conducive to pleasure, nor are they bad *because* they are painful or conducive to pain. But pleasure and pain, though they are thus not the *ratio essendi* of good and evil, are the *ratio cognoscendi* thereof. Pleasure is the infallible sign of heightened vitality, pain is the infallible sign of lowered vitality, and these are the only ultimate good and evil. If a man were born with completely clear ideas and completely active emotions he would, according to Spinoza, have no idea of good or evil. For he would never have felt the pleasure of passing to a higher degree of vitality and mental clearness nor the pain of passing to a lower degree of vitality and to a state of greater mental confusion. Yet he would in fact be in the best state in which a human being could be. But the hypothesis in question is one that could not possibly be realised, for we necessarily start in a state of predominantly confused cognition and predominantly passive emotion. There is just one qualification to be made to the above statements. We must remember the distinction between Well-being and Localised Pleasure, and between Depression and Localised Pain. It is only the first members of these two pairs which are infallible signs of heightened and lowered vitality respectively, and therefore of good and evil.

CHAPTER III

Butler

BUTLER's ethical theories are contained in the *Sermons on Human Nature* which he preached at the Rolls Chapel in London, and in the *Dissertation on the Nature of Virtue* which forms one of the appendices to his famous *Analogy of Religion*. It would be hard to find two writers of such eminence who were so unlike each other as Butler and Spinoza. The writer with whom he has most affinity among those who are treated in this book is Kant, though Hume accepted and emphasised his refutation of psychological egoism. Butler was not, of course, as great a metaphysician as Kant ; but he largely made up for this by his clearness and balance. Kant's work is marred by a mania for neat logical classifications and by a strong trace of moral fanaticism ; whilst Butler has the solid common-sense and the sweet reasonableness of an English bishop of the eighteenth century. He writes about facts with which we are all acquainted in language which we can all understand ; and his work, though it does not pretend to be a complete treatise on ethics, forms one of the best introductions to the subject that exists.

It is necessary to say something at the outset about the ethical and religious tone of the period, because this largely determined the form in which Butler put his arguments. The Christian religion was then going through one of its recurrent phases of dormancy, and has seldom been at a lower ebb in England. Although it has undergone much more serious attacks since Butler's time, I should say (speaking as an outside observer) that it is far more alive now than then. Religion was in a resting stage, worn out with the theological excitements of the seventeenth century and awaiting the revival which was to take place in the latter part of the eighteenth. Butler says in his preface to the *Analogy* : " It is come to be taken for granted by many persons that Christianity is not so much a subject of inquiry, but that it is now at length discovered to be fictitious. And accordingly they treat it as if in the present age this were an agreed point among all people of discernment ; and nothing remained but to set it up as a principal subject of mirth and ridicule, as it were by way of reprisals for its having so long interrupted the pleasures of the world." This would certainly not be an accurate description of the attitude of " people of discernment " at the present time towards religion in general or Christianity in particular. We do indeed meet with such people ; but they strike us as quaint and picturesque survivals of the eighteen-seventies who are rendered all the more amusing by their obviously sincere conviction that they are daringly advanced thinkers.

It was also fashionable in Butler's time to deny the possibility of disinterested action. This doctrine, which was a speculative principle with Hobbes, has always had a certain vogue. It is not without a certain superficial plausibility, and it has naturally been popular both with vicious persons who wanted a philosophical excuse for their own selfishness and with decent people who felt slightly ashamed of their own virtues and wished to be taken for men of the world. One of Butler's great merits is to have pointed out clearly and conclusively the ambiguities of language which make it plausible. As a psychological theory it was killed by Butler; but it still flourishes, I believe, among bookmakers and smart young business men whose claim to know the world is based on an intimate acquaintance with the shadier side of it. In Butler's day the theory moved in higher social and intellectual circles, and it had to be treated more seriously than any philosopher would trouble to treat it now. This change is very largely the result of Butler's work; he killed the theory so thoroughly that he sometimes seems to the modern reader to be flogging dead horses. Still, all good fallacies go to America when they die, and rise again as the latest discoveries of the local professors. So it will always be useful to have Butler's refutation at hand.

After these preliminaries we can consider Butler's ethical theory as a whole. His chief merit is as a moral psychologist. He states with great clearness the principles according to which decent people do feel and act and judge, though they could not state these for themselves. And, in the course of this, he refutes certain plausible fallacies which would not have occurred to common-sense, but which unaided common-sense cannot answer when learned men suggest them to it. His fundamental doctrine is that the human mind is an organised system in which different propensities and principles can be distinguished. But it is not enough to enumerate these without saying how they are related to each other. It would not be an adequate description of a watch to say that it consists of a spring, wheels, hands, etc., nor would it be an adequate description of the British Constitution to say that it consists of the King, Lords, and Commons. We do not understand the nature of a watch until we know that the spring makes the wheels turn, that the balance-wheel controls them, and that the object of the whole arrangement is to record the time. Similarly, we do not understand the British Constitution till we know the precise functions and the mutual relations of the King, the Lords, and the Commons.

Now Butler explicitly compares the nature of man both to a watch and to a constitution. He says that we do not fully understand it till we know what it is for and what are the various functions and relations of the various principles and propensities. According to him none of these is intrinsically evil. Wrong-doing is always the excessive or inappropriate functioning of some principle of action which is right when acting in its due degree and in its proper place. It is like a watch with a spring which is too strong for its balance-wheel, or a constitution in which one of the estates of the realm usurps the functions of another. So the essential thing about man as a moral being is that he is a complex whole of various propensities arranged in a hierarchy. These propensities have a certain right proportion and certain right relations of subordination to each other. But men can go wrong, just as watches and constitutions can do ; and so we must distinguish between the actual relative strength of our various propensities and that which they ought to have. The latter may be called their " moral *authority* ". It may well happen that at times a principle of higher moral authority has less psychological strength than one of lower moral authority. If so the man will be likely to act wrongly. The rightness or wrongness of an action, or even of an intention, can be judged only by viewing it in relation to the whole system in which it is a factor. Thus we judge very differently the same action or intention in a child or a lunatic or a sane grown man. Similarly we do not blame a motor-car for irregularities which would make us regard a watch as worthless. This is because watches and motor-cars are very different systems with very different functions. An actual motor-car must be judged by comparing its behaviour with that of an ideal car, and an actual watch by comparing its behaviour with that of an ideal watch.

It is pretty clear that Butler has hold of a sound and intelligible idea, which is as old as Plato's *Republic*. He chooses to express his theory in the form that virtue consists in acting in accordance with one's nature, and that vice is acting against one's nature. I am not fond of the words "natural" and "unnatural", because they are extremely ambiguous and are commonly used by people to convey a flavour of moral authority to their personal likes and dislikes. Butler fully recognises this ; he sees that in one sense nobody can act against his nature. I think it would be better to say that virtue consists in acting in accordance with the *ideal nature* of man, and that vice consists in acting against it. No man's actual nature is the ideal nature of man. But this raises no special difficulty. We can form the conception of a perfect watch, although no real watches are perfect. And science makes great use of such idealised concepts as perfectly straight lines, perfect circles, perfect gases, etc., though it admits that there are no such objects in Nature.

We must now consider how such concepts are reached, so as to see whether the concept of an ideal human nature is likely to be valid or useful. I think that we commonly reach them in two different ways. In forming the concept of a perfect watch we start with a knowledge of what watches are for. A watch is for telling the time, and a perfect watch would be one that told the time with complete accuracy. Butler often talks as if we could apply this criterion to man, but this does not seem to me to be true. There is no sense in asking what a man is for unless we assume that he has been made by God for a certain purpose. And, even if this were certain, it would not help us ; for we do not know what this purpose may be. But there is another way in which we form ideal concepts, and this is illustrated by the concept of a perfect circle or straight line. We see such things as cakes and biscuits and pennies. On reflection we see that they fall into a series—cake, biscuit, penny—in which a certain attribute is more and more fully realised. Finally we form the concept of a perfect circle as the ideal limit to such a series. Thus we can form the concepts of such ideal limits as circles and straight lines by reflecting on imperfect instances arranged in series ; and here there is no need to know what the objects are for. Intermediate between the ideal watch and the ideal circle, and more closely analogous to what Butler needs for his purpose, would be the biologist's concept of an ideal horse or rabbit. By comparing and contrasting actual horses, all of which are defective in various respects and to various degrees, we can form the notion of an ideal horse. And, although we recognise that it is an anthropomorphic way of speaking and that we must not take it too literally, we are making a statement which has some kind of correspondence to an important fact when we say that Nature is always striving towards such ideals and always falling short of them to some extent.

There are three things to notice about these ideal limits.
(1) There is generally no lower limit to such series. There
is a concept of a perfectly straight line, but there is no
concept of a perfectly crooked one. (2) When we have
formed the concept of an ideal limit we sometimes find
that it is analysable and sometimes that it is not. We
can define " circularity ", but we cannot define " straight-
ness ". Yet we understand just as well what is meant by
one as by the other. (3) We could not reach the concepts
of these ideal limits unless we had the power of reflecting
on series and recognising the characteristic which is more
and more adequately, though still imperfectly, realised in
the higher members of the series.

Now I think that there is an exact analogy to these
three points in forming the concept of an ideal human
nature. (1) There is no concept of a perfectly bad man,
any more than there is a concept of a perfectly crooked
line. (2) If we arrange actual men, including ourselves,
in a series, and reflect on it, we can detect a closer and
closer approximation to an ideal which is not exactly
realised in any of them. But it does not follow that we
can analyse and define this ideal completely. I think that
Butler would say that we can indicate its general outlines
but not its precise details. It certainly involves, as we
shall see, the subordination of particular impulses to the
more general principles of prudence and benevolence. And
it certainly involves the subordination of both these general
principles to the supreme principle of conscience. But just
how far each impulse would be indulged in the ideal man,
and just what compromise he would make between prudence
and benevolence when the two conflict, Butler does not
tell us. And perhaps it is impossible for anyone to tell us.

This margin of vagueness does not, however, make the concept of an ideal human nature either unintelligible or useless. (3) Butler would say that we could not form this concept at all unless we had the power of reflecting upon actions and characters and comparing them in respect of moral worth. Moral worth is evidently a characteristic of a quite peculiar kind. It is not considered by the other sciences; and so the ideal gases of physics or the ideal circles of geometry may be called " purely positive ideals " and must be contrasted with the ideal human nature which is contemplated by ethics. The power of recognising this peculiar characteristic is one which we plainly do have and do constantly use. It is the cognitive aspect of what Butler calls *Conscience*. With these explanations it seems to me that Butler's conception of an ideal human nature is sound, and that it is true to say that virtue consists in acting in accordance with this nature, and that vice is acting against it.

We can now consider in greater detail how Butler supposes human nature to be constituted. In all men he distinguishes four kinds of propensities or springs of action : (1) There are what he calls " particular passions or affections ". These are what we should call impulses to or aversions from particular kinds of objects. Hunger, sexual desire, anger, envy, sympathy, etc., would be examples of these. It is obvious that some of them mainly benefit the agent and that others mainly benefit other people. But we cannot reduce the former to self-love or the latter to benevolence. We shall go more fully into this very important doctrine of Butler's later. (2) There is the general principle of cool self-love. By this Butler means the tendency to seek the maximum happiness for ourselves over the whole course of our lives. It is essentially a rational calculating principle which leads us to check particular impulses and to co-ordinate them with each other in such a way as to maximise our total happiness in the long run. (3) There is the general principle of benevolence. This, again, is a rational calculating principle, which must be sharply distinguished from a mere impulsive sympathy with people whom we see in distress. It is the principle which makes us try to maximise the general happiness according to a rational scheme and without regard to persons. I think it would be fair to say that the ideal of the Charity Organisation Society is benevolence in Butler's sense. (4) There is the principle of Conscience which is supreme over all the rest in authority. In ideal human nature conscience is supreme over self-love and benevolence ; *i.e.*, it determines how far each of these principles is to be carried. Self-love and benevolence in their turn are superior to the particular impulses ; *i.e.*, they determine when and to what extent each shall be gratified. In any actual man self-love may overpower conscience and so spread itself at the expense of benevolence. We then get the coolly selfish man. Or benevolence may overpower conscience and exercise itself at the expense of proper prudence. This happens when a man neglects self-culture and all reasonable care for his health and happiness in order to work for the general welfare. Butler holds that both these excesses are wrong. We do not indeed, as a rule, blame the latter as much as the former. But we do blame it to some extent on calm reflection. We blame the imprudently benevolent man less than the coolly selfish man, partly because his fault is an uncommon one, and partly because it may be beneficial to society to have some men who are too benevolent when there are so many who are not benevolent enough. Butler does not mention this last reason ; but I have no doubt that he would have accepted it, since he holds that the faulty behaviour of individuals is often overruled by Providence for the general good.

Particular impulse, again, may be too strong for self-love or for benevolence or for both. *E.g.*, revenge often leads people to actions which are inconsistent with both benevolence and self-love, and ill-regulated sympathy may have the same effect. In the latter case we have the man who gives excessively to undeserving cases which happen to move his emotions, and who equally violates prudence by the extent of his gifts and benevolence by his neglect of more deserving but less spectacular cases. Butler makes the profoundly true remark that there is far too little self-love in the world ; what we need is not *less self-love* but *more benevolence*. Self-love is continually overcome by particular impulses like pride, envy, anger, etc., and this is disastrous both to the happiness of the individual and to the welfare of society at large. Self-love is not indeed an adequate principle of action. But it is at least rational and coherent so far as it goes ; and, if people really acted on it consistently, taking due account of the pleasures of sympathy and gratitude, and weighing them against those of pride, anger, and lust, their external actions would not differ greatly from those which benevolence would dictate. This seems to me to be perfectly true. Those actions which are most disastrous to others are nearly always such as no person who was clear-sightedly aiming at the maximum amount of happiness for himself would dream of doing. We have an almost perfect example of Butler's contention in the action of France towards Germany since the war of

1914 to 1918. It has been admirably adapted to producing the maximum inconvenience for both parties, and, if the French had acted simply from enlightened self-interest instead of malice and blind fear, they and all other nations would now be far better off.

The ideal human nature, then, consists of particular impulses duly subordinated to self-love and benevolence, and of these general principles in turn duly subordinated to the supreme principle of conscience. This seems to me to be perfectly correct so far as it goes; and I will now consider in rather more detail each of these constituents of human nature.

1. *Particular Impulses.*—Butler's first task is to show that these cannot be reduced to self-love, as many people have thought before and since his time. It is easy to see that he is right. The object of self-love is one's own maximum happiness over the whole course of one's life. The object of hunger is food; the object of revenge is to give pain to someone who we think has injured us; the object of sympathy is to give another man pleasure. Each of these particular impulses has its own particular object, whilst self-love has a general object, viz., one's own maximum happiness. Again, these particular impulses often conflict with self-love, and this is equally true of those which we are inclined to praise and those which we are inclined to blame. Nor is this simply a question of intellectual mistakes about what will make us happy. A man under the influence of a strong particular impulse, such as rage or parental affection, will often do things which he knows at the time to be imprudent.

In a footnote Butler takes as an example Hobbes's definition of " pity " as " fear felt for oneself at the sight of another's distress". His refutation is so short and so annihilating that I will give the substance of it as a model of philosophical reasoning. He points out (*a*) that, on this definition, a sympathetic man is *ipso facto* a man who is nervous about his own safety, and the more sympathetic he is the more cowardly he will be. This is obviously contrary to fact. (*b*) We admire people for being sympathetic to distress ; we have not the least tendency to admire them for being nervously anxious about their own safety. If Hobbes were right admiration for sympathy would involve admiration for timidity. (*c*) Hobbes mentions the fact that we tend specially to sympathise with the troubles of our friends, and he tries to account for it. But, on Hobbes's definition, this would mean that we feel particularly nervous for ourselves when we see a friend in distress. Now, in the first place, it may be doubted whether we do feel any more nervous for ourselves when we see a friend in distress than when we see a stranger in the same situation. On the other hand, it is quite certain that we do feel more sympathy for the distress of a friend than for that of a stranger. Hence it is impossible that sympathy can be what Hobbes says that it is. Butler himself holds that when we see a man in distress our state of mind may be a mixture of three states. One is genuine sympathy, *i.e.*, a direct impulse to relieve his pain. Another is thankfulness at the contrast between our good fortune and his ill luck. A third is the feeling of anxiety about our own future described by Hobbes. These three may be present in varying proportions, and some of them may be wholly absent in a particular case. But it is only the first that any plain man means by " sympathy " or " pity ". Butler makes a very true observation about this theory of Hobbes. He says that it is the kind of mistake which no one but a philosopher would make. Hobbes has a general philosophical theory that all action must necessarily be selfish ; and so he has to force sympathy, which is an apparent exception, into accord with this theory. He thus comes into open conflict with common-sense. But, although common-sense here happens to be right and the philosopher to be wrong, I should say that this is no reason to prefer common-sense to philosophy. Common-sense would *feel* that Hobbes is wrong, but it would be quite unable to say *why* he is wrong. It would have to content itself with calling him names. The only cure for bad philosophy is better philosophy ; a mere return to common-sense is no remedy.

We can now leave Hobbes to his fate, and return to the general question of the relation of our particular impulses to self-love. Why should it seem plausible to reduce particular impulses, like hunger and revenge and sympathy, to self-love ? The plausibility arises, as Butler points out, from two confusions. (i) We confuse the ownership of an impulse with its object. All our impulses, no matter what their objects may be, are *ours*. They all *belong to* the self. This is as true of sympathy, which is directed to others, as of hunger, which is directed to modifying a state of oneself. (ii) Again, the satisfaction of any impulse is *my* satisfaction. *I* get the pleasure of satisfied desire equally whether the desire which I indulge be covetousness or malice or pity. So it is true that all impulses *belong to* a self, and that the carrying out of any impulse as such *gives pleasure to* that self. But it is not true that all impulses have for their objects states of the self whose impulses they are. And it is not true that the object of any of them is the general happiness of the self who owns them. Neither sympathy

nor malice is directed to producing the happiness of the
self who owns these impulses. One is directed to producing
happiness in another person, and the other is directed to
producing misery in another person. Thus there is no
essential contrariety between any impulse and self-love.
The satisfaction of any of my impulses as such gives me
pleasure, and this is a factor in that total happiness of
myself at which self-love aims. And self-love can gain its
end only by allowing the various special impulses to pass
into action. On the other hand, no impulse can be identified
with self-love. The relation of particular impulses to self-
love is that of means to end, or of raw materials to finished
product.

All this is true and very important. But to make it
quite satisfactory it is necessary, I think, to draw some
distinctions which Butler does not. (i) We must distinguish
between those pleasures which consist in the fulfilment of
pre-existing desires and those which do not. Certain sensations are intrinsically pleasant, *e.g.*, the smell of violets or
the taste of sugar. Others are intrinsically unpleasant,
e.g., the smell of sulphuretted hydrogen or the feel of a
burn. We must therefore distinguish between intrinsic
pleasures and pains and the pleasures and pains of satisfied
or frustrated impulse. All fulfilment of impulse is pleasant
for the moment at least ; and all prolonged frustration of
impulse is unpleasant. This kind of pleasure and pain is
quite independent of the object of the impulse. Now these
two kinds of pleasure and pain can be combined in various
ways. Suppose I am hungry and eat some specially nice
food. I have then both the intrinsically pleasant sensation
of taste and also the pleasure of satisfying my hunger.
A shipwrecked sailor who found some putrid meat or dined

off the cabin-boy would enjoy the pleasure of satisfying his hunger accompanied by intrinsically unpleasant sensations of taste. A *bon-vivant* towards the end of a long dinner might get an intrinsically pleasant sensation of taste from his savoury although he was no longer hungry and therefore did not get the pleasures of satisfying his hunger.

(ii) I think that we must distinguish between the object of an impulse, its exciting cause, what will in fact satisfy it, and the collateral effects of satisfying it. Butler lumps together hunger and sympathy, and says that the object of one is food and the object of the other is the distresses of our fellow-men. Now, in the first place, the word " hunger " is ambiguous. It may mean certain organic sensations which are generally caused by lack of food. Or it may mean an impulse to eat which generally accompanies these. Butler evidently uses the word in the latter sense. But, even in this sense, it seems to me inaccurate to say that the object of hunger is food. It would be equally true to say that the object of a butcher going to market is food ; but he may not be hungry. The object or aim of hunger is *to eat food*. The object of the butcher is to buy it as cheaply and sell it as dearly as possible. In fact the object of an impulse is never, strictly speaking, a thing or person ; it is always to change or to preserve some state of a thing or person. So much for the object or aim of an impulse.

Now, as we eat, the impulse of hunger is gradually satisfied, and this is pleasant. If we are continually prevented from eating when we are hungry this continued frustration of the impulse is unpleasant. Lastly, the process of satisfying our hunger has the collateral effect of producing sensations of taste which may be intrinsically pleasant or unpleasant according to the nature of the food and the tastes of the eater. I would say then that the exciting cause of the impulse of hunger is lack of food, accompanied in general by certain characteristic organic sensations ; that its aim or object is the eating of food ; that its collateral effects are sensations of taste ; and that it is accompanied by satisfaction or dissatisfaction according to whether we get food or are unable to do so. Now let us consider pity from the same points of view. The exciting cause is the sight of another person, particularly a friend or relation, in distress. The aim or object of it is to relieve the distress. The collateral effects of its exercise are the gradual relief of the distress, feelings of gratitude in the sufferer's mind, and so on. Lastly, in so far as we are able to exercise the impulse, there is a pleasant feeling of satisfaction in our minds ; and, in so far as we are prevented from doing so, there is an unpleasant feeling of frustration.

Now, in considering the relations between the various particular impulses and the general principles of self-love and benevolence, it is very important to bear these distinctions in mind. Butler says that some particular impulses are more closely connected with self-love and others with benevolence. He gives examples, but he does not carry the analysis further. We can now state the whole case much more fully and clearly. (a) Some impulses have their exciting causes in the agent, some in inanimate objects, and some in other persons. Hunger is excited by one's own lack of food and the organic sensations which accompany it ; covetousness may be excited by the sight of a book or a picture ; pity is excited by another man's distress. (b) Some impulses aim at producing results within the agent himself ; some aim at producing results in other men ; and some aim at effecting changes in inanimate objects. Thus hunger aims at one's own eating ; pity aims at the relief of another man's distress ; and blind rage may aim at smashing plates or furniture. (c) The collateral effects of satisfying an impulse may be in the agent, or in others, or in both. Probably there are always collateral effects in the agent himself, and nearly always in other men too. But sometimes the collateral effects in the agent predominate, and sometimes those produced in other men are much more important. The collateral effects of satisfying hunger are, under ordinary circumstances, almost wholly confined to the agent. The collateral effects of the exercise of pity are mostly in the sufferer and the spectators, though there are always some in the agent. The collateral effects of ambition are divided pretty equally between self and others. Lastly, (d), the pleasures of satisfied impulse and the pains of frustrated impulse are naturally confined to the owner of the impulse.

It is evident that those particular impulses which aim at producing or maintaining states of the agent himself, and those whose collateral effects are mainly confined to the agent, will be of most interest to self-love. Hunger is a typical example. Those impulses which aim at producing or altering or maintaining states in other men, and whose collateral effects are mainly confined to others, will be of most interest to benevolence. Sympathy and resentment are typical examples. There will be some impulses which almost equally concern self-love and benevolence. For it may be that they aim at producing a certain state in others, but that their collateral effects are mainly in the agent ; or conversely. Anger against those whom we cannot hurt is aimed against them but mainly affects ourselves. The

question where the exciting cause of the impulse is situated
is not of much importance for our present purpose, though
it is likely that most impulses whose exciting causes are within
the agent also aim at producing changes in his own state.
The pleasures of satisfaction and the pains of frustration concern self-love alone, since they can be felt only by the agent.

It is important to notice that actions which were
originally done from particular impulses may come to be
done from self-love or from benevolence. As babies we eat
and drink simply because we are hungry or thirsty. But
in course of time we find that the satisfaction of hunger
and thirst is pleasant, and also that the collateral sensations
of eating certain foods and drinking certain wines are
intrinsically pleasant. Self-love may then induce us to
take a great deal of exercise so as to make ourselves
thoroughly hungry and thirsty, and may then make us go
to a restaurant and choose just those dishes and wines
which we know will give intrinsically pleasant sensations
in addition to the agreeable experience of satisfying our
hunger and thirst. Again, a boy may play cricket simply
because he likes it ; but, when he grows older, he may
devote his half-holidays to playing cricket with boy scouts
from benevolence, although he is no longer specially keen
on the game, and although he could enjoy himself more in
other ways.

It sounds to us odd when Butler says that ambition and
hunger are just as disinterested as pity and malice. He is
perfectly right, in his own sense of " disinterested ", and it is
a very important sense. It is true that neither ambition
nor hunger aims at one's own happiness. The object of one
is power over others, the object of the other is to eat food.
True, the satisfaction of either is *my* satisfaction ; but so too

is the satisfaction of pity or malice. If by " disinterested " you mean " not done with the motive of maximising one's own happiness on the whole ", it is quite clear that hunger and ambition can lead only to disinterested actions. The appearance of paradox in Butler's statements is explained by the distinctions which we have drawn. It *is* true that ambition and hunger are more closely connected with self-love than are pity and malice. For they do aim at the production and modification of states of ourselves, although they do not aim at our own greatest happiness ; whereas pity and malice aim at producing and modifying states of other men, and the collateral effects of their exercise are also largely confined to others. Thus both Butler and common-sense are here right, and the apparent difference between them is removed by clearly stating certain distinctions which are liable to be overlooked.

2. *Self-love and Benevolence.*—We can now deal in detail with the two general principles of self-love and benevolence. Butler seems to me to be clearer about the former than about the latter. I have assumed throughout that he regards benevolence as a general principle which impels us to maximise the happiness of humanity without regard to persons, just as he certainly regards self-love as a general principle leading us to maximise our own total happiness. I think that this is what he does mean. But he sometimes tends to drop benevolence, as a general principle co-ordinate with self-love, rather out of sight, and to talk of it as if it were just one of the particular impulses. Thus he says in the *First Sermon* that benevolence undoubtedly exists and is compatible with self-love, but the examples which he gives are in fact particular impulses which aim at the benefit

of some particular person, *e.g.*, paternal and filial affection. He says that, if you grant that paternal and filial affection exist, you must grant that benevolence exists. This is a mistake. He might as well say that, if you grant that hunger exists, you must grant that self-love exists. Really paternal affection is just as much a particular impulse as hunger, and it can no more be identified with benevolence than hunger can be identified with self-love. I think that he makes such apparent mistakes partly because he is anxious to show that benevolence is, as such, no more contrary to self-love than is any of the particular impulses. He shows, *e.g.*, that to gratify the principle of benevolence gives just as much pleasure to the agent as to gratify any particular impulse, such as hunger or revenge. It is true that excessive indulgence in benevolence may conflict with self-love ; but so, as he points out, may excessive indulgence of any particular impulse, such as thirst or anger. In fact benevolence is related to self-love in exactly the same way as any particular impulse is related to self-love. So far he is perfectly right. But this identity of relation seems sometimes to blind Butler to the intrinsic difference between benevolence, which is a general principle, and the particular impulses which aim at producing happiness in certain particular men or classes of men, *e.g.*, patriotism or paternal affection.

I think that there is undoubtedly a general principle of benevolence ; and I think that Butler held this too, though he does not always make this clear. The main business of benevolence is to control and organise those impulses which aim at producing changes in others, or whose collateral effects are mainly in others. Thus it has to do with pity, resentment, paternal affection, and so on. The main business of self-love is to control and organise those impulses which aim at producing states in oneself, or whose collateral effects are largely in oneself. From the point of view of self-love benevolence is simply one impulse among others, like hunger, resentment, etc. But it is equally true that, from the point of view of benevolence, self-love is only one impulse among others. The prudent person may need to check his excessive benevolence towards mankind in general, just as he has to check blind anger or a tendency to over-eating. The benevolent person may need to check his excessive prudence, just as he has to check the special impulse to lose his temper.

There are, however, two respects in which self-love and benevolence seem to me to be not perfectly on a level. Conscience approves both of self-love and of benevolence in their proper degrees. But I think it is clear that conscience rates benevolence higher than self-love. It would hold that it is possible, though not easy, to have too much benevolence, but that you could quite easily have too much self-love, though in fact most people have too little. Again, from a purely psychological point of view, self-love and benevolence are not quite co-ordinate. The putting into action of *any* tendency, including benevolence, is as such pleasant to the agent, and so ministers in its degree to self-love. But the putting into action of our conative tendencies is not as such a source of happiness to others. Others may be affected either pleasurably or painfully according to the nature of the impulse which I exercise. But I get a certain amount of pleasure from the mere fact that I am doing what I want to do, quite apart from whether the object of the action is my own happiness or whether its collateral consequences are pleasant sensations in myself. Thus no action of mine can be *completely* hostile to self-love, though the collateral results of the action may be so unpleasant for me that cool self-love would not on the whole sanction it. But the gratification of many impulses may be completely hostile to benevolence. If I lose my temper and blindly strike a man, self-love gets something out of the transaction, viz., the momentary feeling of satisfaction at fulfilling an impulse, even though the remoter consequences may be so unpleasant for me that cool self-love would have prevented the action. But benevolence gets nothing out of the transaction at all ; it is wholly hostile to it.

As we have said, Butler holds that pure self-love and pure benevolence would lead to very much the same external actions, because the collateral results of most actions really make about as much for the happiness of the agent as for that of others. In this connexion he makes two profoundly true and important observations. (i) If you want to make yourself as happy as possible it is fatal to keep this object constantly before your mind. The happiest people are those who are pretty fully occupied with some activity which they feel to be honourable and useful and which they perform with reasonable success. The most wretched lives are led by men who have nothing to do but think of their own happiness and scheme for it. Happiness which is deliberately sought generally turns out to be disappointing, and the self-conscious egoist divides his time between wanting what he has not and not wanting what he has. (ii) The second point which Butler makes is that the common opinion that there is an inevitable conflict between self-love and benevolence is a fallacy based on the common confusion between enjoyment itself and the means of enjoyment. If I have a certain sum of money, it is evident that the more I spend on myself the less I shall have to spend on others, and conversely. It therefore looks at first sight as if self-love and benevolence must necessarily conflict. But, as Butler says, money and other kinds of property are not themselves happiness; they are only material objects which produce happiness by being used in certain ways. Now it is certain that both spending money on myself and spending it on others may give me happiness. If I already spend a good deal on myself it is quite likely that I shall gain more happiness by spending some of it on others than I shall lose by spending that much less on myself. This is certainly true; and the confusion between happiness and the means to happiness, which Butler here explains, is constantly made. The miser illustrates the typical and exaggerated form of this mistake; but nearly every one makes it to some extent.

I think there is only one point in Butler's theory of the substantial identity of the conduct dictated by self-love and by benevolence which needs criticism. It assumes an isolated purely selfish man in a society of people who are ruled by benevolence as well as by self-love and who have organised their social life accordingly. In such a case it certainly would pay this individual to act very much as the principle of benevolence would dictate. It is not so clear that it would pay to act in this way in a community of men who were all quite devoid of benevolence. All that we can say is that every one in such a society, if it could exist at all, would probably be very miserable; but whether one of them would be rendered less miserable by performing externally benevolent actions it is difficult to say. But, if we suppose Butler to mean that, taking men as they are, and taking the institutions which such men have made for themselves, enlightened self-interest would dictate a line of conduct not very different from that which benevolence would dictate, he seems to be right.

This fact, of course, makes it always difficult to say how far any particular action has been due to benevolence and how far to self-love. What is certain is that both principles exist, and that very few actions are due to one without any admixture of the other. Sometimes we can see pretty clearly which principle has predominated, but this is as far as we can safely go. Exactly the same difficulty arises as Butler points out, over self-love and the particular impulses. It is often impossible to say whether a certain course of action was due to self-love or to a particular impulse for power or money. All that we know for certain is that both principles exist and that they mix in all proportions. Sometimes the onlookers can tell more accurately than the agent what principle predominated, because they are less likely to be biased.

3. *Conscience.*—We come now to Butler's supreme principle of conscience. According to him this has two aspects, a purely cognitive and an authoritative. In addition, I think we must say that it is an active principle ; *i.e.*, that it really does cause, check, and modify actions. In its cognitive aspect it is a principle of reflection. Its subject-matter is the actions, characters, and intentions of men. But it reflects on these from a particular point of view. In one sense we are reflecting on our actions when we merely recall them in memory and note that some turned out fortunately and others unfortunately. But we should not call such reflection an act of conscience, but only an act of retrospection. The peculiarity of conscience is that it

reflects on actions from the point of view of their rightness or wrongness. The very fact that we use words like " right ", " wrong ", " duty ", etc., shows that there is an intellectual faculty within us which recognises the terms denoted by these names. Otherwise such words would be as meaningless to us as the words " black " and " white " to a man born blind. We clearly distinguish between a right action and one that happened to turn out fortunately. And we clearly distinguish between a wrong action and one that happened to turn out unfortunately. Again, we distinguish between mere unintentional hurt and deliberate injury. Conscience is indifferent to the former and condemns the latter. Finally, conscience recognises a certain appropriateness between wrong-doing and pain and between right-doing and happiness ; i.e., it recognises the fact of merit or desert. If we see a man being hurt we judge the situation quite differently according to whether we think that he is innocent or that he is being punished for some wrong act.

So we may say that conscience, on its cognitive side, is a faculty which reflects on characters, actions, and intentions, with a special view to their goodness or badness, rightness or wrongness. And it further judges that pain is appropriate to wrong-doing, and happiness to right-doing. Lastly, we must add that it does not judge of actions or intentions in isolation, but judges them in reference to the ideal nature of the agent. The ideal nature of a child or a lunatic is different from that of a sane grown man, and so conscience takes a different view of the same action when performed by one or the other. Butler apparently assumes that, although the ideal nature of a child or a lunatic is different from that of a sane grown man, the ideal nature of all mature men is identical. No doubt we

have to assume this in practice ; but it seems hardly likely
to be strictly true.   It is hard to draw a perfectly sharp
line between maturity and immaturity, or between sanity
and insanity.

By saying that conscience has supreme authority Butler
means that we regard the pronouncements of conscience,
not simply as interesting or uninteresting statements of
fact, and not simply as reasons to be balanced against
others, but as *conclusive* reasons for or against doing the
actions about which it pronounces.   The fact that conscience
pronounces an act to be wrong is admittedly one motive
against doing it.   But so too is the fact that self-love
condemns it as imprudent, or that benevolence condemns
it as likely to diminish the general happiness.   Thus far
conscience, self-love, and benevolence are all on a level.
They are all capable of providing motives for acting or
abstaining from action.   The difference lies in their respective
authority, *i.e.*, in the relative strength which they *ought* to
have and which they *would* have in an ideal human being.
If self-love and benevolence conflict over some proposed
course of action there is nothing in the nature of either
which gives it authority over the other.   Sometimes it will
be right for self-love to give way to benevolence, and sometimes it will be right for benevolence to give way to self-love.
But conscience is not in this position.   In an ideal man
conscience would not simply take turns with benevolence
and self-love.   If benevolence or self-love conflict with
conscience it is always they, and never it, which should
give way ;   and, if they conflict with each other, it is
conscience, and it alone, which has the right to decide
between them.   In any actual man conscience is often
overpowered by self-love or benevolence, just as they are

often overpowered by particular impulses. But we recognise the *moral right* of conscience to be supreme, even when we find that it lacks the necessary *psychological power*.

I do not think that Butler means to say that every trivial detail of our lives must be solemnly debated before the tribunal of conscience. Just as the man whose aim is to secure his own maximum happiness best secures that end by not constantly thinking about it, so I should say that the man who wants always to act conscientiously will often do best by not making this his explicit motive. So long as our actions are those which conscience would approve, if we carefully considered the question, the supremacy of conscience is preserved, even though we have acted from immediate impulse or self-love or benevolence. Conscience, *e.g.*, approves of a due measure of parental affection ; but it is much better for this affection to be felt spontaneously than to be imposed on a parent by conscience as a duty. In fact the main function of conscience is regulative. The materials both of good and of evil are supplied by the particular impulses. These are organised in the first instance by self-love and benevolence, and these in turn are co-ordinated and regulated by conscience. In a well-bred and well-trained man a great deal of this organisation has become habitual, and in ninety-nine cases out of a hundred he does the right things without having to think whether or why they are right. It is only in the hundredth specially perplexing or specially alluring situation that an explicit appeal to conscience has to be made.

It remains to say something about two rather curious and difficult points in Butler's theory. (1) Although he constantly asserts the supremacy of conscience, yet there are one or two passages in which he seems to make self-love co-ordinate with it. In one place he actually says that no action is consistent with human nature if it violates *either* reasonable self-love or conscience. In another famous passage he seems to admit that, if we reflect coolly, we can justify no course of action which will be contrary to our happiness. The former passage I cannot explain away; it seems to be simply an inconsistency. But the latter occurs in the course of an argument in which he is trying to prove to an objector that there is no real conflict between conscience and enlightened self-love. I think it is clear from the context that he is not here asserting his own view, but is simply making a hypothetical concession to an imaginary opponent. He goes on to argue thus. Even if you grant that it can never be right to go against your own greatest happiness, yet you ought to obey conscience in cases of apparent conflict between it and self-love. For it is very difficult to tell what will make for your own greatest happiness even in this life, and it is always possible that there is another life after this. On the other hand, the dictates of conscience are often quite clear. Thus we can be far more certain about what is right than what is to our own ultimate interest; and therefore, in an apparent conflict between the two, conscience should be followed since we cannot be sure that this is not really to our own interest.

So Butler would probably answer that the question whether conscience is superior to self-love or co-ordinate with it is of merely academic interest. I do not think that this answer can be accepted. In the first place, as moralists we want to know what *should be* the relative positions of conscience and self-love. And it is no answer to this question to say that it is not practically important. Secondly, we may grant all that Butler says about the extreme uncertainty as to what is to our own ultimate interest. But the deliveries of conscience are by no means so certain and unambiguous in most cases as Butler makes out. And even if they were, it is not obvious why they should be assumed to be likely to be a better guide to our own interest than the best opinion that we could reach by reflecting directly on that subject.

(2) The other doubtful point is Butler's view about the value of happiness. In one place he says that it is manifest that nothing can be of consequence to mankind or to any creature but happiness. And he goes on to assert that all common virtues and vices can be traced up to benevolence and the lack of it. Finally, in the same sermon he says that benevolence seems in the strictest sense to include all that is good and worthy. Now, if these statements be accepted at their face-value, Butler was a Utilitarian ; *i.e.*, he thought that happiness is the only intrinsic good and that virtue consists in promoting happiness. But it is to be noted that these remarks occur in the sermon on the *Love of our Neighbour*, where he is specially concerned to recommend benevolence to people who were sadly lacking in it. And even here he adds a footnote in which he distinctly says that there are certain actions and dispositions which are approved altogether apart from their probable effect on general happiness. He asserts this still more strongly in the *Dissertation on Virtue*, which is a later and more formal work. So I think it is clear that his considered opinion is against Utilitarianism.

But in both these works he seems to take the interesting view that God may be a Utilitarian, though this is no reason for our being so. It may be that God's sole ultimate motive is to maximise the total amount of happiness in the universe. But, even if this be the only thing of which he approves as an end, he has so made us that we directly approve of other tendencies beside benevolence, *e.g.*, justice and truth-telling. And he has provided us with the faculty of conscience, which tells us that it is our duty to act in accordance with these principles no matter whether such action seems to us likely to increase the general happiness or not. It is quite possible that God may have given us this direct approval of truth-telling and justice, not because he directly approves of them, but because he knows that it will in fact make for the greatest happiness on the whole if we act justly and speak the truth regardless of the apparent consequences to ourselves and others. If so, that is his business and not ours. Our business is to act in accordance with our consciences, and only to promote the general happiness by such means as conscience approves, even though we may think that we could promote it more in certain cases by lying or partiality. If God does over-rule our conscientious actions in such a way that they do make for the greatest possible happiness even when they seem to us unlikely to have that effect, so much the better. It makes no difference to our duty whether this be so or not.

It is of course plain that Butler leaves undiscussed many questions with which any complete treatise on Ethics ought to deal. We should like to know whether there is any feature common and peculiar to right actions, which we could use as a criterion of rightness and wrongness. And we should like to know how, when the same conscience at different times, or different consciences at the same time, seem to issue conflicting orders, we are to tell which is genuine and which is spurious. To such questions Butler does not attempt to give an answer, whilst the Utilitarians on the one hand and Kant on the other do give their respective very different answers to it. But, though his system is incomplete, it does seem to contain the prolegomena to any system of ethics that can claim to do justice to the facts of moral experience.

CHAPTER IV

Hume

THE best account of Hume's theory of ethics is to be found in his *Enquiry Concerning the Principles of Morals*. This is a treatise specially devoted to ethics. Spinoza's ethical theory is only a part, though a vitally important part, of an elaborate metaphysical theory of the universe. Hume had no such system, and believed it to be impossible for human beings to build one capable of standing. Still, he had certain very definite epistemological principles or prejudices, and these inevitably determined and coloured his ethical theories. The two men were in many ways extremely unlike each other in disposition, outlook, training, and experience ; and the spirit of their respective philosophical writings is profoundly different. Yet, in spite of real and important disagreements, we shall find several points of fundamental similarity between the ethical views of Hume and Spinoza.

It will be best, in the case of Hume, to take first that part of ethical theory which we took last in the case of Spinoza, viz., the question of the meaning and analysis of ethical predicates and propositions. Hume's doctrine is the following. There is a certain specific kind of emotion which nearly all human beings feel from time to time. This is the emotion of *Approval* or *Disapproval*. It is called forth by the contemplation of certain objects, and it is directed towards those objects. Now for Hume the

statement " x is good " *means* the same as the statement
" x is such that the contemplation of it would call forth an
emotion of approval towards it in all or most men ". The
definition of " x is bad " would be the same with " disapproval " substituted for " approval ".

The following points may be noticed at once. (1) It
makes " good " and " bad " to be relational predicates.
Their very meaning involves a relation to the human species.
So far it resembles Spinoza's view. (2) It is a psychological
theory, since it defines " good " and " bad " by reference
to certain kinds of mental state, viz., certain kinds of
emotion. In this it differs from Spinoza's view. " Good "
and " bad ", for him, were definable in terms of specific
powers and activities. No reference to emotion entered
into the *definition,* though he held that the feelings of
pleasure and pain are trustworthy *signs* of the presence of
good and evil respectively. (3) Though Hume's theory is
relational and psychological, in the senses explained, it is
not subjective in the sense that it leaves no room for
argument and refutation in ethical matters. It would be
so if it asserted that " x is good " means " I here and now
have an emotion of approval towards x ". Such statements,
if false, could hardly be refuted ; and all argument about
them would be unprofitable. But Hume's theory is that
" x is good " means that the contemplation of x will call
forth an emotion of approval in all or most men on all or
most occasions. Such statements as this can be argued
about and supported or refuted by observation and collection
of statistics. On Hume's theory a man might quite well
make the judgment that x is good, though the contemplation
of x evoked in him at the time no emotion at all or an
emotion of disapproval. For he might acknowledge that

x evokes in most men at most times when they contemplate it an emotion of approval. I think that it is even possible on Hume's theory for a man *first* to judge that x is good, and then, *in consequence of* this judgment, to begin to feel approval of x. For most of us like to feel the same kind of emotions in given circumstances as others feel, especially if we respect or admire the others. And so the mere fact that I believe that most people have a feeling of approval in contemplating x may cause me to feel an emotion of approval in contemplating x which I should not otherwise have felt. (4) I have laboured these points because it is important to see at the outset that such a theory as Hume's does not inevitably lead to such extreme paradoxes that we can reject it out of hand. But we must not underrate the extent to which Hume's theory conflicts with ordinary views. The common view, though it is never very articulately expressed, is presumably somewhat as follows. Certain things would be good and others would be bad whether the contemplation of them did or did not call forth emotions of approval or disapproval in all or most men. The good things call forth emotions of approval in all or most men *because* they are good and *because* men are so constituted as to feel this kind of emotion towards what they believe to be good. And the same is true, *mutatis mutandis*, of bad things. On Hume's view if men did not feel these emotions nothing would *be* good or bad ; and it is only in the rather exceptional case which I mentioned above that the judgment that x is good might precede and produce in a certain man an emotion of approval towards x.

Hume now passes to the second part of ethical theory, viz., the question : What kinds of thing are good, and what kinds are bad ? This reduces for him to the question :

Is there any characteristic common and peculiar to the things towards which all or most men feel an emotion of approval, beside the fact that they are the objects of this emotion ? Hume holds that such a question can be settled only by ordinary observation followed by an empirical generalisation. The result of his observation is that actions, qualities, and characters which are generally approved by men all fall into two classes, viz.: (1) those which are immediately pleasant either to their possessor or to other men ; and (2) those which are useful, *i.e.*, ultimately and indirectly productive of pleasure, either to their possessor or to other men. Of course these classes are not mutually exclusive. A benevolent act may be directly pleasant to the agent and to spectators whilst it is useful to the person for whose benefit it is done. And an industrious character is useful both to its possessor and to society. Hume also finds that the converse proposition holds ; *i.e.*, everything that falls into one of these classes calls forth an emotion of approval in all or most men who contemplate it. He now generalises these observations by problematic induction, and reaches the conclusion that *all* things which are either directly pleasant or indirectly conducive to pleasure, whether in their owners or in other men, evoke the emotion of approval in all or most men ; and that *only* such things do so.

I will now make some comments on this doctrine. (1) In the first place there are two slight ambiguities to be noticed and removed. The first concerns the distinction between what is immediately pleasant and what is useful. There is an ambiguity in the word " pleasant ", which may be brought out in the following way. We should commonly say both that chocolate is pleasant and that the experience of tasting chocolate is pleasant. But we should not call chocolate itself " a pleasure ", whilst we should call the experience of tasting it " a pleasure ". A pleasure is always a mental event, such as a feeling ; or a whole of which a mental event is an essential constituent, though something non-mental may be contained as object, such as hearing a tune, tasting chocolate, etc. Now the word " pleasant " has a different meaning when applied to an experience and to a non-experience ; and the former meaning is the funda-mental one. In the first sense it denotes a *non-causal* characteristic ; in the second it denotes a *causal* characteristic, *i.e.*, a more or less permanent tendency to produce, in co-operation with other factors, a result of a certain kind. Thus to say that a certain tune is pleasant means that it is such that the experience of hearing it will at most times and in most men be pleasant in the non-causal sense, *i.e.*, will be a pleasure. It must be noted that the same thing may be cognised in several different ways ; *e.g.*, we can see a bit of chocolate instead of tasting it, we can feel a picture instead of seeing it, and so on. Now it will often happen that some of these different modes of cognising a given object are pleasant experiences whilst the others are neutral. But I think that we call an object pleasant if there be *any* way of cognising it which is a pleasant experience to most men at most times.

I can now define the statement that x is " immediately pleasant ". It means that x is either (*a*) a pleasant experience, or (*b*) is such that there is at least one mode of cognising it which is for most men and at most times a pleasant experience. We can now deal with the statement that x is " useful ". A thing is useful without being pleasant when it is not itself a pleasure, and when no mode of cognising it is a pleasure, but when it is a cause-factor in the production of pleasures. It is of course quite possible that one and the same event should be non-causally pleasant, causally pleasant, and useful. Most pleasant experiences are causally pleasant too, since the introspective contemplation of one's own pleasures is itself as a rule a pleasure. And no doubt they are also often cause-factors tending to produce other pleasant experiences in the future, and are thus useful.

The second ambiguity is this. Ought we not to substitute " believed to be " for " are " in Hume's generalisation ? Ought we not to say that the emotion of approval is called forth by all those things and only those things which *are believed* by the observer to be immediately pleasant or useful ? Presumably things would call forth this emotion if they were believed to have the property, even though they did not in fact have it ; and presumably they would not call forth the emotion if they were believed not to have the property, even though they in fact had it. On the other hand, the term " belief " must be taken rather widely if we are not to fall into an opposite error. It must be taken to include what I should call " quasi-belief " ; *i.e.*, cases in which we are not explicitly believing or disbelieving so-and-so, but are acting *as if* we believed it, and, if challenged, would explicitly believe it. I do not think that Hume would have objected to either of these modifications in his doctrine ; and I shall henceforth assume that they have been made.

(2) My second comment is this. If " Hedonism " be defined as the theory that there is a universal and reciprocal connexion between goodness and pleasantness, then Hume is a hedonist. For he has asserted that everything that is good, in his sense, is pleasant or conducive to pleasure ; and that everything which is pleasant or conducive to

pleasure is, in his sense, good. But there are three fundamentally different possible types of hedonism, and Hume's
is perhaps the least usual kind. We may first divide
hedonistic theories into *Analytic* and *Synthetic Hedonism*.
Analytic hedonism asserts that to be " good " *means* to be
" pleasant or conducive to pleasure ". This is plainly not
Hume's view. He is then a synthetic hedonist. But
synthetic hedonism may take two forms, *a priori* and
empirical. The *a priori* synthetic hedonist, whilst denying
that " good " means " pleasant or conducive to pleasure ",
holds that he can see a necessary and reciprocal connexion
between the two characteristics, such as we can see between
the two characteristics of being equilateral and being equiangular in the case of a triangle. Anything that was good
would necessarily be pleasant or conducive to pleasure, and
conversely. This is the view of such a hedonist as Sidgwick ;
but it is plainly not Hume's view. The connexion for him
is contingent, and the evidence for it is observation and
empirical generalisation thereof. He is thus an empirical
hedonist. It is logically possible that all or most men should
have been so constituted as to feel approval when they
contemplated what is painful or conducive to pain in human
beings. If so, character and conduct of this kind would
have been good. Or, again, men might have been so constituted that they simply did not have the emotions of
approval or disapproval at all. If so, nothing would have
been either good or bad.

It is then, according to Hume, an empirical and contingent fact that men are so constituted as to feel approval
and disapproval, and that they are so constituted that their
approvals and disapprovals take the particular direction
which he has found that they do take. I propose to call

the innate disposition to feel emotions of approval and disapproval from time to time the *Moral Sentiment*. In order to account for the particular direction which these emotions take in human beings Hume holds that it is necessary to postulate the existence in them of another sentiment, which he calls that of *Benevolence* or *Humanity*. Men are so constituted that every man tends to feel pleased when he contemplates the happiness of any human being and tends to feel displeased when he thinks of any human being as unhappy. There are four points to notice about this emotional disposition. (i) It is common to all, or nearly all, men, like the sexual instinct. (ii) It is excited by the perception or the thought of *any* human being, as such, in a state of happiness or misery. It thus differs, *e.g.*, from self-love or patriotic sentiment. These are no doubt common to most men ; but the object which evokes them is a certain man or a certain restricted class of men, not any man as such. (iii) The sentiment of humanity determines the particular direction which the emotions of approval and disapproval take in human beings. It is because the happiness of men is, as such, pleasing to most men that most men feel approval for qualities which they believe to be pleasant or conducive to human happiness. And it is because the unhappiness of men is, as such, displeasing to most men that most men feel disapproval for qualities which they believe to be unpleasant or conducive to human misery. (iv) The emotion of approval is itself pleasant and that of disapproval is unpleasant.

Of course Hume admits that the sentiment of humanity is often inhibited and overpowered in particular cases. The special relations in which I stand at a certain moment to a certain other man or group of men may completely inhibit the expression of the sentiment of humanity, which is concerned with them simply as human beings. This obviously happens in the case of jealousy, in war, and so on. Hume also admits that humane emotion may be felt without leading to humane action. All that he asserts is that, in the absence of special causes which excite conflicting sentiments, nearly all men do feel pleased at the thought of a fellow-man in a state of happiness and pained at the thought of a fellow-man in a state of misery. And this seems to be true.

Granted that there is this sentiment of humanity, does it explain the particular direction which the emotions of approval and disapproval take in men? I cannot see that it does. Either the sentiment of humanity is the same as the moral sentiment, or it is not. If it is, then the explanation is merely verbal. This one sentiment is called " the moral sentiment " because it expresses itself in emotions of approval and disapproval, and it is called " the sentiment of humanity " because of the particular direction which these emotions take in men. And, in any case, this identification does not seem to be plausible. To feel moral approval is not the same as to feel sympathetic pleasure, and to feel moral disapproval is not the same as to feel sympathetic pain. Let us then take the other alternative, viz., that there are two different sentiments. If we confine our attention to the positive terms in our pairs of opposites we have now three distinct factors, viz., moral approval, sympathetic pleasure, and something believed to be pleasant or useful to man. The fact to be explained is that the first is directed to the third. The fact alleged as an explanation is that the second exists and is directed to the third. But this explains nothing unless it be assumed that the direction of the first must always be determined by that of the second. And this, whether true or false, is just as ultimate, and as much or as little in need of explanation, as the original fact which we set out to explain. I cannot help thinking that there is here a latent trace of egoistic psychological hedonism in Hume's theory. I suspect that he is tacitly assuming that the fact that I direct a certain emotion on to the supposed pleasure or pain of *another* is intelligible if and only if it be mediated by a feeling of pleasure or pain in *myself*.

Hume has now to defend his theory on three fronts. (1) Against those who would question his identification of what is generally approved with what is believed to be pleasant or conducive to human happiness. (2) Against egoists, like Hobbes and Spinoza, who would object to his postulating an innate sentiment of Humanity or Benevolence, and would claim to be able to explain all the facts on purely egoistic principles. (3) Against those moralists, whom we may roughly classify as " Rationalists," who would altogether reject his analysis of ethical characteristics, and his view that we can and must determine what kinds of thing are good by ordinary observation and empirical generalisation. We will now consider these three points in turn.

(1) Hume sees that the most plausible objection to his identification of what is generally approved with what is believed to be pleasant or conducive to human happiness arises over legal justice. A particular act of justice may be extremely unpleasant to the agent, who may have to deprive his friend of something which the latter values. It may be extremely unpleasant to the person on whom it is exercised. And it may be detrimental to the general happiness. All these conditions might be realised in carrying out the provisions of a will which was correct in point of law. Yet

we should certainly approve of those concerned if they acted in accordance with the law, and disapprove of them if they did not. Hume's general solution of the difficulty is as follows. If we confined our attention to this particular act and its immediate consequences we should disapprove of it. But, as rational beings, we cannot confine our attention to this very restricted object. We shall inevitably tend to think of its remoter consequences, of the consequences of acts like this becoming prevalent, and so on ; and our reaction to this total object may be opposite to that which we should make to the more restricted object which is a part of it.

The application of this general principle to the special case of legal justice is as follows. The happiness of mankind is enormously increased on the whole by there being a set of acknowledged and rigidly enforced rules about the ownership, exchange, and bequest of property. Whatever set of rules be established there will be certain cases in which the enforcement of a rule will lead to worse results than a breach of the rule, if that breach could be taken in isolation. But a breach of an established rule never can in fact be taken in isolation. The whole utility of having rules depends on the fact that they are known to be invariable ; and, if you begin to make exceptions in hard cases, this utility will very soon vanish. Any set of rules about property, however arbitrary, so long as it is generally understood and rigidly enforced, ensures greater happiness than no rules at all or rules which cannot be relied upon.

Hume supports this doctrine of the purely utilitarian sanction for legal justice by the following considerations. It is easy, he says, to conceive of circumstances under which rules of property would be useless ; and we see, on reflection, that in such circumstances all obligation to keep the rules would cease. Three such cases can be imagined. (i) Where there is an unlimited supply of goods available to every one, as there is of air under ordinary conditions ; or where benevolence was unlimited in extension and intensity. (ii) Where there is such an extreme shortage of goods that, if they were equally divided, no one would have enough to be of any use to him. An example would be a ship-wrecked crew with one biscuit. (iii) Where it is certain that others will disobey the rules, and there is no authority to enforce them. An example would be if one were a member of an army which had got out of hand and was retreating in disorder. The actual position in ordinary life differs from all these extreme cases. There is a limited supply of goods, which is enough for all if properly distributed, and which can be increased or diminished by human action. And men are neither perfectly benevolent nor completely selfish. Under these conditions the existence and enforcement of a set of rules about property is of the utmost utility. A breach of these rules is then in general a double injury. It is always a public injury, as tending to upset confidence in a system whose whole utility depends on the confidence which is felt in it. And in most cases it is a private injury, in so far as it disappoints some man's legitimate expectation of continuing to hold such property as is guaranteed to him by the rules of his society.

Hume argues that the only alternative to his theory is that there is a natural instinct about property. This he denies on the ground of the extreme diversity of the rules about property and the extreme complexity of the notions of ownership, inheritance, contract, etc. No single instinct will account for these facts. But the principle of utility accounts both for the diversities of the rules about property

in different times and places, and for what we find common
to all of them. On the one hand, men at different times
and places are in very different situations, and so rules
about property which are useful in one state of society may
be hurtful in another. And, on the other hand, the fundamental needs of men are always the same, and the general
conditions imposed by Nature on their fulfilment are fairly
constant. This contention, I think, may show that no
instinct would be *sufficient* to account for the rules about
property, and that real or fancied utility must play an
important part. But it does not show that such an instinct
may not be *necessary* to account for the facts. The rules
about marriage are as odd as, and even more complicated
than, those about property ; and Hume's argument, if
valid about property, ought to show that the rules of
marriage have nothing to do with the sexual instinct.

Justice, Hume says, is a virtue natural to man, in the
sense that our approval of justice is the inevitable reaction
of a being who is both rational enough to consider the
remote consequences of acts and benevolent enough to
approve of human happiness. And rationality and benevolence are part of the nature of man, in the sense that
they are part of his innate constitution. Again, justice is
certainly not conventional, if this means that it presupposes
an original deliberate contract made among men when they
founded societies. For an essential part of justice is the
keeping of contracts, and so it is circular to deduce justice
from an original contract. It is conventional or artificial
only in the sense that there is no need to postulate a special
instinct for setting up rules about ownership or a special
sentiment which makes us feel disapproval at breaches of
such rules. The obvious utility of having rules of some

kind about ownership, and of rigidly enforcing them, fully explains why men have established them and why they feel strong disapproval at breaches of them. But in the details of the rules at any given time and place there is much that is conventional, traditional, and fanciful.

Hume's theory of Justice thus resembles Spinoza's, except that it is not purely egoistic, and that it is more fully worked out. Is it adequate ? In the first place, it applies at best only to a small part of justice. It professes to account for our approval of the rigid enforcement of an existing set of rules and for our disapproval of breaches of it. Plainly this is not the whole of the matter. We say that one set of rules is, on the whole, " more just " than another. And we may propose to alter some of the existing rules on the ground that they are " unjust ". Now the question whether one set of rules is juster than another seems to be quite different from the question whether the former makes on the whole for greater human happiness than the latter. It seems quite conceivable that one set of rules for distributing property might be far less just than another, and yet that the first might stimulate production so much more than the second that a community would be happier if governed by the first. And I believe that people who were faced with the alternative of introducing one set or the other, or of changing from one to the other, would hesitate between them. For we approve both of justice and of human happiness, and when the two conflict our feelings are mixed.

In this connexion I must add that I question Hume's doctrine that where the utility of justice vanishes our approval of it vanishes too. The truth seems to me to be rather as follows. Where justice and utility conflict, as they may, our feelings are mixed because we approve of both. And cases may arise in which the sacrifice of justice produces so much human happiness or obviates so much human misery that our total reaction is predominantly one of approval. But, where justice has neither utility nor disutility, as in the case of the ship-wrecked sailors with a single biscuit which is not enough to keep even one of them alive, I think it is plain that we should approve of a just distribution of the biscuit and disapprove of a bestial scramble for it. We should all hope that, if we had to starve along with others, we should have the grace to starve decently and in order, and that they would do likewise.

Again, although I heartily agree with all that Hume says about the extreme utility of having rules of some kind about property and strictly enforcing them even in " hard cases ", I am very doubtful whether this fact suffices to explain the original establishment of such rules or the strong feeling of disapproval which we now experience when we contemplate a breach of them. As regards the original establishment of rules about property, it is hard to believe that rather remote and abstract considerations about the happiness of the community as a whole and in the long run would have occurred to the minds of primitive people, or would have had much influence on their conduct unless they had been reinforced by other beliefs and emotions of a less refined kind. As regards our present obedience to such rules in cases where we might profit and escape punishment if we broke them, it seems to me that, if the question of utility comes in at all, it is reinforced by a consideration of justice in the sense which Hume's theory ignores. When I am tempted to do such an act, the question that arises in my mind and sometimes prevents me is this : " Is it *fair* that you should enjoy the advantages which you do, through other men keeping the rules when they would profit by breaking them, whilst you take the liberty to break them when it is to your private advantage to do so ? "

My conclusion then is that Hume's theory of Justice, though it contains much that is true and important, is inadequate. In particular he has failed to answer the objection that our approvals and disapprovals are in part determined by other considerations beside the supposed immediate pleasantness or unpleasantness, utility or disutility, of the object which we are contemplating. Not only the total amount of happiness to be distributed, but also the way in which it is distributed, stirs our emotions of approval and disapproval. And, although the latter may have a profound influence on the former, that is not the only or the main reason why it arouses the moral sentiment.

(2) We can now pass to Hume's defence of his doctrine against psychological Egoists, like Spinoza and Hobbes. The classical refutation of psychological egoism is contained in the works of Bishop Butler, and Hume does not add much to it. But it will be worth while to give a brief account of his arguments, since later writers of great pretensions, such as Green and Bradley, have been psychological egoists, though not psychological hedonists, in spite of Butler and his refutations.

We may divide Hume's contentions into two groups : (i) Positive evidence in favour of his theory, and (ii) a challenge to his opponents. (i) The positive evidence is as follows. (*a*) It is certain that we feel approval and disapproval of actions and sentiments which we know cannot affect our happiness at all ; *e.g.*, the actions of historical persons in the remote past or of fictitious characters in novels or plays. Again, we may approve of the virtues of enemies, although we know that these very virtues make them more dangerous to ourselves. (Hume lived before the gutter-press had shown us a better way.) Now this must be due either to a direct approval of certain types of character and action, as such ; or to a direct approval of human happiness in general, combined with the belief that these types of character and action tend to produce it, even though they affect our own happiness adversely, if at all. Either alternative is inconsistent with psychological egoism. Nor can the facts be explained by saying that we imagine ourselves to be contemporary with the historical characters, or that we imagine the fictitious characters to be real and capable of affecting our happiness. Mere imagination can, no doubt, produce emotion ; but it will not continue to do so when we know all the time that it is *mere* imagination, and that the facts are otherwise. (*b*) It is quite certain that we feel approval of qualities which are agreeable or useful to their possessor, even when they are not useful to anyone else. *E.g.*, we approve of a good taste in literature or painting even in a poor man who cannot be a patron of the arts. How can this be explained on egoistic principles ?

(ii) The challenge is as follows. On the face of it there is such a sentiment as disinterested benevolence, and the egoist must account for this appearance. He may try to do this in two ways. (*a*) He may suggest that the appearance is due to *deliberate* fraud. This alternative Hume rejects as plainly superficial. We might perhaps add that, if every one knows perfectly well that there is no such thing as

disinterested benevolence, it would not be worth anyone's
while to pretend to be benevolent. So we pass to the second
alternative, which Hume calls "the more philosophical
view". (b) This view is that we unwittingly deceive ourselves
by some trick of the imagination, some association of ideas,
or some bit of mistaken reasoning, when we think that we
are feeling an interest in anything but our own happiness.
On this theory Hume makes the following comments.

(α) Even if it were true, the common distinction between
selfish men and actions, on the one hand, and unselfish
men and actions, on the other, would correspond to a fact.
Granted that in all cases self-interest were the only motive,
we must still admit that in some men a certain association
of ideas or trick of the imagination or mistaken reasoning
causes them to do actions which benefit others rather than
themselves. Such men and such actions would be called
"unselfish", and it would be a fact that we approve men
who habitually deceive themselves in this way, and disapprove those who do not.

(β) The affection of animals for each other and for their
masters, the love of parents for their children and of men
for their friends, are instances of emotions which clearly
cannot be reduced to disguised self-interest. There are
two comments to be made on this. In the first place,
granted that these emotions cannot be reduced to self-love,
they are also certainly not instances of general benevolence
or humanity, in Hume's sense. They are instances of what
Butler calls "particular propensities". They might be
admitted to exist, and to be irreducible to self-love, by a
man who denied the existence of a sentiment of general
benevolence. Secondly, the case of animals and young
children would at most prove that apparently disinterested

affection cannot be explained by self-interest and mistaken *reasoning*. It does not prove that self-interest and certain non-rational causes, such as association, might not be adequate to explain the facts.

(γ) He quotes with approval Butler's contention that the possibility of gratifying self-love presupposes the existence of desires for other objects beside one's own happiness. *E.g.*, a revengeful man gratifies his self-love by gaining the pleasures of revenge. But revenge would give him no pleasure if he did not already want to injure his enemy. And this is not a desire for his own happiness, but a desire for another's misery. Hume's argument here appears to be this : " You must admit that we do directly desire some other things beside our own happiness, *e.g.*, the misery of our enemies. If so, why should you deny that we may directly desire the happiness of mankind in general ? " This is a valid *argumentum ad hominem* against the psychological egoist. It does not of course prove that we do in fact directly desire the happiness of mankind in general ; but it does refute the only argument produced by egoists to show that we do not. For their only argument against the existence of general benevolence is that we cannot directly desire *anything* but our own happiness ; and the example of revenge shows that this general principle is false.

(δ) Hume's last argument is characteristically ingenious and plausible, but I believe it to be fallacious. It is this. Not only *has* egoism failed in the past to explain the facts which appear to refute it ; we can be confident that it will be no more successful in the future. In physics very familiar phenomena are often found to be due to very complex and previously unsuspected causes. But in psychology " the simplest and most obvious cause that can be assigned for any phenomenon is probably the true one ". Strong feelings cannot be accounted for by elaborate trains of reasoning. I may feel very strongly about the death of someone who could not possibly have done me any services if he had lived. Self-sophistication might account for my overlooking the presence of self-interest when it is mixed with other motives, but it cannot manufacture strong feelings out of self-interest where, as in the present case, this motive plainly does not come into operation.

I think that there is a tacit assumption and a confusion in this argument of Hume's. The tacit assumption is that all fundamental emotional and conative dispositions which a man owns must be open to introspection by him simply because they are *his*. If this were true there could of course be no question of a mental occurrence being due to some fundamental tendency which we have never yet recognised. But I see no reason to accept the premise. There might be dozens of fundamental tendencies in ourselves which we cannot detect by introspection, just as there is minute structure in matter which we cannot detect by sense-perception. And what cannot be introspected may cause what can be introspected, just as what cannot be perceived by the senses may cause what can be so perceived.

The ambiguity is this. When it is said that strong feelings can never be accounted for by subtle reasonings, this may mean one of two things. It may mean that a strong feeling in A can never be wholly due to a subtle process of reasoning in A's mind. This is no doubt true. And, in any case, strong feelings which are apparently not egoistic are certainly felt by people who are quite incapable of subtle reasoning, whether valid or invalid. But it might mean that B's theory about the causation of A's strong feeling cannot be true if it involves subtle reasoning on B's part. Now I see no reason to accept this. It is obviously possible that the causes of A's strong feeling may be very complex and obscure. In that case any correct theory about the causation of A's strong feeling will necessarily involve subtle reasoning on B's part. The upshot of the matter is this. Any egoistic theory which assumes that apparently non-egoistic emotions are *caused by* a subtle process of reasoning in the mind of the *experient* are certainly false. But we cannot reject off-hand an egoistic theory merely because it asserts that apparently non-egoistic emotions are due to very complex *non-rational* causes which need for their detection and analysis very subtle reasoning on the part of the *psychologist*.

My general conclusion on this whole topic is that psychological egoism is certainly false, and that Butler and Hume between them have refuted it and all the arguments which have been alleged in its favour. But to refute psychological egoism is not the same as to prove that there is a sentiment of general benevolence or humanity. I think it very likely that there is such a sentiment; but I doubt whether Hume has proved that there is.

(3) We come now to what is, from the standpoint of ethics, the most fundamental question of all, viz., " Is Hume's analysis of ethical characteristics correct, and is he right in holding that all general rules about what kinds of thing are good or bad can and must be established by observation and empirical generalisation ? " Hume discusses this question in the form: " What are the respective functions of Reason and Feeling in ethical matters ? "

Unfortunately he never explicitly says what he means by " Reason ". Now " Reason " is a highly ambiguous word, and I suspect that Hume uses it in this discussion in an unduly narrow sense. It will make for clearness if I state what I understand by " Reason " before I begin to deal with Hume's arguments. I ascribe three cognitive functions to Reason : (i) The intuiting of necessary and universal connexions between characteristics, when conjunctions of these characteristics are presented to the mind's attention. *E.g.*, it is an act of Reason, in this sense, when we see by inspection that *any* triangle which is equilateral *must* be equiangular, and conversely. In this way we derive our knowledge of axioms. (ii) The drawing of inferences, demonstrative or problematical, from premises. This activity is, no doubt, closely connected with the former. For it depends on seeing certain formal relations between propositions, and on recognising that such relations justify inference in *any* instance in which they are present. (iii) The formation of *a priori* concepts. This needs explanation. It appears to me that we have concepts of certain characteristics which are neither manifested to us in sensation (as *redness* is) nor synthesised out of characteristics so manifested (as the characteristic of *phœnixhood* is). I believe the concept of *Cause*, and many others, to be of this nature. I have no doubt that certain specific kinds of sensible experience are necessary conditions for the formation of such concepts ; but they are not, strictly speaking, derived from sensible experience, as the concepts of *redness* and *phœnixhood* are. These are what I call " *a priori* concepts ". Some people would deny that there are any such concepts ; and those who would admit them might differ very much about their nature and status. If there be *a priori* concepts, as I believe there are, I ascribe the formation of them to Reason. The three cognitive functions which I assign to Reason may be called respectively "Intuitive Induction", "Ratiocination", and "Formation of *A Priori* Concepts". Now it is an essential principle or prejudice with Hume to deny the possibility of *a priori* concepts ; so naturally he does not include the third function under the head of Reason. But in his other works Hume does admit Intuitive Induction ; for this is involved in what he calls "knowledge of the relations of ideas" and contrasts with "knowledge of matters of fact". Yet here, it seems to me, he ignores this function of Reason altogether, and tacitly reduces Reason to Ratiocination. We are now in a position to consider his arguments.

Hume's general position is the following. The *prima facie* case for the man who thinks that Reason plays an essential part in ethical matters is that we certainly do dispute about questions of right and wrong, and do try to persuade each other on moral questions. Now we do not dispute about mere feelings and emotions. The *prima facie* case for the man who thinks that sentiment and emotion play an essential part in ethical matters is that virtue and vice certainly do move our feelings, and that moral approval and disapproval are undoubtedly motives to action. Now Reason cannot tell us that one quality must attract and another must repel us. This must depend on innate or acquired tastes. And the mere intellectual recognition of the presence or absence of a certain quality or relation neither moves our feelings nor affects our actions.

He concludes that Reason and Sentiment both play an essential part, but that the parts are quite different. Reason is needed to tell us that certain types of character or conduct

tend to produce happiness or misery in the agent or in other
men. When the situation is complex and the consequences
are mixed, Reason is needed to analyse the situation and to
estimate the balance of happiness or misery which is likely to
result. But this knowledge which Reason gives us would lead
neither to approval nor disapproval, action or abstention,
unless the thought of human happiness attracted us and the
thought of human misery repelled us. Now this attraction
and repulsion cannot be due to Reason, but must depend
on the special emotional make-up of the human mind.
The essence of Hume's view then is that Reason is wholly
confined to matters of fact. It will help us to analyse a
situation, to choose means for a given end, and to infer
probable consequences of various alternative courses of
action. But it has nothing whatever to do with our choice
of ends as distinct from means. We desire things as ends
only because they move some emotion in us, and not
because of any objective characteristic in them which
Reason can recognise.

It is evident that there are two different propositions
involved in Hume's doctrine. The first is that Reason, even
if sometimes necessary, is never sufficient to account for
the facts of moral emotion and moral action ; and that
a Sentiment must be postulated in addition to explain
these. The second is that Reason is concerned only with
matters of fact. Now the first of these contentions may be,
and, I believe, is true. But it is little more than a truism ;
and it has no tendency to support the second proposition.
Suppose it were the case that there is a certain quality,
viz., goodness or badness, and certain relations of rightness
or fittingness, which are recognised by Reason and by it
alone. It is still logically possible that a being who was

rational in the cognitive sense, *i.e.*, who recognised these qualities and relations, should be entirely unmoved by the thought of their presence or absence. And it is logically possible that a being who recognised these qualities and relations and felt emotions of approval and disapproval when he thought of their presence or absence should not be moved to do what he approves or to avoid what he disapproves. No doubt we should call such beings " moral lunatics ", and say that they are " not completely rational ". But the fact that they are conceivable, and that they do indeed exist, shows that even the most convinced Rationalist about moral *cognition* must postulate certain emotional and conative dispositions in addition to Reason in order to account for moral *feeling* and moral *action*. Now some Rationalists have written as if they thought that the mere recognition of ethical characteristics by Reason *sufficed* to account for moral feeling and moral action. If any of them really did think this, they were wrong ; and Hume's argument shows that they were. But this has not the faintest tendency to prove that they were wrong in holding that Reason is *necessary* for the recognition of ethical characteristics and for the intuiting of necessary connexions between them and other characteristics. Thus the second part of Hume's contention, viz., that the only business of Reason is with matters of fact, is quite unsupported by the excellent reasons which he gave for the first. Is there any reason to believe it ?

Hume never states very clearly the alternatives to his own theory. I think it will be wise to do this before considering in detail his arguments for it and against its rivals. Let us grant, for the sake of argument, that the judgment " X is good " would never have been made *in the first instance* unless the person who made it had felt an emotion of approval in contemplating X, though it may *now* on occasion be made by a person who is not feeling this emotion. This may be compared with the fact that the judgment " X is red " would never have been made in the first instance unless the person who made it had had a sensation of red on looking at X, though it may now on occasion be made by a person who is not having such a sensation. Now there are two different ways of analysing the latter fact. The first would be to say that " X is red " means simply " Most men will have a sensation of red when they look at X." This may be called the " phenomenalist analysis ". The second would be to say that " X is red " means " There is a certain property in X which causes sensations of red in most men who look at X." This may be called the " causal analysis ". Let us now apply this to the case of goodness. The phenomenalist analysis would be that goodness is the characteristic of *being* generally approved by men. The causal analysis would be that goodness is the property which *causes* a thing to be generally approved by men. It is plain that Hume takes the phenomenalist view about goodness. According to him the property which causes a thing to be generally approved by men is not goodness but supposed direct pleasantness or utility. But he has produced no conclusive reason for preferring the phenomenalist to the causal analysis.

We have now to consider another alternative. As before we will begin with a parallel from non-ethical topics. It is generally held that the judgment " X causes Y " would not have been made in the first instance unless a number of X-like events had been observed and they had all been found to be followed by Y-like events. The phenomenalist analysis of this fact is that " X causes Y " simply means " X-like events will always be followed by Y-like events." But another view is possible. It may be that there is a peculiar relation between X and Y which cannot be manifested through the senses, but which is intuited by the intellect when and only when a number of sequences of X-like and Y-like events have been presented to its attention through the senses. This of course makes the causal relation an *a priori* concept, in the sense defined above. I will therefore call this type of analysis the " *a priori* concept analysis". Now the *a priori* concept analysis of the ethical fact which we are granting to Hume would be as follows. Emotions of approval and disapproval furnish the necessary occasions on which the intellect intuites certain ethical relations, *e.g.*, those of rightness and wrongness, fittingness and unfittingness, which cannot be manifested through the senses. We could not expect Hume to entertain this suggestion, but it is nevertheless a perfectly possible one.

We are now in a position to consider Hume's arguments. He has two arguments against the Rationalist's position, and three in support of his own. (i) Rationalists maintain that actions, intentions, or emotions are right or wrong because of some relation of fittingness or unfittingness to something else, which Reason recognises. Hume says that this relation must either relate the action or emotion to the situation in which it takes place, or it must be the logical relation of falling under or conflicting with some general moral rule. If the former is meant, he challenges the Rationalist to point out exactly what this relation is. If the latter is meant, he argues that the theory is circular. For the general moral rule must have been reached by induction from observed particular cases of right and wrong actions. Particular actions must therefore be recognised to be right or wrong before any general moral rules could have been formulated. Hume's challenge seems to me unfair. Might not the relation in question be absolutely unique and peculiar, and yet perfectly familiar ? If so, any attempt to express it in other terms would necessarily be erroneous or tautologous. On the other hand, his objection to the second form of ethical Rationalism seems fairly conclusive.

(ii) Inanimate objects may have to each other exactly the same kind of relations which would make us approve or condemn human beings. Yet we do not make ethical judgments about inanimate objects. When a young tree destroys the older tree which produced it, the two trees stand in precisely the same relations in which Nero and his mother stood when he murdered her after she had gained him the empire. Yet we blame Nero, and do not blame the young tree, for ingratitude. I do not think that a Rationalist need spend many sleepless nights over this objection. Nero and his mother had minds, whilst we believe that the trees had not. In virtue of this difference Nero and his mother stood in mental relations in which the trees could not have stood. And we condemn Nero in respect of his emotions and intentions towards a person who had had certain emotions and intentions towards him.

We come now to Hume's three arguments for his own view. (i) In geometrical reasoning we first observe certain relations between points, lines, etc., and then proceed to *deduce* other relations which were not before obvious to us. But, when we reflect on a situation in order to pass a moral judgment, *all* the relations must be known *before* we can pass the judgment. Thus Reason must have completed its task before moral judgment can begin, and its task is simply to ascertain the exact facts of the case. All that then remains is for the situation which Reason has analysed to call forth an emotion of approval or disapproval. There are two undoubted truths in this argument of Hume's. (a) I must be fully aware of the non-ethical relations in a situation before I can make a trustworthy judgment on the ethical relations. (b) When I am fully cognisant of the non-ethical relations I cannot infer, from them and them alone, the ethical relations; as I might seem to infer the remaining geometrical relations between a set of points from a selection of their geometrical relations. But, even in the geometrical case, I do not infer the additional geometrical relations *simply* from those which are already known. I infer them from these *together with* the axioms of geometry, which are known by Intuitive Induction. Similarly, it is arguable that I first recognise the co-existence of certain non-ethical relations with certain ethical relations in a particular case; then see by Intuitive Induction that the presence of the former *entails* that of the latter in *any* case; and finally use this as a premise for inferring the presence of these ethical relations in other cases in which I find these non-ethical relations. So the premises of this argument are quite compatible with the view that Reason plays a much more important part in ethics than Hume allows.

(ii) Hume argues that his position is strengthened by the analogy between ethical and æsthetic judgments. The beauty of an object no doubt depends on the relations and proportions of its parts. And these are in many cases recognised only by the exercise of Reason. But the recognition of these relations and proportions is not sufficient to give rise to an æsthetic judgment. A circle would have no beauty unless there were observers so constituted that the recognition of its form calls forth an emotion of admiration in them. Similarly a murder would not be wrong unless there were observers so constituted that this kind of relation between men calls forth an emotion of disapproval. This argument does not, I think, appreciably strengthen Hume's position. Either the situation with regard to æsthetic judgments is, or it is not, exactly analogous to that with regard to moral judgments. If there is exact analogy, we have already shown that the facts in the case of moral judgments are susceptible of two other interpretations beside Hume's. And the same two alternatives would be open in the case of æsthetic judgments. If there is not exact analogy, then the argument from the æsthetic to the moral judgment cannot be relied upon. For the differences might be such as to allow Hume's theory to be true of æsthetic judgments, and to prevent it being true of moral judgments.

(iii) If you press a man as to why he did a certain action there will always come a point at which he can make only a tautologous answer. If you ask him why he plays golf, he may say that it is for the sake of health. If you ask him why he wants to keep in health, he may say that it is because illness is painful. But, if you ask him why he dislikes pain, and he still has patience to answer you at all, he can only make the tautologous answer : " Because I do." This, Hume thinks, shows that Reason is concerned only with means and with relative ends, never with ultimate ends. Now virtue is admitted to be an ultimate end, desirable for its own sake. Therefore there must be some sentiment in men to which virtue appeals, and it must derive its value from this and this alone. The weakness of this argument will best be seen by taking a parallel case. In any chain of reasoning whatever we eventually get back to premises for which we can give no reason, in the sense that we cannot mention any other proposition from which they are deducible. But this does not show that our acceptance of these ultimate premises must be irrational. It may of course happen to be so. But it may be that we accept them because Reason perceives directly that their subjects and their predicates are necessarily connected. Similarly, in explaining why we acted in a certain way, we come eventually to ends which are valued for themselves and not as means to anything else. But it does not follow that our recognition of their value does not depend on rational insight into their nature.

The upshot of the matter is that, on this vitally important point, Hume has neither proved his own case nor refuted that of his opponents. But it remains possible that he is right and they are wrong. I cannot profess to decide the question here ; but I will end by pointing out one consequence of Hume's view. This is that every dispute on questions of right and wrong is capable of being settled completely by the simple method of collecting statistics. Suppose that A thinks that X is right, and B thinks that X is wrong. We have first to make sure that A and B agree as to the non-ethical facts about X, *i.e.*, as to its non-ethical qualities and relations to other things, as to what effects it will have and what effects other things which might have been substituted for it would have had, and so on. Suppose that, when all differences and confusions on these non-ethical matters have been removed, A still thinks that X is right and B still thinks that it is wrong. If Hume's theory be true, this means that A thinks that most men would feel an emotion of approval on contemplating X, whilst B thinks that most men would feel an emotion of disapproval on contemplating X. Now this is a question which can be settled by experiment, observation, collection of statistics, and empirical generalisation. This seems to me simply incredible. I should accept the view that there is a point in any ethical dispute between A and B beyond which further argument becomes futile. This would not, of course, prove that the difference has been reduced to a mere difference of taste ; for it might be that A's intellect was obtuse or warped, as compared with B's, in respect to certain quite objective qualities or relations. But, as I have just pointed out, the logical consequence of Hume's theory is not that in disputes on moral questions there comes a point beyond which we can only say " *de gustibus non est disputandum*." The logical consequence of his theory is that all such disputes *could* be settled, and that the way to settle them is to collect statistics of how people in fact do feel. And to me this kind of answer seems utterly irrelevant to this kind of question. If I am right in this, Hume's theory must be false.

CHAPTER V
Kant

KANT's theory of ethics differs from Spinoza's and Hume's far more radically than these differ from each other. The most fundamental point of divergence is the following. For Spinoza and Hume the notions of good and evil are primary, those of right and wrong are derived from them, whilst that of duty or obligation is barely mentioned. A right action or intention is simply one that leads or is likely to lead to a good result. For Kant the notion of duty or obligation and the notions of right and wrong are fundamental. A good man is one who habitually acts rightly, and a right action is one that is done from a sense of duty. There is a second absolutely fundamental difference between Kant and Hume, at any rate, which may be mentioned at once. Ethics for Hume is concerned simply with mankind. It deals with the purely contingent fact that men have a disposition to feel emotions of approval and disapproval, and the equally contingent fact that in men this disposition is excited by contemplating the happiness or misery of human beings. Kant, on the other hand, holds that the fundamental laws of morality are the same for every rational being, whether man, angel, or God, since the ultimate criterion of rightness is deducible from the concept of a rational being as such. The relation of Kant to Spinoza on this point cannot be stated briefly ; it will suffice to say here that both, in their very different ways, thought that the double nature of man, as being partly instinctive and partly rational, was of vital importance in human ethics. After these preliminaries I will now give a critical account of Kant's theory.

The theory may be summed up in the following propositions. (1) Nothing is intrinsically good but a good will. Kant tries to prove this by taking other alleged intrinsic goods, such as happiness, intellectual eminence, etc., and showing that each may be worthless or positively evil when not combined with a good will. This argument is fallacious. If we accept the alleged facts they prove only that a good will is a *necessary constituent* of any whole which is intrinsically good. It does not follow, though it may of course be true, that a good will has itself any intrinsic value.

(2) A good will is one that habitually wills rightly.

(3) The rightness or wrongness of a volition depends wholly on the nature of its motive. It does not depend on its actual consequences. And it does not depend on its intended consequences except in so far as the expectation of these forms part of the motive. Of course a mere idle wish is of no moral value. But, provided we genuinely try to carry out our intention, and provided our motive is right, then the volition is right no matter what its consequences may be.

(4) The next question that arises is therefore : " What is the criterion of rightness of motive ? " Before answering this question we must draw some distinctions among voluntary actions. In the first place we may divide them into *Actions on Impulse* and *Actions on Principle*. I will begin by illustrating this distinction. Suppose that I want to relieve a certain man who is in distress, simply because

I like him personally or because the sight of his distress makes me feel uncomfortable. Then I might not want to relieve a precisely similar man in a precisely similar situation if I did not happen to like him or if his distress were not thrust under my nose. This kind of voluntary action is impulsive. No doubt it has *causes*; there is something in the particular case which excites some conative disposition in me. But it is not, strictly speaking, done for a *reason* or on any *principle* which goes beyond this particular case. Now contrast this with the case of a member of the Charity Organisation Society giving relief to a complete stranger. He analyses the situation to see whether it does or does not come under a certain rule or principle of action which he has accepted. If it does, he gives relief ; if it does not, he refuses it. And he would treat in exactly the same way any other man whose case had the same features. This is an example of action on principle. The agent had a *reason* for his action. And, if he stated his reason, his statement would always take the following form : " This case has such and such characteristics ; and *any* case having these characteristics ought to be treated in such and such a way." Now Kant holds that an action cannot be right unless it is done on some general principle, which the agent accepts.

(5) This, however, is not a sufficient criterion of rightness. Kant divides principles or maxims of conduct into two classes, which he calls *Hypothetical* and *Categorical Imperatives*. A hypothetical imperative is a principle of conduct which is accepted, not on its own merits, but simply as a rule for gaining some desired end. Suppose that I refuse to make a certain statement on a certain occasion, for the reason that it would be a lie, and that lies ought not to be

told. Suppose that my ground for believing that lies ought not to be told is that they undermine confidence and thus reduce human happiness. Then the principle that lies ought not to be told would be, for me, a merely hypothetical imperative. It is accepted as a rule for maintaining human happiness, and not on its own merits. It is thus both contingent and derivative. It is contingent, because conditions are conceivable in which lying would not reduce human happiness, and in such conditions I should no longer accept the principle. And it is derivative, because my acceptance of it in existing circumstances depends on my desire for human happiness. The latter is my ultimate motive for not lying. A categorical imperative would be one that is accepted on its own merits, and not as a rule for gaining some desired end. If an action were done on a principle which is a categorical imperative we might say that it was done *for* a principle, and not merely *on* a principle. In fact we can distinguish three cases, viz., action *in accordance with*, action *on*, and action *for* a principle. An impulsive action might happen to be in accordance with a principle, though it could not be done on principle nor for principle. Now Kant holds that there are categorical as well as hypothetical imperatives ; a view which many philosophers would reject. And he holds that an action is right if and only if it is done on a principle which is a categorical imperative, *i.e.*, if it is done *for* a principle.

Why did Kant hold this view ? His reason appears to be this. It seems evident to him that any action which, in a given situation, is right or wrong at all must be right or wrong, in that situation, for *any* rational being whatever, no matter what his particular tastes and inclinations may be. Now any hypothetical imperative presupposes a desire for some particular kind of object. But different rational beings, or different species of rational beings, might like different kinds of objects. All men, *e.g.*, dislike the kind of sensation which we call toothache. But this fact has no necessary connexion with their rationality. There is nothing impossible in the supposition that there might be rational beings who liked the sensation of toothache as much as most men like the scent of roses. And it is conceivable that there might be rational beings who have no sensations at all ; indeed many people would hold that this possibility is realised in the case of angels. Therefore no hypothetical imperative would be accepted by all rational beings as such. Hence, if there be any principles of conduct which would be accepted by all rational beings as such, they must be accepted on their own merits and must therefore be categorical imperatives.

(6) We come now to the final question : " What characteristic must a principle of conduct have in order to be accepted on its own merits by every rational being as such ? " Kant's answer is that the feature which is common and peculiar to such principles must be a certain characteristic *form*, and not anything characteristic in their *content*. And the formal criterion is this. It is necessary and sufficient that the principle shall be such that anyone who accepts it as *his* principle of conduct can consistently desire that every one else should also make it *their* principle of conduct and should act upon it. This supreme criterion Kant often calls " *the* Categorical Imperative " or " *the* Moral Law ". It would be better to call it the " Supreme Principle of Categorical Imperatives ". For it is a second-order principle which states the necessary and sufficient conditions that must be fulfilled by any first-order principle if the latter is

to be a categorical imperative and action determined by it is to be morally right.

We may now sum up the theory. An action is right if and only if the agent's sufficient motive in doing it is the fact that he recognises it to be required in the circumstances by a right principle of conduct. A principle of conduct is right if and only if it would be accepted on its own merits by any rational being, no matter what his special tastes and inclinations might be. It must therefore be a principle which is acceptable to rational beings simply because of its intrinsic form, and not because it is a rule for gaining some desired end. And a principle will be acceptable to all rational beings if and only if each could consistently will that all should adopt it and act on it. This is the essence of Kant's theory, as I understand it; and I will now make some explanations and criticisms before considering the further developments of the theory. I will begin with some explanations.

(1) What are we to say about actions which are determined by a mixture of causes? Suppose I refrain from telling a lie to a certain man on a certain occasion. All the following three causes may be moving me in the same direction. I may have a special feeling of love or respect for him. I may desire human happiness, and believe that lying under the given circumstances would tend to diminish it. And I may accept the principle that lies ought not to be told as a categorical imperative. Does my action cease to be right because the first two cause-factors are present and are moving me in the same direction as the third? Kant certainly talks as if this were so. But I do not think that he need have taken this extreme view if he had recognised a certain ambiguity in the notion of " mixed

motives ". Suppose that three cause-factors, x, y, and z, are all moving me in the same direction. It may be that they are severally necessary and jointly sufficient to determine my action. If so, the situation would properly be described by saying that I have a *single* motive which is *internally complex*. On the other hand, it may be that one of these motive-factors, *e.g.*, x, would have sufficed to determine my action even if the others had been absent. Now all that Kant needs to maintain is that, when there is a plurality of cause-factors all moving the agent in the same direction, the action would be right if and only if it *would still* have been done for a principle even though the other factors had been absent.

(2) Kant has sometimes been counted as an extreme advocate of the infallibility of the individual conscience. This is a peculiarly foolish accusation. He nowhere suggests that a single first-order moral principle is self-evident. On the contrary the essence of his theory is to offer a single necessary and sufficient criterion by which every suggested principle of conduct must be tested and judged before it can rightly be accepted and acted upon.

(3) Kant has sometimes been blamed because no particular rules of conduct can be deduced from his general principle. It is said to be " empty ", " sterile ", and " merely formal ". Since Kant was perfectly well aware that his general principle is merely formal, and since he plainly regarded this as its great merit, we may assume that this objection rests on a misunderstanding. The relation of the Moral Law to particular Categorical Imperatives, such as " Lies ought not to be told ", is not supposed to be like the relation of the Law of Gravitation to Kepler's Laws of Planetary Motion. It is much more like the relation of the general principle : " All

arguments of the form ' all M is P and all S is M entail all S is P ' are valid " to a particular bit of reasoning of that form, such as : " All men are mortal and all Greeks are men, therefore all Greeks are mortal." You cannot deduce any particular argument from the general principle of the syllogism ; but, if any particular argument in syllogistic form claims to be valid, you can test its claims by seeing whether it does or does not have the formal structure required by the general principle. Kant would say, I think, that it is no more the business of ethics to provide rules of conduct than it is the business of logic to provide arguments. The business of ethics is to provide a test for rules of conduct, just as it is the business of logic to provide a test for arguments.

I have now, I hope, removed the more obvious mis-understandings that may arise about Kant's theory. Let me then begin to criticise it. (1) We must admit at once, as a plain matter of fact, that certain principles are accepted and acted upon by many people who do not accept or act upon them simply as hypothetical imperatives. It is perfectly certain that many people accept and act on the principle that lies ought not to be told, without thinking of whether the results of lying are desirable or undesirable. There are then imperatives which are here and now cate-gorical for certain persons, and there is action for the sake of principles. To this extent Kant is right, and he has pointed out an important psychological fact which moralists like Spinoza and Hume tend to ignore. The utmost that a Utilitarian could honestly say of such facts is that the imperatives which are now categorical for Smith must once have been merely hypothetical, either for Smith himself or for earlier members of his society or race. Accepted originally only as rules for gaining some desired end, they have now acquired such prestige that Smith accepts them for their own sake without thinking of their consequences. I am not at present concerned to criticise this theory of the origin of categorical imperatives. I wish simply to point out that there are imperatives which are here and now categorical for certain persons.

(2) We saw that the premise which is alleged to entail the most characteristic parts of Kant's theory is the following. Any action which, in a given situation, is right or wrong at all would be right or wrong for *any* rational being whatever in that situation, no matter what his special tastes and inclinations might be. Now this premise seems to me plainly false. I think it is true that *some* actions would be right, and that *some* would be wrong, in a given situation, quite independently of the tastes and inclinations of the agent. *E.g.*, if he were a member of a board of electors it would be his business to ignore his personal liking or disliking for any of the candidates. But it is equally certain that some actions would be right if done by an agent with one set of tastes and inclinations and wrong if done in precisely the same situation by an agent with certain other tastes and inclinations. If the agent, instead of having to decide whether to choose A or B for a professorship, had to decide whether to make a proposal of marriage to A or to B, it is perfectly obvious that his personal likings and dislikings would be relevant to the rightness of his action.

This conclusion may perhaps be reinforced by the following consideration. Every one admits that what is right or wrong for a given agent at a given moment depends

in part on the nature of the situation in which he is placed
at the moment of acting. Now among the factors in the
situation are the tastes and inclinations of the other rational
beings with whom the agent is concerned. And, although
these are not relevant to the rightness or wrongness of *some*
actions, they quite certainly are relevant to the rightness
or wrongness of others. Now it seems very far-fetched to
suppose that, whilst the tastes and inclinations of all other
rational beings are often ethically relevant, those of the
agent are never so.

The most then that I could admit is that there may be
some actions which would be right and some which would
be wrong in a given situation no matter what might be the
tastes and inclinations of the agent. Since there are certainly
others of which this is not true, Kant's theory of ethics
must at best be incomplete. For his criterion at best will
apply only to this department of morality and not to
morality as a whole. Perhaps this is the only part of morality
for which any general criterion can be given ; but that is
another matter.

(3) Supposing that there are some actions which would
be right and some which would be wrong in a given situation
for *any* rational/ being, does it follow that the principles on
which such actions are done must be categorical and not
hypothetical imperatives ? Kant's ground for asserting this
is, as we have seen, that a hypothetical imperative is accepted
only as a rule for gaining some desired end ; and that there
is no end which all rational beings as such must desire.
This seems highly plausible. But it is necessary to draw
a distinction between two different questions. (*a*) Is there
any end which all rational beings who contemplated it
would judge to be desirable ? And (*b*) is there any end

such that one could infer from the concept of a rational being that any such being must judge it to be desirable ?

The answer to the second question is, no doubt, in the negative. The concept of a rational being is the concept of a being who is capable of intuiting necessary connexions, of making inferences both deductive and problematic, and of forming *a priori* concepts. It is quite impossible to see directly or to infer deductively that such a being would find anything desirable, still less that it would find so-and-so—*e.g.*, general happiness—desirable. We could, how-ever, infer the hypothetical proposition that, *if* anything—*e.g.*, general happiness—be intrinsically desirable, *then* such a being would be able to see this if he contemplated the notion of general happiness. For this hypothetical pro-position does follow from the premise that the being is capable of intuiting necessary connexions, and this is part of the definition of a rational being.

It should now be evident that the negative answer which we have had to give to the second question has no bearing whatever on the first question. Let us take a parallel case from mathematics. We could not infer from the concept of a rational being that all rational beings are capable of seeing that the square-root of 2 is an irrational number. We could infer only that, *if* this be a necessary proposition, *then* all rational beings will be capable of seeing its truth and necessity. Yet, in point of fact, the proposition that the square-root of 2 is an irrational number *is* a necessary truth, and all rational beings who are properly trained and pay attention to the very simple proof of it can see this for themselves. In exactly the same way it might, *e.g.*, be the case that general happiness is intrinsically desirable. In that case every rational being who contemplated the notion of general happiness with enough attention would be able to see that it is desirable, though it is certainly not deducible from the notion of a rational being that he should find general happiness desirable.

We see then that it is perfectly possible that there may be ends which every rational being who contemplated them *would in fact* recognise to be intrinsically desirable, although there are no ends with regard to which it could be *inferred* from the concept of a rational being that he would find them desirable. It is therefore possible that even those actions which would be right or wrong in a given situation regardless of the special tastes and inclinations of the agent may be done on principles which are accepted as hypothetical, and not as categorical, imperatives.

(4) Let us suppose, however, that there are some principles which are accepted by all rational beings as categorical, and not merely as hypothetical, imperatives. Kant, as we know, claims to infer from the concept of a rational being the necessary and sufficient conditions which such a principle must fulfil. Can this be done ? It seems perfectly clear to me that it cannot. It appears possible only so long as the concept of a rational being is left unanalysed in an atmosphere misty with the incense of adoration. When it is brought into the common light of day and analysed, as we have done to it, we see that one can no more infer that a rational being would recognise any principle as right than that it would recognise any end as desirable. Still less could we infer from the concept of a rational being that it would accept all those principles and only those which answered to a certain formal condition.

Why did Kant imagine that he could infer such a criterion from the concept of a rational being ? Presumably his mind

must have moved in the following way. If there be anything
which a rational being as such might be expected to dislike,
it will be logical inconsistency. So a rational being would
reject any principle whose acceptance *would* involve him in
logical inconsistency. Then Kant must have jumped, in
some way which I cannot pretend to explain, from this
proposition to the proposition that a rational being would
accept any principle whose acceptance would *not* involve
him in logical inconsistency. This is of course absolutely
indefensible, and charity bids us turn our eyes from the
painful spectacle.

The truth on this matter seems to me to be the following.
There may be principles which would be accepted as categorical imperatives by all rational beings. But, if so, each
is accepted because of its special content, and not because
of any peculiarity in its form. I think that the principle
that gratitude is due to our benefactors is a plausible example
of such a principle. Now, if this would be accepted by any
rational being who understood the meaning of the terms
" gratitude " and " benefactor ", it is because there is an
intrinsic relation of *fittingness* between the former kind of
emotion and the latter kind of object. It is accepted
then, if at all, because a rational being can see that
a certain relation necessarily relates those two special
terms. It is not accepted because of anything in its general
form.

Again, it is possible that there may be some characteristic
which is common and peculiar to all the principles which
would be accepted as categorical imperatives by all rational
beings. If so, this characteristic might be abstracted and
used in future as a test for any principle which claimed to
be a categorical imperative acceptable to all rational beings.

But it is quite certain that such a criterion, even if it exists, could not be deduced from the concept of a rational being. If it exists and can be discovered at all, its discovery and establishment must take place in the following way. We should have to compare a number of admittedly categorical imperatives with each other, and contrast them with a number of principles which were admittedly not categorical imperatives. We might then discover that there is a certain characteristic common and peculiar to the former. Finally we might be able to see by an act of intuitive induction that *any* principle which had this characteristic would necessarily be a categorical imperative, and that the converse of this is also necessarily true.

(5) Let us now consider Kant's criterion in greater detail. The criterion is that a principle must be such that any rational being who proposes to accept it could consistently will that it should be accepted and acted upon by every one. As Kant points out, a principle might fail to pass this test in two different ways. In the first place, the very supposition of every one acting in a certain manner in certain circumstances might be self-contradictory. This case, he thinks, would be illustrated by the principle that every one should refuse to pay back money which was originally lent to him on promise of repayment. Secondly, the supposition of every one acting in a certain way in certain circumstances might not be self-contradictory, but it might be that the consequence of other people acting on this principle would be to hinder me from acting on it. In that case I could not consistently will that the principle should be generally accepted and acted upon. Kant thinks that this case would be illustrated by the principle that every one should seek to make himself as happy as possible

without regard to the happiness of any other man except in so far as this subserves his own happiness.

It is very difficult to think of any principle which would strictly be self-contradictory when generalised. I cannot see that Kant's example of promise-breaking is a case in point. If the principle were generally acted upon people in difficulties would, no doubt, soon cease to be able to get help from others by promises of repayment. So the real position is that the desire that every one who has got out of a difficulty by making a promise shall be allowed to break the promise afterwards is incompatible with the desire that every one who is in difficulties shall be able to get out of them by making promises. The incompatibility consists in the fact that, human memory and human motives being what they are, the fulfilment of the former desire would prevent that of the latter. In fact human nature is so constituted that, if the principle were generally acted upon, there would very soon be no more cases for it to apply to. This is plainly not, as it ought to be on Kant's theory, a case of *self*-contradiction or purely *formal* inconsistency.

The example of the second case is equally unfortunate, though in a different way. If it is to be relevant at all we must suppose that the principle of Egoism is accepted as a *categorical* imperative, and not as a mere rule for gaining maximum personal happiness. My acceptance of the principle therefore does not presuppose a desire for my own happiness or a belief that this is the most effective way to secure it. Now all that Kant shows is that the acceptance of this principle by others would be likely to lead to consequences detrimental to my happiness. Thus he shows only that my desire that every one should accept and act on the principle of Egoism would be inconsistent with my desire for my own maximum happiness. And this is wholly irrelevant. For we ought to be testing the claims of Egoism to be a *categorical* imperative ; and, as such, it does not pre-suppose the existence of a desire for my own happiness. And, so far as I can see, if anyone did propose to accept the principle of Egoism as a categorical, and not as a hypo-thetical, imperative, there would be no way of refuting him. I should claim to see by inspection that he was mistaken ; but there I should have to leave the matter.

The only importance of Kant's criterion is as a means of avoiding personal bias. If I feel inclined to approve a certain action by myself in a certain situation it is always desirable to consider what I should think if the same kind of action were done in the same situation by another man. If I find that I should condemn it in another, and yet can see no relevant differences between him and me, the chances are that my approval of the action in my own case is due to some personal bias. But it is important to notice that this principle, like the Principle of Indifference in Probability, cannot be used mechanically. I have to judge for myself what differences between me and another are, and what are not, ethically relevant to this kind of action in this kind of situation. And, beyond a certain point, this cannot be reduced to general rules.

I have now criticised the most fundamental points in Kant's theory. I will therefore pass to the further develop-ments of it. (1) Kant gives two other forms of the Supreme Principle of Morality. The second form is : " Treat every rational being, including yourself, always as an end and never as a mere means." The third form is : " A principle of conduct is morally binding on me if and only if I can regard it as a law which I impose on myself." He regards the three forms of the Moral Law as logically equivalent, but thinks that each emphasises a different aspect of it. I cannot see that the three forms are logically equivalent ; but the two additional principles are interesting, and deserve some slight comment.

(a) The second formula plainly contains an important truth, but it stands in need of some qualification. In the first place, so far from being thought wrong, it is thought to be an act of specially heroic virtue in certain circumstances for a soldier to sacrifice his life for his country, or for a doctor to do so for his patients, or for a scientist to do so for the advancement of knowledge. It must be admitted, however, that, although we thus admire people in certain circumstances for treating *themselves* as mere means, we should not feel justified in treating them in that way without their consent. Again, there seem to be cases in which you must either treat A or treat B, not as an end, but as a means. If we isolate a man who is a carrier of typhoid, we are *pro tanto* treating him merely as a cause of infection to others. But, if we refuse to isolate him, we are treating other people *pro tanto* merely as means to his comfort and culture. The fact which this formula exaggerates seems to be the following. Every rational being (and, I should add, every sentient being) has as such certain claims to consideration which it is always wrong to ignore. But, although such claims must always be *considered*, they need not, and indeed cannot, all be *satisfied* in full. For they may conflict with each other, and then some compromise must be struck between them. And in certain cases we approve a man for voluntarily abating or renouncing his claims, though we should not judge it right to impose this abatement or renunciation on him in the circumstances.

(b) The third formula also contains an important truth expressed in an exaggerated form. It is not necessary that a principle of conduct should be " self-imposed " ; indeed it is doubtful whether any clear meaning can be attached to this notion. But it is true that an action done for a principle has no moral value unless the agent freely and wittingly accepts the principle for which it is done. It is important to notice, however, that a principle may be freely and wittingly accepted in two quite different ways. (i) I may accept it directly, because, on inspection, I persuade myself that it is right to act in such and such a way in such and such circumstances. (ii) I may not be able to see this directly. But I may be told that it is so by someone whom I believe to have greater moral insight in general or in this special department of conduct than I have. Or, again, I might believe that it had been ordained by a good God for reasons which I cannot understand but which are certainly adequate. In such cases it would be my duty to accept the principle and act on it, even though I could not see its truth by direct inspection of the terms. The kind of case which Kant's third formula is meant to cut out is where the principle is accepted *merely* on tradition, or *merely* from the fear that God will punish me if I do not act in accordance with it. In such cases actions done from this principle would plainly have no moral value.

(2) Kant draws a very important distinction between the *intrinsically* good (*Summum Bonum*) and the *complete* good (*Bonum Consummatum*). As we have seen, he holds that a will which habitually wills rightly is intrinsically good and that nothing else is so. Pleasure and pain, *e.g.*, by

themselves are neither good nor bad. Nevertheless pleasure and pain are capable of adding to or detracting from the total value of a situation. A being who wills rightly *deserves* a certain degree of happiness, and one who wills wrongly deserves a certain degree of unhappiness. The *moral* value of each being who wills rightly is of course quite independent of whether he gets the amount of happiness which his right willing deserves. But the *total* value of a universe in which each being who willed rightly did get the amount and kind of happiness which his right willing deserved would plainly be greater than that of an otherwise similar universe in which happiness was absent or was not distributed on this principle. If we adopt a useful distinction of M'Taggart's we may say that the total value *in* the universe would be the same in both cases; but the total value *of* the universe would be greater in the first case than in the second. The *complete* good would be a system of perfectly virtuous beings, each enjoying that amount and kind of happiness which his virtue deserved; although the only *intrinsic* good is right willing, and although an action is never right if it be done *for the sake of* a reward.

This doctrine of Kant's is perfectly consistent, and I agree with a large part of it. I accept the notion of desert, and I agree that it is better that there should be virtue with the appropriate amount of happiness than the same degree of virtue with less happiness. I am not, however, convinced that pleasure and pain have no intrinsic value; though I am more inclined to think that pain is intrinsically evil than that pleasure is intrinsically good. Doubts on these points would introduce many complications into the elegant simplicity of Kant's doctrine; and it would be out of place to pursue the subject further here.

(3) The last point to be noticed is Kant's theory of Moral Obligation. Kant, like Spinoza, is greatly impressed with the double nature of man, as being partly a creature of passion, impulse, instinct, and sensation, and partly a rational being. Kant and Spinoza both held that the rational aspect of man's nature is the more fundamental. Neither of them gave a satisfactory account of the relations between the two ; but for this no other philosopher is in a position to cast stones at them. Kant's theory is, roughly, that the non-rational aspect of a human mind is the way in which such a mind inevitably appears to itself. It is needless to waste much time over this theory. Either the human mind, as it really is, is purely active and rational or it is not. If it is not, the problem of the relation between the active rational side and the passive, emotional, and sensuous side remains where it was. But, if it is purely active and rational, the problem of how it comes to appear to itself as partly passive, emotional, and sensuous arises at once and is plainly insoluble. Most of Kant's theory of freedom consists of a rapid shuffle between one and the other horn of this dilemma, and resembles an unskilful performance of the three-card trick rather than a serious philosophical argument.

Still, the double nature of man remains a fact, whatever may be the right explanation of it. And both Kant and Spinoza held that the characteristic experiences of obligation and moral struggle are closely bound up with it. It will be remembered that Spinoza said that, if, *per impossibile*, a man were born with nothing but clear ideas and active emotions, he would not know the meaning of good and evil though he would in fact enjoy the highest good. Now Kant distinguishes between what he calls the *Good Will* and the

Holy Will. And he ascribes the experience of moral obligation in human beings to the fact that their wills are good, but not holy. A good will is one which always has the power to act on right principles, but is also susceptible to other kinds of solicitation, *e.g.*, special impulses and passions, desires for certain ends, and so on. The wills of human beings, in this life at any rate, are in this state. They *need* never act on these other solicitations, but they are always subject to them. A holy will would be one in which every tendency to action except for the sake of a right principle was absent. Such a will must be ascribed to God, and it may perhaps belong to angels and to just men made perfect. Now, in the case of a holy will, there is no question of duty or obligation. All obligation is the obligation of a being whose will is good, but not holy, to act *as if* its will were holy ; *i.e.*, never to act on any motive but right principle, although other motives do in fact solicit it. Kant holds that the fact that we are under an obligation to act in this way implies that we always *could* have done so even in those cases where we in fact did not. If you ask him how this is possible his answer is that, as we really are, we are purely rational active beings and therefore can always behave as such. The particular inclinations, impulses, and passions are only aspects under which a being who is purely active and rational appears to itself.

I have already shown that this solution is metaphysically impossible. It is equally unsatisfactory from an ethical point of view. Either what appear to me as my passive emotions and irrational impulses are *purely* delusive appearances, or they correspond to something in my real self. If it be a pure delusion that I have irrational impulses it must be a pure delusion that I ever act on them, and therefore a pure delusion that I ever act wrongly. If, on the other hand, these appearances do correspond to something in my real self, then it is indeed possible that I should really act wrongly at times. But my self will *really* be mixed ; and there is no explanation why a self which is in fact of mixed nature should always be able to act as if its nature were purely rational. The truth is that Kant takes the mixture to be real when he is dealing with purely ethical questions, and takes it to be delusive when he is trying to give a rational theory of the metaphysical consequences which he thinks are entailed by the ethical facts.

In Kant's theological works there are traces of a different, but no more satisfactory, theory. If it be admitted that the notion of duty has any application it must be admitted that some actions which I actually have done are actions that I ought not to have done, and that some which I failed to do ought to have been done by me. But to say that I did X but ought not to have done it implies that I could have avoided doing X. And to say that I omitted X but ought to have done it implies that I could have done it. It must therefore be admitted that the fact of duty and moral obligation implies that my present actions are not completely determined by my present character and situation. Yet my actions are events in time, and Kant claims to have proved in the *Critique of Pure Reason* that all events in time are completely determined. The solution is to distinguish between me as a noumenon and me as a phenomenon. Every act of mine could be predicted by a person who knew enough about my circumstances, my innate dispositions, my past actions, and the laws of empirical psychology. But, on the other hand, the whole series of my acts, emotions, etc., is the manifestation of a single noumenal self which is not in time. Suppose now that my empirical self contains, among other events, certain wrong actions. These, as we have seen, must be so connected with the other events in my empirical self and the rest of the empirical world that they could have been predicted with complete certainty by anyone who had enough knowledge of empirical facts and laws. Nevertheless I am responsible for them. For my noumenal self *could have* manifested itself in time as an empirical self which did not contain these wrong actions but contained right actions instead. And I cannot disclaim responsibility for the fact that my noumenal self chose to appear as an empirical self which contains wrong actions rather than as an empirical self which contains nothing but right actions. For it is my real self ; and the whole series of events which make up my empirical self is just one possible manifestation of my noumenal self, which the latter freely and timelessly chooses in preference to other possible manifestations.

This theory has at least the merit of admitting that the noumenal self can really choose wrongly. But the notion of a timeless and undetermined choice by a noumenon of the series of phenomena by which it shall be manifested in time is quite unintelligible. And there is a further difficulty. We have to suppose that each noumenon independently of all the rest makes an undetermined choice of the series of phenomena by which it shall be manifested in time. Yet these various independently chosen series of phenomena must all fit into each other in such a way that the whole phenomenal world forms a single system in which even the minutest items are subject to invariable rules of sequence and co-existence. This seems absolutely incredible. And so both Kant's attempts to reconcile complete determinism in the empirical self with the possibility of real wrong and right doing seem to break down.

Nevertheless, from a purely ethical point of view, Kant's theory of moral obligation seems highly plausible, if we put it in the form that " duty " and " obligation " have meaning and application only to beings who are fundamentally, and yet not wholly, rational. And he is right in holding that an obligation to do or to abstain implies power to do or abstain. But it is a very difficult problem to say what precise meaning is to be given to the two highly ambiguous words " fundamentally " and " power " ; and it is certain that Kant has failed to answer this question satisfactorily.

Kant holds that there is a peculiar kind of emotion which a being who has a good, but not a holy, will experiences when he contemplates moral purity. This emotion, which he calls *Achtung*, is a species of awe. On such occasions the being, who from his mixed nature belongs both to the world of sense and to the supersensible world, is getting a peep, and the only direct peep which he can get in this life, into the latter. This glimpse humbles and even frightens him, in so far as his nature is partly animal and sensuous ; yet, at the same time, it exalts him, in so far as his nature is fundamentally rational, by reminding him that he is a citizen of the supersensible world. Here again it seems clear that Kant is describing a genuine fact in terms which most of us can understand and accept in outline, even though we might hesitate to follow him in points of detail.

It remains to say something about Kant's ethical arguments for immortality and for the existence of God. The argument for immortality is as follows. We are under a moral obligation, not merely to act rightly on all occasions, but also to make ourselves perfect. Now we should not be perfect until we had no inclination to act wrongly. And we shall never cease to have the inclination to act wrongly unless we become purely rational, and the sensuous, impulsive, passive side of our nature is completely eliminated. Now, in terms of time, this would take an infinite time to accomplish. But, since we are morally obliged to aim at this result, it must be possible to reach it. Therefore we must be immortal to allow us time to do so.

The following criticisms must be made on this argument : (a) The command to make ourselves perfect is not to be taken literally. It is merely a rhetorical way of saying : " Never be contented with your present level of moral achievement." No doubt we always can improve our moral characters so long as we are alive. But this does not imply that we shall ever be able to make them perfect. (b) Kant's premises are really inconsistent with each other. One premise is that moral perfection must be attainable or it could not be our duty to seek it. The other premise is that it is attainable only after an unending time. And this is surely equivalent to saying that it is not attainable at all.

The ethical argument for the existence of God is as follows. Nothing is intrinsically good except virtue, which consists in doing right without any ulterior motive. Every one can always act virtuously whether God exists or not. But, although virtue is the only *intrinsic* good, it is not, as we have seen, the *complete* good. The complete good is composed of virtue with the appropriate amount of happiness. Now we can say of the complete good that it *ought* to exist. But what ought to be must be possible, and therefore the necessary conditions of its possibility must be actual. Now there is no necessary connexion between virtue and happiness either logically or by way of ordinary natural causation. There is no logical connexion, because virtue cannot be defined in terms of happiness, and there are many other kinds of happiness beside the feeling of satisfaction with one's own virtue. And there is no causal connexion by the ordinary laws of Nature. Virtue depends wholly on oneself, and, on Kant's view, can always be realised no matter how unfavourable the conditions may be. But happiness depends largely on one's innate tastes and dispositions, on the state of one's bodily health, and on external circumstances. And a perfectly virtuous man has no more control over these than a vicious one. The position then is this. The complete good must be capable of existing, since it ought to exist. One of its factors, viz., perfect virtue, is possible under all circumstances. But the other factor, viz., the deserved amount of happiness, will be realised only if the course of Nature be deliberately overruled so as to secure it. And the only way in which we can conceive this happening is by supposing that Nature is dependent on a powerful, benevolent, and moral being, who arranges that in the long run virtue shall be rewarded by the appropriate amount of happiness.

This argument is open to the following criticisms : (1) There are two different senses of " ought ", and one of these involves factual possibility whilst the other involves only logical possibility. If I say : " You ought to do so and so," I do imply that you *could* do so and so in some sense which is not merely that there is no logical contradiction in the notion of your doing it. But, if I say : " So and so ought to exist," I imply only that it would involve no logical contradiction, and that any being who could bring it about ought to try to do so. But it does not imply that there actually is any such being. Thus Kant is entitled only to the hypothetical proposition: " If a perfect God existed he would order the course of Nature so that virtue would receive its appropriate reward in happiness." He is not entitled to the categorical conclusion that such a being exists. (2) It seems to me that there is a certain inconsistency between Kant's position in this argument and his position in the argument for immortality. In the latter it is assumed that we shall not be morally perfect until we have completely got rid of the passive, sensuous, and emotional side of our nature. In the argument about God it is assumed that the happiness, which is an essential feature in the supreme good, is not the mere consciousness of virtue, but is something further added as a reward of virtue. But how could we feel any such happiness if we had no sensations or emotions left ?

CHAPTER VI

Sidgwick

SIDGWICK'S *Methods of Ethics* seems to me to be on the whole the best treatise on moral theory that has ever been written, and to be one of the English philosophical classics. This does not of course imply that Sidgwick was a better man or an acuter thinker than the other writers with whose theories we have been dealing ; for he inherited the results of their labours, and he thus had over them an advantage of the kind which any contemporary student of mathematics or physics has over Newton and Faraday. But, even when this advantage has been discounted, Sidgwick must continue to rank extremely high. He combined deep moral earnestness with complete coolness and absence of moral fanaticism. His capacity for seeing all sides of a question and estimating their relative importance was unrivalled ; his power of analysis was very great ; and he never allowed the natural desire to make up one's mind on important questions to hurry him into a decision where the evidence seemed inadequate or conflicting. Those who, like the present writer, never had the privilege of meeting Sidgwick can infer from his writings, and still more from the characteristic philosophic merits of such pupils of his as M'Taggart and Moore, how acute and painstaking a thinker and how inspiring a teacher he must have been. Yet he has grave defects as a writer which have certainly detracted from his fame. His style is heavy and involved, and he seldom allowed that strong sense of humour, which is said to have made him a delightful conversationalist, to relieve the uniform dull dignity of his writing. He incessantly refines, qualifies, raises objections, answers them, and then finds further objections to the answers. Each of these objections, rebuttals, rejoinders, and surrejoinders is in itself admirable, and does infinite credit to the acuteness and candour of the author. But the reader is apt to become impatient ; to lose the thread of the argument ; and to rise from his desk finding that he has read a great deal with constant admiration and now remembers little or nothing. The result is that Sidgwick probably has far less influence at present than he ought to have, and less than many writers, such as Bradley, who were as superior to him in literary style as he was to them in ethical and philosophical acumen. Even a thoroughly second-rate thinker like T. H. Green, by diffusing a grateful and comforting aroma of ethical " uplift ", has probably made far more undergraduates into prigs than Sidgwick will ever make into philosophers. If I can give in my own words an intelligible critical account of Sidgwick's main argument, which will induce some people to read or re-read the *Methods of Ethics* and will furnish them with a guide to it, I shall have done a useful bit of work. They will then be able to study at leisure and without confusion the admirable details, and to fill in those lights and shades which are so important and so characteristic of Sidgwick but are necessarily omitted in the sketch which I offer them.

I will begin with a synopsis of the work, taking the topics in my own order and stating the conclusions in my own words. I shall then give a more detailed critical discussion of each of the main points in the synopsis.

(A) *Logical Analysis of Ethical Terms.*—We constantly make judgments which involve the terms *right, wrong, ought, good, bad,* etc. These may be called " Ethical Judgments ". We must begin by seeing whether the terms *right* and *ought,* on the one hand, and *good,* on the other, are analysable into simpler factors or are logically ultimate. (1) In the case of *ought* we must distinguish between a merely hypothetical and a categorical sense. We certainly do seem to use " ought " in a categorical sense sometimes, and all attempts to define it when used in this sense have failed. It is therefore likely that the categorical ought is a logically primitive term, though it may well be that the *notion of it* has arisen in the course of human history or pre-history from psychological pre-conditions in which it was not present. (2) In the case of *good* we must distinguish between good-as-means and good-as-end, and we may confine our discussion to the latter. There is a long and complex argument, which is not easy to summarise, on the question whether good-as-end is logically analysable. The upshot seems to be that it can be defined in a very complicated way by means of relations to hypothetical desires, and that it does not involve in its analysis any obligation to seek it.

(B) *Epistemological Questions.*—The main question here is as to which of our cognitive faculties is involved in the cognition of ethical terms and propositions. From the discussion of the term *ought* it appears probable that this is an *a priori* concept. Now the recognition of *a priori* concepts and the making of judgments which involve such terms have always been ascribed to Reason. Again, although we no doubt start with singular ethical judgments, such as " That act is wrong ", we never regard them as ultimate and as neither needing nor being capable of justification. On the contrary we should always expect to be able to justify our singular judgment by a statement of the form : " That act has such and such a characteristic, and *any* act which had that characteristic would *ipso facto* be wrong." These universal ethical judgments are derived by intuitive induction from inspecting the particular cases which are described in the singular judgments. And this process of seeing that a particular conjunction of characteristics is an instance of a universal and necessary connexion between characteristics has always been ascribed to Reason. So Reason plays an essential part in ethical cognition.

(C) *Psychological Questions about Motives and Volitions.*— (1) Can Reason affect our actions in any other way than by suggesting new means to already desired ends and by calling attention to remote probable consequences ? Sidgwick holds that there is a perfectly definite way, in addition to these two, in which Reason can and does affect our actions. Human beings have an impulse or desire to do what they judge to be right and to shun what they believe to be wrong as such. It is only one motive among others, and it may be, and often is, overcome by others. But it exists and it affects our actions. And it is a motive which could act only on a rational being ; for only such a being could have the *a priori* concept of right or ought. (2) As he holds this view, it is important for him to refute a certain psychological theory which is inconsistent with it and which has been very widely held. This is the doctrine called *Psychological Hedonism.* According to this theory the only motive which can move any human being is the expectation of pleasure or of pain. Sidgwick first clearly distinguishes this from the theory called *Ethical Hedonism,* which asserts that pleasantness and painfulness are the only characteristics in virtue of which any state of affairs is intrinsically good or bad. He discusses the relations between the two wholly different theories, and shows that Ethical Hedonism cannot be inferred from Psychological Hedonism and can be held consistently by a man who denies Psychological Hedonism. He then discusses and refutes Psychological Hedonism itself.

(D) *Free-will and Determinism.*—The question of motives naturally leads us to that of freedom and determinism. For ethics the question comes to this : " Is there always a possibility of my choosing to act in the manner which I now judge to be reasonable and right, whatever my past actions and experiences may have been ? " There are two points to be considered. (1) What is the right answer to the question ? (2) To what extent is ethics concerned with the question and its answer ? On the first point Sidgwick contends that all argument and analogy is in favour of the determinist view, but that direct inspection is in favour of free-will. Although every yielding to temptation makes it harder to do what one judges to be right, yet at the moment of choice between an alternative which he judges to be right and one which he judges not to be so he cannot doubt that he can choose the former. " The difficulty seems to be separated from impossibility by an impassible gulf." On the second point his view is that a deterministic answer to the question would make very little ethical difference in practice, far less than libertarians have thought. But it would be inconsistent with certain elements in the common - sense notions of merit and demerit, praise and blame, reward and punishment, and remorse for wrong-doing.

(E) *Classification of the Methods of Ethics.*—The subjects which have so far been mentioned are common to all types of ethical theory, though different theories might give different answers to some of the questions which have been raised. We come now to the main purpose of the book, viz., a discussion of the most important Methods of Ethics. By a " Method of Ethics " Sidgwick means roughly any type of general theory which claims to unify our various ethical judgments into a coherent system on some principle which is claimed to be self-evident. In the end he comes to the conclusion that the really important methods of ethics reduce to three, which he calls *Intuitionism, Egoistic Hedonism,* and *Utilitarianism* or *Universalistic Hedonism.* (In this context of course " hedonism " is to be understood as " ethical ", not as " psychological ", hedonism.) I think that there is a good deal to be criticised in this classification, but I must reserve my criticisms for the present. Intuition-ism is, roughly speaking, the view that there are a number of fairly concrete ethical axioms of the general form : " Any action of such and such a kind, done in such and such a kind of situation, would be right (or wrong) no matter whether its consequences were good, bad, or indifferent." *E.g.,* common sense would hold that any action which was an instance of deliberate ingratitude to a benefactor would *ipso facto* be wrong, and that this can be seen by direct inspection without any consideration of the consequences of *this* action or of the prevalence of *similar* actions.

Egoistic and Universalistic Hedonism agree in rejecting the view that there are such concrete self-evident ethical axioms as these. Sidgwick points out, what most Egoists and Utilitarians seem to have failed to notice, that Egoism and Utilitarianism cannot do without self-evident ethical propositions altogether. Both would hold it to be self-evident that nothing is ultimately worth aiming at but pleasure and absence of pain. The Egoist finds it self-evident that an individual ought to aim at a maximum balance of happiness for himself, and that, if necessary, he ought to be ready to sacrifice any amount of other men's happiness in order to produce the slightest nett increase in his own. The Utilitarian, on the other hand, finds it self-evident that each individual ought to aim at the maximum balance of happiness for all sentient beings present and future, and that, if necessary, he ought to be ready to sacrifice any amount of his own happiness provided that he will thereby produce the slightest nett increase in the general happiness. And there might be other very general principles, mainly about the proper distribution of a given amount of happiness, which either Egoists or Utilitarians or both would accept as self-evident. But neither Egoists nor Utilitarians would admit more concrete ethical intuitions than these. Those specific ethical principles, such as the principles of truth-speaking, gratitude to benefactors, etc., which common-sense regards as self-evident and independent of consequences, would be regarded by Egoists and Utilitarians as mere empirical generalisations which tell us what types of action have been found on the whole to maximise individual or general happiness in various commonly recurring types of circumstances. They are thus hypothetical, and not categorical, imperatives ; and, when obedience to them would clearly involve a nett sacrifice of individual or general happiness as compared with the results of breaking them, it is our duty to break them.

(F) *Detailed Discussion of each of the Three Methods.*— Each of the three methods is discussed, so far as possible by itself. The order which Sidgwick takes is Egoism, Intuitionism, and Utilitarianism. This does not seem to me to be the best order, since a great deal of the argument that is used in connexion with Egoistic Hedonism has to be assumed in dealing with Universalistic Hedonism, and the reader is rather liable to forget what has been established in connexion with the former when he emerges into the latter after the very long and complicated discussion on Intuitionism which is sandwiched between the two. I prefer the order (1) *Intuitionism*, and (2) *Hedonism*. The latter can then be subdivided into (2, 1) *Hedonism in General*, (2, 2) *Egoistic Hedonism*, and (2, 3) *Universalistic Hedonism*.

(1) *Intuitionism*.—The treatment of this method begins with a discussion of certain general questions, of which the following are the most important. What is the nature of ethical intuitions, and do they in fact occur ? What relation, if any, is there between the psycho-genetic history of the occurrence of intuitions and their validity when they have occurred ? What is the subject-matter of ethical judgments ; are they about acts or intentions or motives or character ? Sidgwick then undertakes an extremely elaborate detailed investigation into the morality of common-sense. He takes in turn those types of action which seem to common-sense to be self-evidently right (or wrong) without regard to consequences in certain types of situation ; his object being to see whether critical reflexion can extract from common-sense morality a coherent system of self-evident principles connected with each other in a logically satisfactory way. The upshot of the discussion is that, so long as we confine our attention to fairly normal cases and do not try to analyse our terms very carefully, there is a great deal of agreement about what ought and what ought not to be

done in given types of situation, and our duties seem self-evident. But no sooner do we bring the principles of common-sense morality face to face with difficult and unusual situations than this agreement and this apparent self-evidence vanish. Terms which seemed clear and simple are found to cover a multitude of alternatives ; and, when these alternatives are explicitly introduced into the statement of an alleged self-evident principle, the latter is liable to reduce to a tautology or to cease to be self-evident, according to which alternative we substitute. Then again the axioms of common-sense morality seem to conflict with each other in marginal cases. If we try to enunciate higher principles, which will harmonise the lower ones in a rational way when they conflict and will tell us how far each is to be followed in such cases, we find either that we cannot do it, or that the higher principle is so complicated that we should hesitate to ascribe self-evidence to it, or that we are frankly beginning to take account of remote consequences and thus deserting pure Intuitionism.

As we have already remarked, Sidgwick himself holds that *every* method of ethics must involve at least one intuition ; for at any rate the judgment that we ought to aim at so and so as an ultimate end must be intuitive. In addition to such intuitions as these he recognised as self-evident a few very abstract principles about the right distribution of happiness. But these few highly abstract *a priori* principles serve only to delimit an enormous field outside which no action can be right, just as the Conservation of Energy only sets limits to the changes that are physically possible. Within this field innumerable alternative courses of action are possible, just as there are innumerable possible changes which would satisfy the Conservation of Energy.

To determine which of these alternatives is right we need supplementary and more concrete ethical principles, just as we need the specific laws of physics and mechanics to determine which of the changes compatible with the Conservation of Energy will actually happen. And, on Sidgwick's view, no such concrete ethical principles are intrinsically necessary and self-evident. They are, as Egoism and Utilitarianism teach, mere hypothetical imperatives, to be accepted only as general prescriptions for gaining ends which are judged to be intrinsically desirable.

(2, 1) *Hedonism in General.*—Under this heading two very different questions have to be discussed. One is purely ethical, the other is purely factual and mainly psychological.

(2, 11) *The Ethical Problem.* It seems intuitively certain that we ought to aim at realising the greatest nett balance of good that we can. But this at once leads to the question : " In virtue of what characteristics is a thing, or person, or event, or state of affairs intrinsically good ? " *Prima facie* there would seem to be several characteristics which give intrinsic value to anything that has them. *E.g.*, it would be plausible to hold that a virtuous character has intrinsic value in respect of its virtue, that an acute intellect has intrinsic value in respect of its acuteness, that a beautiful person has intrinsic value in respect of his beauty, and so on. Now the pure ethical hedonist has to show that this is a mistake. He has to show that nothing is intrinsically good or bad except experiences, that no characteristic of an experience has any bearing on its intrinsic value except its pleasantness or painfulness, and that the measure of its intrinsic value is the nett balance of pleasantness over painfulness which characterises it. Sidgwick claims that, when all the numerous sources of illusion which tend to cloud the issue have been removed and we view the alternatives quite clearly, we are bound to agree with the ethical hedonist.

(2, 12) *The Factual Problem.* Even if ethical hedonism be in fact true, it will be of no use as a practical guide to right conduct unless we can compare pleasures and pains with a fair degree of accuracy and can reach fairly accurate estimates of the nett balance of pleasure in various alternative future experiences which we can initiate by our present choice of action. For the Egoistic Hedonist the problem is confined to his own future experiences during the rest of his life. The Utilitarian is faced with all the problems of the Egoistic Hedonist and with others in addition. For he has to consider how his actions will affect the happiness of all present and future sentient beings throughout the whole of their lives from now onwards. Sidgwick discusses the alleged and the real difficulties of such estimation very elaborately. The uncertainties of direct comparison are very great ; and he concludes that various indirect methods which have been suggested as easier and more accurate cannot dispense with the direct method and have difficulties of their own. Still, we all do make such comparisons and estimates constantly in ordinary life, and we do regard them as reasonably trustworthy when due precautions have been taken. And ethical hedonism only asks us to do in connexion with *all* our conduct what we admittedly do in connexion with a large part of it.

The greater part of Sidgwick's discussion of (2, 2) *Egoistic Hedonism* is concerned with this problem of estimation, which is really common to it and to Universalistic Hedonism.

(2, 3) *Universalistic Hedonism.*—Sidgwick's arguments

for Utilitarianism are of two different kinds. The first is an abstract argument from principles which claim to be self-evident. The second is based on his criticisms of the morality of common sense.

The essence of the direct abstract argument is this. (a) There is a *Total* or *Universal Good*. This is composed of the Goods which reside in individuals and their experiences, and it has no other components. (b) Our primary duty is to aim at maximising this Universal Good. We can of course do this only by affecting the amount of Good which resides in this, that, or the other individual. But we ought to aim at the Good of any individual *only* as a factor in the Universal Good. It can therefore never be right to increase the amount of Good which resides in a certain individual or group of individuals if this can be done only at the expense of a reduction in the Universal Good. (c) Now it has been argued in connexion with Hedonism in general that nothing is intrinsically good except pleasant experiences, and that the intrinsic goodness of any experience is determined simply by the nett balance of pleasantness over painfulness in it. (d) It is therefore my primary duty to aim at increasing the total amount and intensity of pleasant experience and decreasing the total amount and intensity of unpleasant experience in the universe as much as I can. I can do this only by affecting the nett balance of happiness in this, that, and the other individual, including myself. But I must recognise that the happiness of any individual (*e.g.*, myself) or of any group of individuals (*e.g.*, my family or country-men) is to be aimed at *only* as a component of the Universal Happiness ; and that, as such, it is in no way to be preferred to the equal happiness of any other individual or group of individuals. Consequently it is never right to increase the nett happiness of an individual or a limited group at the expense of a reduction in universal happiness.

It will be seen that in the above argument (*a*) and (*b*) are directed against Egoists, whilst (*c*) is addressed to people who take a non-hedonistic or a not purely hedonistic view of Good. It remains to deal with Intuitionists, in the sense of people who hold that we can see directly that certain types of action would *ipso facto* be right (or wrong) in certain types of situation without regard to the goodness or badness of their consequences. Sidgwick does this by following up his negative treatment of the claims of common-sense morality to furnish a coherent system of self-evident ethical principles with an equally detailed positive discussion of these principles regarded as rules for maximising general happiness in constantly recurring types of situation. The conclusion which he reaches after a very careful examination is that the resemblance between the rules accepted as intuitively certain by common-sense and those which would be reasonable on Utilitarian grounds is close and detailed. In the ordinary cases, where common-sense feels no doubts about its principles, the Utilitarian grounds for the rule are strong and obvious. In the marginal cases, where common-sense begins to feel doubtful about a principle, there are nearly always strong Utilitarian grounds both for obeying the rule and for breaking it. In such cases the Utilitarian solution seems to be generally in accord with the vague instincts of common-sense, and common-sense often explicitly appeals to Utilitarian considerations in such difficulties. Again, the differences between the moral judgments of men of different races or periods about the same type of action can often be explained by Utilitarian considerations. On the whole too the relative importance which common-sense ascribes to the various virtues is the same as that which would be ascribed to them on Utilitarian grounds.

Sidgwick does not conclude from these facts that our remote ancestors were consciously and deliberately Utilitarians, and that they laboriously derived by observation, induction, and hedonic calculation those general rules which now seem to us directly self-evident. On the contrary, the further we go back in the course of history the less trace do we find of deliberate Utilitarian calculation and inference, and the more immediate and direct do moral judgments become. Still, the distribution of praise, blame, admiration, etc., for character and conduct is very accurately proportional to its apparent effect on general happiness. It seems fair to conclude that common-sense has always been implicitly and unconsciously Utilitarian, and that it tends to become more and more explicitly so as intelligence, sympathy, and experience grow.

This extensive and detailed agreement between Utilitarianism and the morality of common-sense should no doubt help to give us confidence in the former. But, on the present hypothesis, the rules of common-sense morality are traditional prescriptions for maximising general happiness which grew up among our remote ancestors and have been handed down to us. The circumstances under which they arose must have been widely different from those in which we live ; the persons among whom they grew up did not consciously aim at the Utilitarian end ; and, even if they had done so, they must have had a very limited insight into remote consequences, a very restricted range of sympathy, and many superstitious beliefs which would affect their estimates of the happiness to be gained from various courses of action. It is therefore most unlikely that there would be complete agreement between the rules of common-sense morality and those which an enlightened Utilitarian would lay down at the present day in Western Europe. And, if one is persuaded of the truth of Utilitarianism, one will naturally hold that, where the morality of common-sense differs from that of Utilitarianism, the former is mistaken and ought to be corrected.

It had been fashionable with Utilitarians before Sidgwick's time to insist with a good deal of fervour on this point, and to talk as if Utilitarianism could and should produce a new ethical heaven and earth at very short notice. Sidgwick examines with extreme care and subtlety the duty of a Utilitarian living in a society of non-Utilitarians and convinced that certain of the rules of the current morality are out of accord with his principles. He pours buckets of cold water on the reforming fires of such Utilitarians. When all relevant facts are taken into consideration it will scarcely ever be right on Utilitarian grounds for a Utilitarian openly to break or to recommend others to break the rules of morality commonly accepted in his society.

(G) *The Relations between the Three Methods.*—Sidgwick thinks that in the daily practice of ordinary men all three methods are accepted and used in turn to justify and correlate moral judgments. And it is vaguely assumed that they are mutually consistent, that " honesty in the long run is the best policy ", and that on the whole I shall find my greatest happiness in what produces the greatest happiness for every one. These comfortable assumptions have no doubt a good deal of truth in them so long as one is living a normal life in peaceful times in a well-organised society with fairly decent laws and a fairly enlightened public opinion. But even in these circumstances cases arise from time to time in which the alternative which would be right according to one method would be wrong according to another. And in less favourable conditions such conflicts might be frequent and glaring. Now, as regards possible conflicts between Intuitionism and Utilitarianism, Sidgwick has no difficulty in deciding. He accepts no moral principles as self-evident except the general principle of Ethical Hedonism and a few highly abstract rules about the right distribution of happiness. The morality of common-sense, so far as it can be justified, must be justified by the Utilitarian method ; and, where it cannot be thus justified, it must be rejected by the moralist in his private thinking, though not necessarily or usually in his public speaking or overt action. If then the choice had lain simply between Intuitionism and Utilitarianism, Sidgwick would definitely have been a Utilitarian, though his Utilitarianism would have involved a few highly abstract intuitions.

But unfortunately the position for him was not so simple as this. He had also to consider the relation between Egoistic and Universalistic Ethical Hedonism, and here he finds an insuperable difficulty. If it be admitted that there is a Total or Universal Good, then it is no doubt my duty to aim at maximising this and to regard the Good which resides in me and my experiences as important only in so far as it is a part of the Total Good. In that case I must be prepared to sacrifice some or all of my Good if by that means and by that only I can increase the Total Good. But the consistent Egoist will not admit that there is a Total or Universal Good. There is my Good and your Good, but they are not parts of a Total Good, on his view. My duty is to aim at maximising my Good, and to consider the effects of my actions on your Good only in so far as they may indirectly affect mine. Your duty is to aim at maximising your Good, and to consider the effects of your actions on my Good only in so far as they may indirectly affect yours. It is plain that there is no logical inconsistency in this doctrine. And Sidgwick goes further. He says that it is plain that X is concerned with the quality of X's experiences in a way in which he is not concerned with the quality of Y's experiences, whoever Y may be. And it is impossible to feel certain that this distinction is not ethically fundamental. Thus Sidgwick is left in the unfortunate position that there are two principles, each of which separately seems to him self-evident, but which when taken together seem to be mutually inconsistent.

To this logical difficulty he does not, so far as I can see, profess to be able to give any solution. For he proceeds to discuss what is clearly a different point, viz., whether there is any way of convincing an Egoist that he ought always to act *as if* he were a Utilitarian. Even if this could be done, it would of course be no disproof of the truth of Egoism. Nor would it alter or explain the fact that there are two fundamental ethical principles which are mutually incompatible though each seems self-evident. The only sense in which Egoism and Utilitarianism would have been " reconciled " would be that we should have shown that the fundamental theoretical difference between the two should make no difference in practice. We must show that the Universe is so constituted that, whenever obedience to Utilitarian principles would seem to demand a greater sacrifice of happiness on the part of an agent than dis-obedience to them, this sacrifice is recouped from some source of happiness which escapes the notice of the super-ficial observer. Such attempted " reconciliations " have

taken two forms, viz. : (1) *Psychological,* and (2) *Metaphysical.*
Each is discussed by Sidgwick.

The psychological attempt at reconciliation has been
based on the pleasures and pains of sympathy. Sidgwick
discusses this solution elaborately and reaches the conclusion
that, whilst sympathetic pleasures and pains are extremely
important and would go far towards making Egoistic and
Utilitarian conduct coincide, yet they will not produce
complete identity. Indeed there are certain respects in
which the growing intensity of sympathy, when combined
with its inevitable limitation of range, would increase the
divergence between Egoistic and Utilitarian conduct.

The metaphysical attempt at reconciliation has in
Western Europe generally taken the theistic form that
there is an all-powerful God who desires the greatest
Total Good of all living beings. By rewards and punishments in a future life he will make it worth the Egoist's
while to act in such a way as to subserve this end, even
when, if this life alone be considered, it would be his duty
to act otherwise. Sidgwick recognises that it is not essential
that the metaphysical reconciliation should take this theistic
form ; it would be secured equally well by the Buddhist
doctrine of reincarnation. Sidgwick puts aside, as out of
place in an ethical treatise, the question whether the
existence of a celestial Jeremy Bentham (if we may use
the expression with becoming reverence) has been revealed
supernaturally or can be established by reasoning from
non-ethical premises. But he thinks that it is in place to
consider whether anything can be determined on this subject
from purely ethical premises. His conclusion seems to be as
follows. The hypothesis that the universe is so constituted
that to act as a Utilitarian will always be consistent with

the dictates of Egoism is necessary and sufficient to avoid a contradiction in ethics, which is a fundamental department of human thought. Is this any ground for accepting the hypothesis ? If we hold that, in other departments of human thought, it is reasonable to accept certain general principles (*e.g.*, the Uniformity of Nature), which are not self-evident nor capable of proof by problematic induction, simply because they introduce order and coherence which would otherwise be lacking, then it would seem to be inconsistent to object to moralists for doing likewise. But Sidgwick expresses no opinion here as to whether in other departments of thought men do *in fact* assume such principles ; or whether, *if* they do, they are justified.

*   *   *

I have now completed what I hope is a fair and clear account of the main contents of Sidgwick's *Methods of Ethics*. I have refrained from all criticism, and I have not entered into the details of his arguments. I propose now to take the main points of the synopsis in order; to give a somewhat more detailed account of Sidgwick's views on each ; and to make such criticisms or comments as seem to me desirable.

(A) LOGICAL ANALYSIS OF ETHICAL TERMS : (1) *Ought and Right*. The main discussion on this subject is to be found in *Book I, Chap. III*.

(1, 1) We must begin by distinguishing a narrower and a wider sense of " ought ". In its narrower sense it applies only to actions which an agent could do if he willed. But there is a wider sense in which there is no such implication. We can say that sorrow ought to have been felt by a certain man at the death of a certain relation, though it was not in his power to feel sorrow at will. And we can say that virtue ought to be rewarded.

(1, 2) There is another distinction to be drawn between what I will call the *deontological*, the *teleological*, and the *logical* application of " ought ". Some people judge that there are certain types of action which ought to be done (or avoided) in all or in certain types of situation, regardless of the goodness or badness of the probable consequences. This is what I call the " deontological " application of " ought ". Now there are people who would deny that they ever make such judgments as these. But such people may, nevertheless, make the judgment that every one ought to aim at certain ends without any ulterior motive, *e.g.*, at his own greatest happiness, at the greatest happiness of all sentient beings, and so on. This is what I call the " teleo-logical " application of " ought ". Sidgwick suggests that many people who say that they have no notion of un-conditional obligation merely mean that they never use " ought " in the deontological application though they may quite well use it in the teleological application. Lastly, it is conceivable that there are people who not only do not recognise any types of action as being obligatory apart from all consideration of the goodness of their consequences, but also do not recognise that there are any ends which every one ought to aim at. Every one must admit indeed that there are ends which are *in fact* ultimate for a given individual, *i.e.*, things that he does in fact desire directly and not merely as a means to something else. But it might be said that there is nothing of which it could be held that every one *ought* to desire it as an end. Even so, as Sidgwick points out, there is an application of " ought " which such people would make. If a certain man does in fact take a certain end as ultimate for him then he *ought* to be consistent about it. He ought to take such means as he believes will tend to bring it into being, and he ought not to do things which he believes will be inconsistent with its realisation. That people can and do will ends and then fail to will what they believe to be the right means to them is certain. And we do say that no one ought to act in this inconsistent way. This is the logical application of " ought ".

It will be noted that I have been careful to talk of three different *applications*, and not of three different *meanings*, of " ought ". We have now to consider whether these different applications do involve different meanings, and also how they are related to the distinction which we have already drawn between the wider and the narrower sense of " ought ". The position seems to me to be as follows : (*a*) " Ought ", when used in its teleological application, is used in its wider sense. For in this application we say that every one ought to desire so-and-so as an ultimate end. Now it is plain that we cannot desire this or that at will, any more than we can love this or that person at will. Thus to say that each ought to desire the happiness of all is like saying that every one ought to love his parents and is not like saying that every one ought to speak the truth. (*b*) " Ought ", when used in its logical application, would seem to be used in its narrower sense. For we believe that it is within the power of any sane human being to be consistent if he tries. Thus to say that anyone who adopts an end as ultimate for him ought to adopt what he believes to be the means to it is like saying that every one ought to tell the truth and is not like saying that every one ought to love his parents. In fact it seems to me that the logical ought is just a special case of the deontological ought. Its main interest is that it is recognised by people who would not admit that they could recognise any other instance of the deontological ought.

(1, 3) We must now say something about the relations between " right " and " ought ". This will enable us to say something further about the relations between the narrower and the wider senses of " ought ". (*a*) Any action that I ought to do would be right for me to do. But there might be several alternative actions open to me all of which were equally right. In that case it cannot be said of any one of them that I ought to do *it*; it could only be said that I ought to do *one or other* of these actions, and that it was indifferent which I did. (*b*) Even if only one course of action open to me were right, or if one alternative were more right than any of the others, we should not necessarily say that I ought to do that action. We tend to confine the word " ought ", in its narrower sense, to cases where we believe that there are motives and inclinations against doing the rightest action open to the agent. Thus, as Sidgwick points out, we should hardly say of an ordinary healthy man that he *ought*, in the narrower sense, to take adequate nourishment ; though we might say this of an invalid with a disinclination to take food or of a miser. And, although we hold that God acts rightly, we should hesitate to say that he always does as he ought or does his duty. Such notions would seem inappropriate to a being who is supposed to have no inclinations to do what is wrong or to leave undone what is right. (*c*) It seems to me that, when I speak of anything as " right ", I am always thinking of it as a factor in a certain wider total situation, and that I mean that it is " appropriately " or " fittingly " related to the rest of this situation. When I speak of anything as " wrong " I am thinking of it as " inappropriately " or " unfittingly "

related to the rest of the situation. This is quite explicit
when we say that love is the right emotion to feel to one's
parents, or that pity and help are the right kinds of emotion
and action in presence of undeserved suffering. This
relational character of rightness and wrongness tends to be
disguised by the fact that some types of action are commonly
thought to be wrong absolutely ; but this, I think, means
only that they are held to be unfitting to *all* situations.
What I have just asserted is not, and does not pretend to
be, an analytical *definition* of " right " and " wrong ". It
does bring out their relational character, and it correlates
them with certain other notions. But the kind of appropriateness and inappropriateness which is implied in the
notions of " right " and " wrong " is, so far as I can see,
specific and unanalysable.

Now, so far as I can see, the wider sense of " ought "
reduces to that of right, together with the associated notion
that, if the right state of affairs were in the power of anyone
to produce, he ought to produce it. Take, *e.g.*, the statement that virtue ought to be rewarded. This means
primarily that it is right that virtue should be accompanied
by happiness, that the one is fitting to the other. In so
far as it means more than this the further implication is
that anyone who had it in his power to make the virtuous
happy would be under an obligation to do so. I think
therefore that there is no need to hold that " ought-to-be "
is a third independent notion in addition to " right " and
" ought-to-do ". For it seems that " ought-to-be " can be
analysed in terms of " right " together with a hypothetical
reference to what a being who had it in his power to produce
the right state of affairs " ought to do ".

(*d*) " Ought ", in the narrower sense in which in future

I propose to use it, seems to be bound up with the following facts. (i) That a man's belief that a certain action which is in his power is right is a motive for doing it, and that his belief that a certain state of affairs which he could help to bring about would be good is a motive for aiming at it. (ii) That human beings are subject to other motives which may and often do conflict with this one. And (iii) that, in cases of conflict, it is right that this motive should win. When such a conflict is actually taking place we have a peculiar emotional experience which may be called a " feeling of obligation ".

(I, 4) In the above discussion I have in places wandered far from Sidgwick, though I do not know that I have said anything that he would deny. We come now to a question which he discusses very fully : " Can the term ' right ' be analysed into a combination of other, and not specifically ethical, terms ? " To hold that it can is to hold a naturalistic theory as regards right. Sidgwick's method is to take the most plausible of the naturalistic analyses, and to try to show that they are inadequate. It of course remains possible that some day some more subtle naturalistic analysis may be proposed, and that this will be immune to Sidgwick's criticisms. But this has not in fact happened up to now. The objections have often been ignored, but they have never been answered.

Sidgwick takes four suggested analyses for discussion. (*a*) It might be suggested that when I say that X is right I mean simply that it excites in me a certain kind of feeling of approval. Since people certainly argue with each other about right and wrong, this can hardly be their primary meaning. But it might be said that this is all that they ever have any *ground* for asserting ; and that they carelessly put their judgment in an impersonal form, as a man might do if he said that the taste of onions is nasty, though he really means no more than that he dislikes the taste of onions. I think it is obvious that this extremely subjective view will not fit the facts. At the very least I must mean that X would evoke a feeling of approval in all or most people on all or most occasions when they contemplated it.

It is clear that the theory could be most satisfactorily refuted if it could be shown that I sometimes reverse the judgment about X whilst my emotion towards it remains unchanged, or that my emotion towards X sometimes changes its determinate form whilst my judgment about X remains unchanged. Sidgwick, however, does not claim that this happens. What he says is that my judgment may change from " X is wrong " to " X is right ", and I may still feel towards X an emotion which resembles that which I formerly felt. But, on careful introspection, it is found to be no longer moral disapproval but a " *quasi*-moral feeling of repugnance ". This fact is important in so far as it enables us to distinguish the feeling of moral approval and disapproval from other pairs of opposed emotions which often accompany that feeling and are liable to be mistaken for it. It is, *e.g.*, clear that, in the case of unusual sexual practices, the majority of normal people constantly mistake what is in fact a *quasi*-moral feeling of repugnance for a genuine feeling of moral disapproval. But I cannot see that the fact is incompatible with the theory of the meaning of " right " which Sidgwick is attacking. For in his example it is surely possible that at first I feel moral disapproval mixed with *quasi*-moral repugnance, and that later I feel moral approval mixed with *quasi*-moral repugnance. And the supporters of the present theory could say that my first judgment expressed the fact that I was feeling moral disapproval; my second expresses the fact that I am feeling moral approval; and the constant factor of *quasi*-moral repugnance does not enter into either judgment. Sidgwick's conclusion that the moral emotion is *causally determined* by the moral judgment, and therefore cannot be the *subject-matter* of the judgment, is compatible with the facts but is not necessitated by them.

(*b*) The second analysis is that when I say that X is right I mean that I have a feeling of approval towards it and also sympathetic representations of other men's similar feelings. To this Sidgwick answers that I may begin to feel moral disapproval of an action which I once approved, whilst my fellow-men continue to feel moral approval of it. Or, again, I might go on feeling moral approval after other men had begun to feel moral disapproval. In such cases the sympathetic representation of other men's similar feelings has ceased. Nevertheless I should begin to judge that the action is wrong in the first case, and I should continue to judge that it is right in the second case. It is of course true that the sympathetic representation of the similar feelings of others generally accompanies and supports my moral judgments. But this is because my judgments generally agree with those of others, and this agreement increases my conviction of the truth of my own judgments.

(*c*) The third analysis is that when I say that X is right I mean that other men will feel approval towards *me* if I do X and will feel disapproval towards *me* if I omit to do X. This theory, as Sidgwick says, does bring out a certain analogy between moral and legal right. An action is legally wrong if it will be punished by the law; and, on this theory, it is morally wrong if it will be punished by the pains of public disapprobation. But it is plain that the analogy is only partial, and that the theory is inadequate. For we admit that there are things which it is right to do, but which will call forth public disapproval; and conversely. We often hold that public opinion distributes its approvals and disapprovals *wrongly*; and it seems clear that such judgments involve a sense of " wrong " which cannot be analysed in terms of public approval and disapproval. Lastly, if I say to a man : " You will be wrong if you do so and so, and public opinion will be against you," the second part of my admonition is clearly not a mere repetition of the first, as it should be on the present theory. It is true that there are *quasi*-moral judgments, just as there are *quasi*-moral emotions. The words " right " and " wrong " in such judgments *do* mean no more than " evoking social approval " and " evoking social disapproval " respectively. The codes of honour, of fashion, etc., consist of such judgments. And unreflective people do not sharply distinguish them from genuine moral judgments. But, when we reflect, we do seem to see that there is a fundamental difference between the *quasi*-moral judgment : " It is wrong to wear brown boots with a morning-coat " and the genuinely moral judgment : " It is wrong to inflict pain on innocent persons except as a means to removing some greater evil." The distinction becomes most clear when one and the same action is the object of moral approval and *quasi*-moral disapproval, or conversely. This difference seems plainly to exist within my experience ; but I cannot help being somewhat perturbed to find that there are important departments of conduct in which judgments which seem to most people to be clearly moral seem to me equally clearly to be only *quasi*-moral. I have no doubt that *they* are mistaken in thinking these judgments moral (though it is of course possible that I suffer from moral obtuseness), but I cannot help wondering whether the few judgments which seem to me so clearly moral may not really be only *quasi*-moral judgments which have so far resisted my attempts at ethical scepticism.

(*d*) The fourth analysis is that to say that X is right or that it is wrong means respectively that one will be rewarded or punished by God if one does it. To this Sidgwick answers that people certainly make moral judgments and feel moral emotions without holding this particular form of theism. Moreover, those who believe that God will in fact reward certain actions and punish certain others generally believe that he will do so *because* the former are independently right and the latter independently wrong. Lastly, although we should not say that it is God's *duty* to act justly, because we think of him as not subject to any opposing impulses, we should say that it is *right* for him to do so. And we certainly do not mean that he will be punished by himself if he does not.

Sidgwick concludes that the notions of right and wrong are probably logically simple and so incapable of analysis. Even if his list of attempted analyses covers all the possibilities, which we cannot safely assume, there remains a point of formal logic to be mentioned. Strictly speaking, he has shown only that " right " does not *always* mean any *one* of these. It remains logically possible that it always means *one or other* of them, sometimes one and sometimes another. If so, it is a fundamentally ambiguous word. What he needs to show is that there is a meaning of " right " which does not coincide with any of these alternatives, and that it is used with this sense in ethical judgments. I am inclined to think that this is true ; but Sidgwick's argument does not strictly suffice to prove it.

(1, 5) It remains to be noticed that Sidgwick clearly points out that the logical simplicity of the term *right* neither entails nor is incompatible with the psychological primitiveness of the notion of right in the human mind. It is quite possible that the notion may have arisen in the course of evolution, and that we can point out the other notions which have preceded it. Some people have imagined that, if this could be done, it would follow that *right* cannot be logically simple but must be composed of the terms which are the objects of these psychologically earlier notions. This, as Sidgwick remarks, is to carry over to psychology the chemical theory that the resultant of the interaction of several elements is composed of those elements, still persisting in a disguised form, and of nothing else. Even in chemistry this is a bit of highly speculative metaphysics, if taken literally. But at least it is a convenient way of summing up certain important observable facts, such as the constancy of mass, the fact that a compound can be repeatedly generated by the disappearance of its elements and the elements be regenerated by the destruction of the compound, and so on. There are absolutely no facts in psychology which bear the least analogy to these ; and so there is no justification for treating the products of psychological development as if they were compounds containing their antecedents as elements.

(2) *Good.* Sidgwick does not treat the term *Good* until *Book I, Chap. IX* is reached. But this seems to be the proper place to deal with it.

(2, 1) The first question to be considered is whether " goodness " can be defined in terms of pleasantness. In this discussion it will be well to remember the distinction which I drew, in connexion with Hume's theory, between non-causal pleasantness, which can belong only to experiences and which makes such experiences pleasures, and causal pleasantness, which can belong to other things beside experiences. It will be remembered that the statement that X is " causally pleasant " means that there is at least one mode of cognising X which is at most times and for most men a pleasant experience.

Now, when we talk of " good " wine or " good " pictures, it does seem at first sight that we mean simply wine which is pleasant to taste or pictures which are pleasant to see. And so it seems as if " goodness ", in these cases at any rate, could be identified with causal pleasantness. But, even when we confine ourselves to such things as wines and pictures, there are serious difficulties, which Sidgwick points out, in this view. We distinguish between good and bad *taste* in such matters. A " good " picture could hardly be defined as one which most men at most times find it pleasant to contemplate. We should rather be inclined to say that it is one which persons *of good taste* in such matters find it pleasant to contemplate. But then we are defining " goodness ", as applied to pictures, not simply in terms of causal pleasantness, but in terms of this and " goodness " as applied to taste. And it seems as if " goodness ", in the latter sense, involved some reference to a supposed objective standard, and could not itself be defined in terms of causal pleasantness. Then, again, it must be admitted that a bad picture or wine may not only please more people than a better one, but may also give more intense pleasure to those whom it pleases. The *blasé* expert may get very little pleasure from seeing pictures or tasting wines which he recognises to be very good, whilst he may get acute discomfort from wines and pictures which give intense pleasure to less sophisticated people of crude tastes and strong susceptibilities.

Suppose now that we pass regretfully from wines and pictures to character and conduct. If we say that a " good " character means one which spectators find it pleasant to contemplate, we shall be back in the difficulties which arose over wines and pictures. We shall have to say that the pleasure must be of a certain specific kind, that it will be felt only by people of good moral taste, and that even in them it may not excite a degree of pleasure proportional to its goodness. It seems almost certain that the contemplation of the character and conduct of the heroes and heroines of the films has given far more intense and widespread pleasure than the contemplation of the character and conduct of Socrates or St. Paul. If, on the other hand, we take a wider definition, and say that " good " character or conduct *means* character or conduct which is either immediately pleasant or productive of pleasure on the whole and in the long run, we seem to be asserting that the fundamental doctrine of Hedonism is a tautology like the statement that the rich and only the rich are wealthy. Now Hedonism, whether true or false, has seldom seemed to its supporters and never to its opponents to be a mere tautology which is true *ex vi termini*.

I am not prepared to accept this last argument of Sidgwick's, for I believe that it rests on a very common confusion between analytical propositions and verbal or tautological propositions. It seems clear to me that a term may in fact be complex and in fact have a certain analysis, and that people may yet use it in the main correctly without recognising that it is complex or knowing the right analysis of it. In that case the proposition which asserts that it has such and such an analysis will be analytic, but will not be tautologous. It therefore seems to me that " good " might *mean* immediately pleasant or conducive to pleasure in the long run, and yet that people who use the word " good " correctly might quite well fail to recognise that this is the right analysis of the term which the word denotes. I agree with Sidgwick in thinking that this is not in fact the meaning of the word " good ", but I deny that his argument proves his conclusion.

(2, 2) We pass now to a second suggestion, viz., that " good " can be defined in terms of desire. In this connexion Sidgwick makes a very important point which he hardly stresses enough, so that the reader may easily overlook it. I will therefore begin by making this point quite explicit. It concerns the ambiguity of the word " desirable." In criticising Mill at our mother's knee we all learnt one ambiguity of this word, viz., that it may mean *capable of being desired* or *fit to be* desired. The first meaning might be called the " purely positive meaning " and the second might be called the " ethically ideal meaning ". The important point which Sidgwick makes is that there is a third sense, which might be called the "positively ideal meaning". In this sense " X has such and such a degree of desirability for me " means that I *should* desire X with such and such an intensity *if* I knew that it were attainable by voluntary action and *if* I could forecast with complete accuracy what my experience would be on attaining X. We must now notice that what is highly desirable, in this sense, if it could be got apart from its consequences, might have highly undesirable results. Among these results is the fact that

the indulgence of desire A may strengthen it and cause
desire B to weaken or vanish ; and yet B may be a more
desirable desire, in the sense defined, than A. We thus
come to the notion of " the most desirable future for me on
the whole from now on ".

This, according to Sidgwick, may be defined as that state
of affairs which I should now choose in preference to any
other that I could initiate at the time, provided that I had
completely accurate knowledge of this and of all practically
possible alternatives, and provided that I could accurately
forecast what my experiences would be on the supposition
that each alternative were realised. It will be noted that
this would involve a knowledge of how my desires and
feelings are going to alter in the course of my life, either
as a result of my present choice or from causes outside my
control. It is evident that this notion is "ideal", in the
sense in which the notion of a perfect gas or a frictionless
fluid is ideal. But, like those notions, it is purely positive ;
it involves in its analysis no reference to obligation or
fittingness. The suggestion is that this is what is meant by
"my good on the whole". He says that it seems paradoxical
to suppose that " my good on the whole " can mean anything
so complicated as this. And yet (*Methods of Ethics*, Sixth
Edition, p. 112) he seems inclined to think that this may
be the correct analysis of the term. And, for reasons
which I have already given, I see no objection to the
view that a term with which we are quite familiar
may in fact have a very complicated and unfamiliar
analysis.

In the second paragraph of the same page he goes on to
say : " It seems to me, however, more in accordance with
common-sense to recognise, as Butler does, that the calm

desire for my good on the whole is *authoritative*; and therefore carries with it implicitly a rational dictate to aim at this end, if in any case a conflicting desire urges the will in an opposite direction." It is not perfectly clear to me what he wishes us to infer from this statement. He might mean (*a*) that the purely positive, though ideal, definition of " my greatest good on the whole " is adequate ; but that it is a *synthetic* and necessary proposition that I *ought* to desire my greatest good on the whole, thus defined. Or (*b*) he might mean that the purely positive definition is not adequate, and that " good " cannot be *defined* without reference to the ethical notion of " ought " or " right ". It seems fairly clear from the latter part of this paragraph that he takes the second view. " My greatest good on the whole " is what I *ought* to desire, assuming that only my own existence were to be considered. And " *the* greatest good on the whole " is what I *ought* to desire when I give the *right* amount of importance to all other individuals as well as myself. (Sidgwick says " *equal* importance ". But this prejudges the question whether equality is the right relative importance of myself and others.)

This seems to be Sidgwick's conclusion, but I must confess that I find his discussion very complicated and the result not very clearly stated. Assuming this to be the right interpretation, there remains one further question to be raised. It follows, no doubt, that a purely positive definition of " good " has been found to be impossible. But is *any* definition possible ? Granted that the two propositions " X is the greatest good on the whole for me " and " X is what I ought to desire when I take account only of my own existence " are *logically equivalent,* is the second *an analysis of* the first ? This does not seem to me at all

obvious. It is surely possible that both " good " and
" right " are indefinable, as both " shape " and " size " are,
and yet that there is a synthetic, necessary, and mutual
relation between them, as there is between shape and size.

(B) EPISTEMOLOGICAL QUESTIONS. I have discussed the
epistemology of ethics very fully in connexion with Hume,
and can therefore afford to be brief here. Sidgwick's
argument begins in the last paragraph of p. 33 in the Sixth
Edition. It may be summarised as follows. We have
come to the conclusion that there are judgments which use
certain specific and indefinable ethical notions, such as
right and *ought*. We may ascribe such judgments to a
faculty of Moral Cognition, without thereby assuming that
any of them are true. Can this faculty be identified with,
or regarded as a species of, any of the familiar cognitive
faculties which deal with non-ethical matters ? In particular,
is it analogous to Sense or to Reason ? It is not plausible
to suppose that all moral judgments are the results of
reason*ing* from self-evident general principles to particular
cases. On the contrary it is quite plausible to hold that
the faculty of Moral Cognition primarily pronounces singular
judgments on particular cases as they arise. And this
might make it appear that this faculty is more analogous
to Sense than to Reason. But (*a*) this suggests that it
involves sensations or feelings, which might vary from man
to man, and that there could be no question of truth or
falsity and no real differences of opinion on ethical matters.
And (*b*) even if we start with singular ethical judgments,
we never remain content with them or regard them as
ultimate. If I judge that X is wrong I always think it
reasonable to be asked for a ground for my assertion. And

the ground would always take the form : " X has certain non-ethical characteristics C, and it is evident that anything which had these characteristics would be wrong." These general principles are reached from particular cases by acts of intuitive induction, and this is a typical act of Reason. Moreover, there are certain very abstract general principles which form an essential part of Ethics, though they do not suffice to tell us our duties in particular cases. An example is that it is wrong to give benefits to or impose sacrifices on A rather than B unless there be some ground, other than the mere numerical difference between A and B, for treating them differently. Such principles can be grasped only by Reason.

After what I have said in connexion with Hume I need make only the following comments. (*a*) The essential point is that Ethics involves both *a priori* concepts and *a priori* judgments ; and these, by definition, are the work of Reason. We may therefore admit that Reason is essential in ethical cognition. But (*b*) analogy would suggest that it is not sufficient. In other departments of knowledge Reason does not form *a priori* concepts unless and until it is presented with suitable materials to reflect upon by Sense-perception. Thus, *e.g.*, it may well be that, unless our sensations had very often come in recurrent bundles, we should never have reached the *a priori* concept of Substance ; and that, unless there had been a good deal of regularity in sense-perception, we should never have reached the *a priori* concept of Cause. It therefore seems likely that something analogous to sense-perception is necessary, though not sufficient, in ethical cognition. It is difficult to suppose that ordinary sense-perception can play the required part. But it does seem to me plausible to suppose that this part may be played by emotions of moral approval and disapproval. The statement that X is wrong is not, in my opinion, a statement *about* my own or other men's emotions of disapproval ; just as the statement that X causes Y is not, in my opinion, a statement *about* the regular sequence of Y-like events on X-like events. But it seems to me arguable that *wrongness* would never have been recognised by Reason without the stimulus and suggestion of the emotion of disapproval, and that *causation* would never have been recognised by Reason without the stimulus and suggestion of perceived regular sequence. I do not think that this is in any way incompatible with the fact that *now*, in many cases, the judgment that so-and-so is wrong may precede and causally determine an emotion of moral disapproval towards so-and-so.

(C) PSYCHOLOGICAL QUESTIONS ABOUT MOTIVES AND VOLITIONS : (1) *Reason as Motive.* Here again, after what I have said in connexion with Hume and with Kant, there is very little for me to add. It is a fact that in most human beings the belief that a certain course of action is right, whatever their criterion of rightness may be, is *pro tanto* a motive for doing it ; and it is a fact the belief that a certain course of action is wrong is *pro tanto* a motive against doing it. We are perfectly familiar with this motive and can watch its conflict with other motives. It is a further fact that, when it does conflict with other motives, we judge that it is right that it and not they should prevail. This, I take it, is what is meant by the "authority" of this motive, which moralists insist upon and which Butler contrasts with its actual psychological power. Now rightness and wrongness, as we have seen, are characteristics which can be grasped only by a rational being, since the concepts of them are *a priori*. It follows that this kind of motive can act *only* on a rational being. It does not follow that it *must* act on every rational being, as such ; unless you choose to define " rational being " in such a way as to include the property of being susceptible to this motive. With these explanations and qualifications it seems clear to me that " Reason is a motive," though I think that this is an abominably loose way of expressing the very important facts which it is meant to convey.

(2) *Psychological Hedonism*. This is the doctrine that my volitions are determined wholly and solely by my pleasures and pains, present and prospective. It is thus a particular species of Psychological Egoism. It is not the only species ; one might quite well be a Psychological Egoist without being a Psychological Hedonist, and, so far as I can see, T. H. Green in his *Prolegomena to Ethics* and Bradley in his *Ethical Studies* are non-hedonistic psychological egoists. It is plain that any refutation of the generic doctrine of Psychological Egoism would, *ipso facto*, be a refutation of its specifically hedonistic form, whilst the converse would not be true. We have already considered at some length attempted refutations of Psychological Egoism by Butler and by Hume. But Sidgwick's is probably the best discussion of the whole subject that exists. We have to deal with two questions, viz. : (2, 1) the relation or want of relation between Psychological and Ethical Hedonism, and (2, 2) the truth or falsehood of Psychological Hedonism itself.

(2, 1) Since Ethical Hedonism can take either an egoistic or a universalistic form, we must consider in turn the relation of Psychological Hedonism to (2, 11) Egoistic Ethical Hedonism, and (2, 12) Universalistic Ethical Hedonism or

Utilitarianism. Sidgwick discusses the first point in *Book I, Chap. IV, Sect.* 1 of the *Methods of Ethics*. He discusses the second rather briefly in *Book III, Chap. XIII, Sect.* 5.

(2, 11) Egoistic Ethical Hedonism is the doctrine that it is my duty to aim at the greatest possible amount of happiness in my own life, and to treat all other objects as subservient to this end. Now, Sidgwick argues, it cannot be my duty to aim at anything which it would be psychologically impossible for me to aim at. So, if Psychological Hedonism implies that it is psychologically impossible for me to aim at anything but my own greatest happiness, it implies that any ethical theory which says that it is my duty to aim at any other end must be false. It would thus entail the *rejection* of all *rival* ethical theories, though not necessarily the *acceptance* of Egoistic Ethical Hedonism. On the other hand, it can hardly be said to be my duty to aim at my own greatest happiness unless it be psychologically possible for me to aim at something else instead. For duty seems to imply the existence of motives which may conflict with the one which it is a duty to obey. It seems to follow that Psychological Hedonism, if taken to mean that I can aim only at my own greatest happiness, is incompatible with *every* ethical theory, including Egoistic Ethical Hedonism. If, however, Psychological Hedonism, whilst holding that nothing can act on my will except my present and prospective pleasures and pains, admits that I may wittingly or unwittingly prefer what will give me less pleasure or more pain to what will give me more pleasure or less pain, this conclusion will not follow. Although, even in this form, it will not *entail* Egoistic Ethical Hedonism (for no purely psychological theory could entail any purely ethical theory), still Egoistic Ethical Hedonism might fairly be regarded as the only reasonable ethical theory to hold in the circumstances.

This is the gist of Sidgwick's doctrine of the connexion or lack of connexion between the two theories. It may be remarked that, if it be valid, it would apply equally to *any* psychological theory which asserted that there is one and only one object which I can desire as an end. For I could be under no obligation to aim at any *other* end, since this would be psychologically impossible for me. And I could be under no obligation to aim at *this* end, since there could be no motives conflicting with my desire for it. But, although the notion of *duty* or *obligation* would have ceased to apply, the notion of *right* might still have application. It might be the case that the only end which I *can* desire is also the end which it is *right* or appropriate or fitting for me to desire. I should simply be in the position of God, who is assumed to be incapable by nature of desiring anything but what is right for him to desire.

Even if Psychological Hedonism be put in the extreme form that I can desire nothing but my greatest happiness on the whole, this must presumably mean that I shall always choose at any moment that course which then *seems to me* to involve most private happiness. This may differ from the course which would *in fact* involve most private happiness. Thus, even on this interpretation of Psychological Hedonism, the agent might diverge from the ideal of Egoistic Ethical Hedonism through intellectual defects, though not through succumbing to the influence of rival motives. But, on the more usual interpretation, he can also diverge from the ideal of Egoistic Ethical Hedonism through volitional and emotional defects. Though nothing can move him but the expectation of private pleasure or pain, he may prefer a nearer, shorter, and intenser pleasure to a more distant, longer, and more diffused pleasure, though he recognises that the latter is greater than the former. Or he may refuse to purchase what he recognises to be a more than equivalent future pleasure at the cost of suffering a present short intense pain. In deciding whether to have a tooth stopped or not we may be moved by none but hedonistic considerations, and we may recognise that there will be a nett balance of happiness in having it stopped ; and yet the prospect of immediate intense pain may prevent us from going to the dentist. Such a decision will certainly be wrong on the theory of Egoistic Ethical Hedonism, and we can say that the agent *ought* to have gone to the dentist if we accept this milder form of Psychological Hedonism.

(2, 12) Universalistic Ethical Hedonism is the doctrine that it is the duty of each to aim at the maximum happiness of all, and to subordinate everything else to this end. It is perfectly plain that this ethical theory is incompatible with *any* form of Psychological Egoism, and therefore with Psychological Hedonism. For Psychological Egoism denies that anyone can desire as an end anything but some state of himself, *e.g.*, his own happiness or the greatest development of all his faculties. And if, as would follow, no one can desire as an end the happiness of humanity in general, this cannot be the right or fitting object of anyone's desire, nor can it be anyone's duty to aim at this end.

Yet Mill, in his *Utilitarianism*, professed to deduce Universalistic Hedonism from Psychological Hedonism. Mill starts by assuming that " desirable " means " desired by someone." Though this rests on a confusion which we have already noted, there is no need to insist on that fact here.

For Mill's argument involves another fallacy which would invalidate it even though the above premise were granted. The argument may be put as follows. If Psychological Hedonism be true, each man's happiness is desired by someone, viz., by himself. Therefore each man's happiness is desirable. But the happiness of humanity is simply the whole composed of the happinesses of each man and of nothing else. Mill concludes that the happiness of humanity is desirable. But the only legitimate conclusion from these premises is that the happiness of humanity is a whole composed of a set of parts each one of which is desirable. It does not follow from this that the happiness of humanity is itself desirable. For, on Mill's definition of "desirable", this would mean that the happiness of humanity is desired by someone. And it does not follow from the fact that every part of this whole is desired by someone that the whole itself is desired by anyone. On the contrary, it would follow from the premise that no one can desire anything but his own happiness, that no one can desire the happiness of humanity ; and therefore, on Mill's definition, that the happiness of humanity is *not* desirable.

(2, 2) Having now considered the relation of Psychological Hedonism to the two forms of Ethical Hedonism, we can deal with the question whether Psychological Hedonism be itself true. Let us begin with certain undoubted facts which must be admitted. The belief that a future experience will be pleasant is *pro tanto* a motive for trying to get it, and the belief that it will be painful is *pro tanto* a motive for trying to avoid it. Again, the felt pleasantness of a present pleasant experience is *pro tanto* a motive for trying to make it last, whilst the felt painfulness of a present experience is *pro tanto* a motive for trying to make it stop.

The question is whether the expected pleasantness of a future experience is the only feature in it which can make us want to get it, whether the felt pleasantness of a present experience is the only feature in it which can make us want to prolong it, whether the expected painfulness of a future experience is the only feature in it which can make us want to avoid it, and whether the felt painfulness of a present experience is the only feature in it which can make us want to get rid of it.

I must begin with one explanatory remark which is necessary if the above proposition is to be taken as a perfectly accurate statement of Psychological Hedonism. No sane Psychological Hedonist would deny that a pleasure which is believed to be longer and less intense may be preferred for its greater duration to one which is believed to be shorter and more intense. Nor would he deny that a nearer and less intense pleasure may be preferred for its greater nearness to a more intense but remoter pleasure. And this implies that duration and remoteness are in some sense factors which affect our desires as well as pleasantness and painfulness. This complication may be dealt with as follows. There are certain determinable characteristics which every event, as such, must have. Date of beginning and duration are examples. There are others which an event may or may not have. Pleasantness, colour, and so on, are examples. Let us for the present call them respectively "categorial" and "non-categorial" determinable characteristics of events. Then the accurate statement of Psychological Hedonism would be as follows. No non-categorial characteristic of a present or prospective experience can move our desires for or against it except its hedonic quality ; but, granted that it has hedonic quality, the effect on our desires is determined jointly by the determinate form of this and by the determinate forms of its categorial characteristics.

Now, so far as I am aware, no argument has ever been given for Psychological Hedonism except an obviously fallacious one which Mill produces in his *Utilitarianism.* He says there that " to desire " anything and " to find " that thing " pleasant " are just two different ways of stating the same fact. Yet he also appeals to careful introspection in support of Psychological Hedonism. Sidgwick points out that, if Mill's statement were true, there would be no more need of introspection to decide in favour of the doctrine than there is need for introspection to decide that " to be rich " and " to be wealthy " are two different expressions for the same fact. But, as he also points out, Mill is deceived by a verbal ambiguity. There is a sense of " please " in English in which the two phrases " X pleases me " and " I desire X " stand for the same fact. But the verb " to please " and the phrase " to be pleasant " are not equivalent in English. In the sense in which " X pleases me " is equivalent to " I desire X " it is not equivalent to " I find X pleasant ". If I decide to be martyred rather than to live in comfort at the expense of concealing my opinions, there is a sense in which martyrdom must " please me " more than living in comfort under these conditions. But it certainly does not follow *ex vi termini* that I believe that martyrdom will be " more pleasant " than a comfortable life of external conformity. I do not think that " pleasantness " can be defined, or even described unambiguously by reference to its relations to desire. But I think we can give a fairly satisfactory ostensive definition of it as that characteristic which is common to the experience of smelling roses, of tasting chocolate, of requited affection, and so on, and which is opposed to the characteristic which is common to the experiences of smelling sulphuretted hydrogen, of hearing a squeaky slate-pencil, of being burnt, of unrequited affection, and so on. And it is certainly not self-evident that I can desire *only* experiences which have the characteristic thus ostensively defined.

I think that there is no doubt that Psychological Hedonism has been rendered plausible by another confusion. The experience of having a desire fulfilled is always *pro tanto* and for the moment pleasant. So, whenever I desire anything, I foresee that if I get it I shall have the pleasure of fulfilled desire. It is easy to slip from this into the view that my motive for desiring X is the pleasure of fulfilled desire which I foresee that I shall enjoy if I get X. It is clear that this will not do. I have no reason to anticipate the pleasure of fulfilled desire on getting X unless I already desire X itself. It is evident then that there must be *some* desires which are not for the pleasures of fulfilled desire. Let us call them "primary desires", and the others "secondary". Butler has abundantly shown that there must be some primary desires. But, as Sidgwick rightly points out, he has gone to extremes in the matter which are not logically justified. The fact that there must be primary desires is quite compatible with Psychological Hedonism, since it is quite compatible with the view that all primary desires are for primary pleasures, *i.e.*, for pleasures of taste, touch, smell, etc., as distinct from the pleasures of fulfilled desire. Still, introspection shows that this is not in fact so. The ordinary man at most times plainly desires quite directly to eat when he is hungry. In so doing he incidentally gets primary pleasures of taste and the secondary pleasure of fulfilled desire. Eventually he may become a *gourmand*. He will then eat because he desires the pleasures of taste, and he may even make himself hungry in order to enjoy the pleasures of fulfilled desire.

There is a special form of Psychological Hedonism of which Locke is the main exponent. This holds that all desire can be reduced to the desire to remove pain or uneasiness. The one conative experience is aversion to present pain, not desire for future pleasure. The position is as follows. When I am said to desire some future state X this means that the contemplation by me of my non-possession of X is painful. I feel an aversion to this pain and try to remove it by trying to get X. Since in the case of some things the contemplation of my non-possession of them is painful, whilst in the case of others it is neutral or pleasant, the question would still have to be raised as to why there are these differences. Perhaps the theory under discussion should not be counted as a form of Psychological Hedonism unless it holds that my awareness of the absence of X is painful if and only if I believe that the possession of X would be pleasant. This is in fact Locke's view, though he adds the proviso that my uneasiness at the absence of X is not necessarily proportional to the pleasure which I believe I should get from the possession of X. We will therefore take the theory in this form.

As regards the first part of the theory Sidgwick points out that desire is not usually a painful experience, unless it be very intense and be continually frustrated. No doubt desire is an unrestful state, in the sense that it tends to make us change our present condition. It shares this characteristic with genuine pain. But the difference is profound. When I feel aversion to a present pain I simply try to get rid of it.

When I feel the unrest of desire for a certain object I do not simply try to get rid of the uneasiness ; I try to get that particular object. I could often get rid of the feeling far more easily by diverting my attention from the object than by the tedious and uncertain process of trying to gain possession of it. As regards the second part of the theory, it seems plain on inspection that I may feel uneasiness at the absence of some contemplated object for other reasons than that I believe that the possession of it would be pleasant. I might feel uncomfortable at the fact that I am selfish, and desire to be less selfish, without for a moment believing that I should be happier if I were more unselfish.

The Psychological Hedonist, at this stage, has two more lines of defence : (a) He may say that we unwittingly desire things only in respect of their hedonic qualities, but that we deceive ourselves and think that we desire some things directly or in respect of other qualities. It is plain that this assertion cannot be proved ; and, unless there be some positive reason to accept Psychological Hedonism, there is not the faintest reason to believe it. (b) He may say that our desires were originally determined wholly and solely by the hedonic qualities of objects ; but that now, by association and other causes, we have come to desire certain things directly or for other reasons. The case of the miser who has come by association to desire money for itself, though he originally desired it only for its use, is commonly quoted in support of this view. Mill, in his *Utilitarianism*, deals with the disinterested love of virtue on these lines. Sidgwick makes the following important observations on this contention. In the first place it must be sharply distinguished from the doctrine that the original *causes* of all our desires were previous pleasant and painful experiences. The question is what were the original *objects* and *motives* of desire, not what kind of previous experiences may have *produced* our present desires. Secondly, the important question for ethics is what we desire here and now, not what we may have desired in infancy or in that pre-natal state about which the Psycho-analysts, who appear to be as familiar with the inside of their mother's womb as with the back of their own hands, have so much to tell us. If Ethical Hedonism be the true doctrine of the good, it is no excuse for the miser or the disinterested lover of virtue that they were sound Utilitarians while they were still trailing clouds of glory behind them. Lastly, such observations as we can make on young children point in exactly the opposite direction. They seem to be much more liable to desire things directly and for no reason than grown people. No doubt, as we go further back it becomes harder to distinguish between self-regarding and other impulses. But there is no ground for identifying the vague matrix out of which both grow with one rather than with the other.

I think that we may accept Sidgwick's argument here, subject to one explanation. It may well be the case that what very young children desire is on the whole what will in fact give them immediate pleasure, and that what they shun is what will in fact give them immediate pain ; though there are plenty of exceptions even to this. But there is no ground to suppose that they think of the former things as likely to be pleasant, and desire them *for that reason* ; or that they think of the latter things as likely to be painful, and shun them *for that reason*. It is unlikely that they have the experience of desiring and shunning for a reason at all at the early stages. And, if this be so, their experiences

are irrelevant to Psychological Hedonism, which is essentially
a theory about the reasons or motives of desire.

(2, 3) Psychological Hedonism is now refuted, and the
confusions which have made it plausible have been cleared
up. It remains to notice a few important general facts
about the relations of pleasure and desire and of pain and
aversion. (a) Just as we distinguished between the pleasure
of fulfilled desire and other pleasures, such as the smell of
roses, so we must distinguish between the pain of frustrated
desire and other pains, such as being burnt. And just as
there are secondary desires for the pleasures of fulfilled
desire, so there are secondary aversions for the pain of
frustrated desire. Secondary aversions presuppose the
existence of primary aversions, and it is logically possible
that all primary aversions might be directed to pains. But
inspection shows that this is not in fact the case. (b) Among
those pleasures which do not consist in the experience of
fulfilled desire a distinction must be drawn between passive
pleasures, such as the experience of smelling a rose, and the
pleasures of pursuit. A great part of human happiness
consists in the experience of pursuing some desired object
and successfully overcoming difficulties in doing so. The
relations of this kind of pleasure to desire are somewhat
complicated. The pleasure of pursuit will not be enjoyed
unless we start with at least some faint desire for the
pursued end. But the intensity of the pleasure of pursuit
may be out of all proportion to the initial intensity of the
desire for the end. As the pursuit goes on the desire to
attain the end grows in intensity, and so, if we attain it,
we may have enjoyed not only the pleasure of pursuit but
also the pleasure of fulfilling a desire which has become
very strong. All these facts are illustrated by the playing

of games, and it is often prudent to try to create a desire for an end in order to enjoy the pleasures of pursuit. As Sidgwick points out, too great a concentration on the thought of the pleasure to be gained by pursuing an end will diminish the desire for the end and thus diminish the pleasure of pursuit. If you want to get most pleasure from pursuing X you will do best to try to forget that this is your object and to concentrate directly on aiming at X. This fact he calls " the Paradox of Hedonism."

It seems to me that the facts which we have been describing have a most important bearing on the question of Optimism and Pessimism. If this question be discussed, as it generally is, simply with regard to the prospects of human happiness or misery in this life, and account be taken only of passive pleasures and pains and the pleasures and pains of fulfilled or frustrated desire, it is difficult to justify anything but a most gloomy answer to it. But it is possible to take a much more cheerful view if we include, as we ought to do, the pleasures of pursuit. From a hedonistic standpoint, it seems to me that in human affairs the means generally have to justify the end ; that ends are inferior carrots dangled before our noses to make us exercise those activities from which we gain most of our pleasures ; and that the secret of a tolerably happy life may be summed up in a parody of Hegel's famous epigram about the Infinite End,* viz., " the attainment of the Infinite End just consists in preserving the illusion that there is an End to be attained."

(D) FREE-WILL AND DETERMINISM. Sidgwick discusses this topic in *Book I, Chap. V* of the *Methods of Ethics*. The general question can, I think, be stated as follows :

* *Die Vollführung des unendlichen Zwecks ist so nur die Täuschung aufzuheben, als ob er noch nicht vollführt sei.*

" Granted that a certain man at a certain moment did in fact deliberately choose the alternative X and deliberately reject the alternative Y, could the very same man have instead chosen Y and rejected X even though everything in his own past history and present dispositions and everything in the past history and present dispositions of the rest of the universe had been precisely as it in fact was ? " Ethics is interested mainly in a particular case of this general problem, viz., when the alternative X is wrong and the alternative Y is right. Granted that I did at a certain moment deliberately choose the wrong alternative and reject the right one, could I at that moment have instead chosen the right and rejected the wrong one, even though everything in my past history and present dispositions and in those of the rest of the universe had been precisely as it in fact was ?

Sidgwick confines himself to this special case of the more general problem. He mentions a number of empirical facts which seem to support determinism, but he deliberately refrains from going into the metaphysics of the question. In this, though rather reluctantly, I shall follow him. But this much I must say. Physical substances and events are so utterly different in kind from minds and mental events that, even if complete determinism were certainly true of the former, any argument by analogy to a like conclusion about the latter would be most unreliable. Again, the kind of causation which applies to mental events in general, and particularly to those mental events which are characteristic of the rational level, such as inference and deliberate choice, is so utterly unlike physical or even physiological causation, that it would be most dangerous to transfer any proposition which involves the latter to the former. No doubt apparent exceptions to complete mental determinism can always be theoretically reconciled with it if we are ready to postulate *ad hoc* for each case enough non-introspectible mental processes and enough hitherto latent mental dispositions. But we must confess that we have no clear idea of what we are postulating when we do this.   And the whole procedure is painfully reminiscent of Molière's physicians and of the less reputable kind of company-promoter. The essential question is whether we can give any clear meaning to indeterminism, and whether with any meaning that we give to it it can be made consistent with certain fundamental principles of logic and metaphysics which seem to be self-evident.   This leads at once into some of the hardest problems of philosophy ; *e.g.*, the meanings of "possibility", the analysis of the notions of cause and substance and the relations between the two, the notions of variable states and permanent dispositions, and so on.   The devils who discussed the subject in Pandemonium soon discovered, as Milton tells us, that there is no end to what may plausibly be said on both sides of the question.   They, it will be remembered, very wisely reverted to purely ethical problems ; and in this, if in no other respect, Sidgwick followed their example.

Sidgwick is content to record his immediate conviction that, at the moment when he has to decide between two alternatives one of which he believes to be right and the other to be wrong, he can always choose the former.   It should be noticed that what seems so certain to Sidgwick is not what has sometimes been called " freaks of unmotived volition ".   The choice is determined in the end by the actual motives in their actual strength.   But one impulse, viz., the desire to do what is believed to be right, is held to be in a peculiar position. It is held that this desire always *could have been* strong enough to overcome all opposing desires even though in fact it was so weak that opposing desires overcame it. The possibility which is contemplated by indeterminism is, not that a decision might have taken place without a complete cause, but that a certain one of the factors in this complete cause could have been of different strength though everything else in the universe up to the time of the decision had been exactly as it in fact was.

Now, as regards this statement, all that I can say is this. It does seem to me to express some proposition or other which I believe and cannot help believing. And yet, whenever I try to give any definite meaning to " could " in it, it seems either no longer to express what I believe or to express something which conflicts with other principles which seem to me to be self-evident. And in this unsatisfactory state I must leave the matter.

Indeterminism, in the sense described above, is, I think, quite compatible with the obvious fact that making frequent wrong decisions under certain circumstances in the past diminishes the likelihood of making right decisions in similar circumstances in the future. Even if it always remains *possible* for the desire to do what is believed to be right to exceed a certain assigned strength, it may still be the case that habitual indulgence of opposed desires makes this less and less *probable*. But this is not the whole of the matter. It is certain that the habitual indulgence of opposed desires makes *their* intensity greater. Now the decision in any case will be determined by the relative intensities of the desire to do what is believed to be right and of these opposed desires. Consequently the desire to do what is believed to be right will have to be present in greater and greater strength if a right decision is to be made after repeated indulgence of opposed desires. Now, even if the desire to do what is believed to be right *could* reach the necessary degree of intensity, and even if the probability of its reaching an assigned degree be in no way affected by the habitual indulgence of opposed desires, it may still be the case that there is a certain average degree which it is most likely to reach. And it may be that the more the required degree exceeds this average the less likely it is to be reached.

I agree with Sidgwick that a belief in determinism or a belief in indeterminism ought to make hardly any difference to our practice. On either view I have to act on probability. On neither can I be absolutely certain what I or any other man will do in given circumstances, and on both I can in the same cases make a fairly accurate guess. No means which it would be reasonable on one theory to choose for securing a given end would be unreasonable to choose on the other. On either view it is certain that a present resolve to act rightly in future, and the building up of certain habits in the meanwhile, increase the probability that I shall decide rightly in future. No doubt a dishonest determinist, who does not really want to give up a bad habit, will be tempted to say : " It is no use trying to give it up, for my character is such that I shall certainly fail." But a dishonest indeterminist in the same situation will be tempted to say : " There is no harm in indulging to-day ; for I shall always be able to stop to-morrow."

Would any end which it is right for a human being to desire on the one view cease to be right for him to desire on the other ? So far as I can see, the statement that it is right to desire so-and-so as an end means that there is a

certain appropriateness between the nature of this object
and the attitude of desire for it. But I think that this
may over-simplify the situation. Perhaps we should rather
say that there is a certain appropriateness between the
nature of this object and the attitude of desire for it when
felt by a being of such and such a nature. Now, so far as
the appropriateness concerns only the object and the mental
attitude, there seems no reason to think that the question
of determinism or indeterminism would be relevant. Determinists and indeterminists ascribe precisely the same desires
to human beings ; they differ only in that indeterminists
assert that a certain one of these desires always could have
been strong enough to overcome the rest even when in fact
it was overcome by the rest. Still, this difference may
fairly be called a difference of opinion about the nature of
the human mind ; and it is conceivable that this difference
of nature might be relevant at this point. It might be
fitting for a mind of the nature which indeterminists ascribe
to the human mind to feel desire for a certain object, whilst
it would not be fitting for a mind of the nature which determinists ascribe to the human mind to feel desire for such
an object. Whether there would in fact be this difference
can be decided only by inspection in the case of each
suggested end in turn.

Sidgwick confines his attention to the two ends of
Happiness and Perfection. It seems clear that, if it be
fitting to desire the maximum happiness either of oneself
or of humanity in general as an end, it will be equally
fitting to do so whether determinism or indeterminism be
the truth about the nature of one's mind. The case is not
so simple in regard to Perfection. In so far as the notion
of Perfection contains factors which involve undetermined

free-will it cannot be a suitable object of desire if determinism be true. For it cannot be fitting for anyone to desire what is or involves a logical or metaphysical impossibility. But, even if the notion of Perfection does contain such factors, it is certain that it contains many others which do not involve undetermined free-will, *e.g.*, intelligence, courage, kindness, etc. If it be fitting to desire these as ends at all, it will be fitting to do so even if determinism be the truth about the human mind.

Are there then any points at which the difference between determinism and indeterminism becomes practically relevant in ethical matters ? Sidgwick holds that the ordinary notion of Merit and Demerit is bound up with indeterminism, and that Remorse and Retributory Punishment are bound up with Merit and Demerit in this sense. Let us first consider what a determinist can consistently say and do in this connexion. (*a*) It is obvious that he can talk of " good " and " bad " men in a perfectly definite sense. A " good " man will be one whose character is such that, even in conditions under which many men would be determined to make wrong choices, he will be determined to make right ones. And a " bad " man could be defined in the same way *mutatis mutandis*. It may be objected that in this sense of " good " and " bad " they mean exactly what they would mean when we talk of a good watch or a bad motor-bicycle, and that it is plain that we ascribe goodness and badness to men in some other sense beside this. This is no doubt true ; but there are, even on the determinist view, profound differences between men and material systems, and between the causal determination of mental and of physical events. And it may be that these differences, rather than the difference between indeterminism and determinism, account for the fact that we feel it unsatisfactory to equate a good man and a good motor. There are at least three points here which are, I think, important.

(i) Common-sense draws a distinction between the good man who was born with a happy balance of innate tendencies, who enjoyed a sound education, and who has generally done right without any moral struggle, and the good man who has been less fortunate in his moral inheritance and training but has managed to make himself virtuous with considerable difficulty. It is inclined to ascribe " merit " to the second, and to say of the first that " it is no particular credit to him to be good ". Now this distinction might, at first sight, seem to be bound up with indeterminism ; but it is perfectly possible for a determinist to admit it, so far as it is tenable, and to account for it. The second type of good man has shown clearly that he possesses in a high degree the desire to do what is right ; we have a measure of its strength in the obstacles which it has overcome. This is a guarantee that he will probably continue to act rightly. The first type of good man *may* have this desire in an equally high degree ; but, since he has had little occasion to exercise it, we cannot possibly *know* that he has. It is therefore possible that, if circumstances were to change considerably, he would no longer habitually act rightly. It must be noted that common-sense keeps its admiration of the second type of good man within bounds, and that the bounds are such as would be reasonable on the determinist view. We should not particularly admire a man who had continually to struggle against impulses to commit murder, rape, and incest on the most trivial occasions, even though his struggles were always successful. There is something wrong with a man who has to be perpetually performing hair-raising feats of moral acrobatics, though we may admire the strength and skill displayed in the performance.

(ii) Complete determinism involves two different propositions which it is important to distinguish. The first is that a man's present choices are completely determined by his original character and the influences to which it has since been subjected. The second is that the man himself began to exist at a certain moment of time, and that his coming into existence at that moment with such and such an original character was completely determined by the nature, relations, and history of pre-existing substances. Either proposition can be held without the other. *E.g.*, many indeterminists have held that human minds are created by God at the moment of conception ; *i.e.*, they hold the second proposition and reject the first. And some determinists, *e.g.*, M'Taggart, hold that no human mind has ever come into existence. What is determined is simply that it shall begin to animate a certain body at a certain moment. Such determinists hold the first proposition and reject the second. We might call the two propositions respectively " determinism of mental events " and " determinism of mental substances ". I think that Sidgwick always assumes that, if there be the first kind of determinism, there must also be the second.

Now, in the first place, I want to point out that determinism of mental substances involves a perfectly unique kind of causation which we cannot pretend to understand even in the sense of finding it familiar. There is one and only one sense in which we can understand the origin of a " new substance ". This is when the " substance " is a compound of pre-existing simpler substances. Its " originating " simply means that these simpler substances at a certain moment came into more intimate mutual relations, that the whole thus formed is relatively stable, and that it has characteristic properties. Now, if minds come into *existence*, as distinct from merely beginning to manifest themselves through bodies, at all, they certainly cannot be conceived to do so in this way. I submit that we literally " do not know what we are talking about " when we speak of the coming into existence of a mind. If such substances do originate in the course of history, and if their origination be causally determined, the kind of causation involved must presumably be quite different from that with which we are familiar in the determination of events in pre-existing substances by each other. Now I think that it has been held that the notion of " merit ", in the strict sense, vanishes on the determinist view because my original character is completely determined by substances and events which existed before I began to exist. My actions and decisions are completely determined in the end by my original character and subsequent circumstances, and I can take no credit for the goodness of my original character, if it be good, because it owes its being and nature to other things. Even if this be admitted, it does not follow that the notion of " merit " would vanish on all forms of determinist theory. A theory like M'Taggart's, which accepts determinism of mental events and denies that mental substances ever originated, would be untouched by this kind of objection.

But, secondly, it seems to me that the above contention errs through a confusion between joint partial responsibility and remote total responsibility. If X and Y be two cause-factors which together are sufficient and severally are necessary to produce the effect E, we can say that the responsibility for E is divided between them. The credit or discredit of each is thus reduced. But suppose that D is the immediate total cause of E and that C is the immediate total cause of D. Then, although we can say that C is indirectly totally responsible for E, this does not in the least alter or diminish D's responsibility for E. If God deliberately makes a mind which will inevitably choose wrongly under the conditions in which it will be placed, this does not in the least alter the fact that this mind is bad and merits disapproval. The fact that God also merits disapproval for making such a mind is simply a supplementary fact, not a plea in mitigation.

(iii) Watches and motor-cycles are called " good " or " bad " simply as means to the end for which they are constructed and used. It would be held by many people that these adjectives are applied to men as ends and not as means to anything else. But, whether this be so or not, it has nothing to do with the difference between determinism and indeterminism. An indeterminist might hold that a man can be called " good " or " bad " only as a means to producing good or bad results. And a determinist might hold that a character in which certain conative and emotional tendencies are present in certain proportions and in due relation to the desire to do what is right is an intrinsically admirable thing. The fact that a watch or a motor-car cannot be regarded as intrinsically good or bad does not depend on the fact that all its behaviour is determined, or even on the fact that it was constructed out of pre-existing materials by a pre-existing mind. It depends on the fact that it is a mere material mechanism. Now the human mind is not supposed to be of this nature by any determinist whose opinions are worth a moment's consideration.

On the whole then I am inclined to think that much

more remains to the determinist of the notion of Merit and Demerit than Sidgwick will admit.

(b) Let us turn next to the question of Remorse. A determinist can obviously regret that his character was such that he behaved badly on a past occasion, and can reasonably take such steps as experience has shown to be likely to amend it in the respect in which it has proved faulty. But, if remorse be a feeling of regret for a past bad action, which is bound up with the belief that my desire to do what is right could have been strong enough to conquer the other desires which led me astray, it is plainly not an emotion which a determinist can reasonably feel. It does not follow that he will not continue to feel it, as a person who disbelieves in ghosts might feel frightened in a house reputed to be haunted. Whether remorse does essentially involve the indeterminist view of oneself I am not quite sure. It seems to me that regret for past wrong-doing amounts to remorse when two conditions are fulfilled, viz., when no reparation can be made by me owing, e.g., to the death of the injured party, and when I feel that I might so easily have done better. The first condition is obviously independent of determinism or indeterminism. As regards the second it must be remembered that there are a great many senses of " could ", in which the statement that I could so easily have done better would be compatible with determinism. E.g., it may mean that nothing but a slightly stronger desire to do right was needed, and that a man who had used my opportunities better than I had done would have had this stronger desire.

(c) We come now to Praise and Blame. And here we must distinguish between privately feeling and publicly expressing approbation and disapprobation. The determinist has the same motive for the latter as the indeterminist, viz., the motive which makes us oil a bit of machinery. It is found that the public expression of approval of an action is a strong incentive to the agent to do similar actions in the future, and that the public expression of disapprobation is a strong incentive to him to avoid such actions. If the determinist can give a meaning to goodness and badness of character and conduct, and if it is appropriate to feel approval of good and disapproval of bad character and conduct in the determinist sense, a determinist is justified in privately praising or blaming men and their actions. I have already argued that both these conditions are fulfilled.

(d) Lastly, we have to consider Reward and Punishment. The expression of praise and blame is really a particular case of this. Sidgwick's position is as follows. The determinist can justify punishment on reformatory and deterrent grounds ; and in practice these are the only grounds that anyone can use in apportioning rewards and punishments. He cannot justify retributive punishment ; but it is doubtful whether this is justifiable even on the indeterminist view. I agree with the positive parts of Sidgwick's statement, but am inclined to disagree with the negative part, viz., that, if retributive punishment can be defended at all, it can be defended only on the indeterminist view. The fundamental question in connexion with retributive punishment is whether a combination of two evils, viz., wrong-doing and pain, can be a more desirable state of affairs than one of these evils, viz., wrong-doing, without the other. The general answer is that there is no logical impossibility in this because the value of a whole depends largely on the relations between its constituents as well as on the natures of the constituents themselves. And the contention of the believers in retributive punishment is that there is a certain appropriateness of pain to wrong-doing which, unless the pain be altogether excessive in duration and intensity, makes the whole state of affairs less bad than it would be if the wrong-doing were unpunished.

This opinion seems to me to be true in spite of being old-fashioned. And there is nothing in it which could not be accepted by a determinist. Determinists can admit that there are bad men and wrong actions ; and they can admit the general principle that a whole composed of two evils suitably related may be less bad, owing the appropriateness of the one evil to the other, than one would be without the other. The question that remains is whether pain would be appropriate only to wrong-doing which is undetermined in the sense already defined. It is of course admitted that an action would not deserve punishment if it were involuntary, or contra-voluntary, or were done under an honest misapprehension of the circumstances. But this is irrelevant for the present purpose. The only question now at issue is this : " Suppose that at a certain moment I deliberately made a wrong choice simply because my desire to do what is right was not strong enough as compared with my other desires at the time. Should I not deserve punishment unless my desire to do right *could* at that moment have been strong enough to conquer my other desires even though everything in my past history and present circumstances had been exactly as it in fact was ? " The reader must answer this question for himself, after inspecting as carefully as he can. It is certainly not obvious to me that I should not deserve punishment unless the condition mentioned above were fulfilled.

(E) CLASSIFICATION OF THE METHODS OF ETHICS. As we have seen in the Synopsis, Sidgwick reduces the fundamental types of ethical theory to three, viz., *Intuitionism, Egoistic Hedonism,* and *Utilitarianism.* The only criticism that I wish to make at this point is that his division does not seem to rest on any very clear principle. The name " Intuitionism " seems to suggest an epistemic principle of classification, and the opposite of it would seem to be " Empiricism ". On the other hand, the opposition of Egoistic and Universalistic Hedonism to Intuitionism rests on a quite different basis, viz., on whether some types of action are *intrinsically* right or wrong or whether the rightness or wrongness of actions always depends on their conduciveness to certain *ends.* This of course is not an epistemic question at all. And this cross-division leads to needless complications in Sidgwick's exposition. He has to recognise that, from an epistemic point of view, all three types of theory involve ethical intuitions. For the two types of Hedonism involve at least the intuition that pleasure, and nothing else, is intrinsically desirable. He thus has to distinguish between a wider and a narrower sense of " Intuitionism ". All this seems rather untidy and unsatisfactory. I would therefore propose the following amendments. I would first divide ethical theories into two classes, which I will call respectively *deontological* and *teleological.*

Deontological theories hold that there are ethical propositions of the form : " Such and such a kind of action would always be right (or wrong) in such and such circumstances, no matter what its consequences might be." This division corresponds with Sidgwick's Intuitionism in the narrower sense. Teleological theories hold that the rightness or wrongness of an action is always determined by its

tendency to produce certain consequences which are intrinsically good or bad. Hedonism is a form of teleological theory.
It is plain that teleological theories can be subdivided into
monistic and *pluralistic* varieties. A monistic theory would
hold that there is one and only one characteristic which
makes a state of affairs good or bad intrinsically. A
pluralistic theory would hold that there are several independent characteristics of this kind. Hedonism is a monistic
teleological theory. I think that a similar subdivision could
be made among deontological theories. It might be held
that all the various moral rules recognised by a deontological
theory are determinate forms of a single rule, or at any
rate that they all answer to a single necessary and sufficient
criterion. This seems to have been Kant's view. Such
a theory is monistic. A deontological theory which held
that there is a number of independent moral rules would be
pluralistic.

Both kinds of teleological theory can now be divided on
a new principle. The end to be aimed at is of course never
a characteristic in the abstract ; it is always a concrete
state of affairs in which a certain characteristic, or characteristics, is manifested. And the question arises whether it
is the agent's duty to aim at the manifestation of this
desirable characteristic in himself only or in a larger circle.
We thus get a subdivision into *egoistic* and *non-egoistic* types
of teleological theory. Utilitarianism, *e.g.*, may be described
as a non-egoistic form of monistic teleological theory.

The principles of division which I have suggested are
clear in outline, and they have the advantage of not introducing epistemological considerations. We must remember,
however, that *purely* deontological and *purely* teleological
theories are rather ideal limits than real existents. Most

actual theories are mixed, some being predominantly deontological and others predominantly teleological. Sidgwick,
e.g., is definitely a Hedonist, and so far a monistic teleologist,
though he cannot make up his mind as between the egoistic
and the non-egoistic forms of hedonism. But this is not the
whole truth about his position. He also accepts as self-
evident certain abstract principles about the right way of
distributing a given amount of happiness. These modes of
distribution ought to be followed, on his view, because they
are *intrinsically* right, and not merely because they are
likely to increase the amount of happiness to be distributed
in future. To this extent Sidgwick's theory must be counted
as deontological. When, as with Sidgwick, the *only* deontological principles which the moralist accepts are about the
right *distribution* of something which is held to be intrinsically
desirable, his system must be regarded as almost purely
teleological.

(F) DETAILED DISCUSSION OF EACH OF THE THREE
METHODS. (1) *Intuitionism.* We may divide Sidgwick's
discussion of this subject into two main parts, viz. : (1, 1) a
general treatment of the subject, and (1, 2) a detailed
analysis and criticism of the alleged moral intuitions of
common-sense. The former is contained in *Book I, Chap.
VIII*, and *Book III, Chaps. I* and *XIII*. The latter is
contained in *Book III, Chaps. III* to *XI* inclusive.

(1, 1) We must begin by stating more definitely what is
the subject-matter of moral judgments. So far we have
said that Intuitionism, in the narrower sense to which we
are now confining the term, holds that certain types of
action are intrinsically right or wrong without regard to
their consequences. This statement must now be made

more accurate. In order to do this let us take a concrete example. It is held by many people that it is always wrong to tell a lie, no matter how disastrous the consequences of telling the truth might be. We are not at present concerned with the correctness of this doctrine, but only with its precise meaning. Now it is plain that an action cannot be called a " lie " without reference to certain of the consequences which the agent expects that it will have. He must expect that his action will produce certain beliefs, and he must hold that these beliefs will be false.

The action, then, is judged to be wrong because the agent expects it to have consequences of a certain kind. But, if so, it may be asked, how does Intuitionism differ from a teleological type of ethical theory, such as Utilitarianism? Does not Utilitarianism also condemn lying because it is likely to have consequences of a certain kind?

To deal with this question let us begin by defining a " lie " as a statement made by an agent with the intention of producing a false belief. This definition would presumably be accepted both by Intuitionists and by Utilitarians. It will be seen that the definition includes a reference to certain consequences (viz., the production of a belief) and to a certain characteristic of these consequences (viz., the falsity of this belief). In any particular case both the Utilitarian and the Intuitionist will know, or reasonably suspect, that there will be other consequences beside the production of a belief, and that the belief will have other characteristics beside falsity. These, however, form no part of the definition of a " lie ", though they do form part of the intention of the person who tells a lie. Now the fundamental difference between the Teleologist and the Intuitionist in this case seems to be the following : The Teleologist is interested only in the *goodness* or *badness* of the intended consequences. For he recognises only what I have called earlier in this chapter the teleological and the logical senses of " ought ". When he says : " I ought to do X ", he always means simply and solely : (*a*) " I ought (in the teleological sense) to desire Y " ; (*b*) " So far as I can see X is the most suitable means open to me for producing Y " ; and (*c*) " I ought (in the logical sense) to choose the most suitable means open to me for producing what I ought (in the teleological sense) to desire." The Teleologist will therefore take into account *all* the intended consequences, whether they be included in the definition of the action as a " lie " or not. And he will take into account *all* those characteristics, and *only* those characteristics, of the intended consequences which he holds to be relevant to their goodness or badness. These may include other characteristics beside those involved in the definition of the act as a " lie " ; and they may not include that particular characteristic at all. Thus, *e.g.*, a Utilitarian would *not* consider the characteristic of falsity, which is involved in the definition, to be directly relevant ; whilst he *would* consider that another characteristic which is not involved in the definition, viz., the tendency to diminish human happiness, is directly relevant. It is of course quite possible to imagine a non-hedonistic Teleologist who held that true belief is intrinsically good, and that it is therefore our duty to produce as much true belief as possible. Such a Teleologist would still differ fundamentally from an Intuitionist about lying. An Intuitionist need not hold that true belief is intrinsically good and false belief intrinsically bad, and he certainly will not hold that truth-telling is right and lying wrong simply because the former tends to increase and the latter to diminish the amount of true belief in the world. Cases might easily arise in which it would be almost certain that more true belief would be produced by telling a lie than by telling the truth. In such cases a Teleologist of the kind just described would consider it his duty to tell a lie, whilst an Intuitionist about lying would still hold that it is wrong to do so.

The fundamental difference between the Intuitionist and the Teleologist is that the former does, and the latter does not, recognise a sense of " right " which applies to actions and intentions and is not analysable into " conducive to *good* consequences ". It is not true to say that the Intuitionist takes no account of intended consequences when judging of the rightness or wrongness of an action. What is true is that he takes no account of the *goodness* or *badness* of the intended consequences. For him a lie is wrong simply and solely because it is intended to produce a *false* belief, and not because a false belief is an intrinsically bad state of mind. For the Teleologist the other characteristics of the consequences are relevant only in so far as they make the consequences intrinsically *good* or *bad*, and to say that a lie is wrong simply means that its consequences will on the whole be bad.

There is a further difference, which is not, I think, so fundamental, but which certainly has existed between most Intuitionists and most Teleologists. A Teleologist cannot reasonably take into account anything less than the whole of the consequences intended by the agent. For he has to consider the conduciveness of the action to good or evil results, and it would seem quite arbitrary to exclude from his survey any part of the consequences which the agent foresaw and desired or tolerated. But many Intuitionists have held that the rightness or wrongness of an action was completely determined by certain characteristics of a certain restricted part of its total intended consequences. If, *e.g.*, its immediate consequences had a certain characteristic, then it would be right (or wrong) no matter what might be its remoter consequences and no matter what might be the other characteristics of its immediate consequences. *E.g.*, some Intuitionists would hold that, if I were asked a question about a certain matter, it would be my duty to make such a statement as would produce a true belief on that matter, even though I knew that its remoter consequences would be false beliefs on other matters, and even though the belief which I produce would be intensely painful to my hearer in addition to being true.

I do not think that there is any logical necessity for a person who admits that there is a sense of " right " which applies to actions and intentions and is not analysable into " conducive to good consequences " to go to these extremes. He might reasonably hold that the rightness or wrongness of an action was determined by certain of the characteristics of all its intended consequences. But I think it is true that certain forms of Intuitionism could hardly be held if this view were taken. The point is this. Teleological theories would make all statements about the rightness or wrongness of classes of action into empirical propositions about general tendencies. We might be able to conclude by induction from past experience that lying generally has bad consequences ; but we could not be sure that *every* lie, under existing circumstances, or *any* lie, under certain conceivable circumstances, would have such consequences. Hence, on a teleological theory, there could be no propositions of the form : " Such and such a type of action would always be right (or wrong)." Now most Intuitionists have claimed to know some propositions of this kind by direct insight into the terms. Now it is difficult to see how they could possibly do this unless they knew that all but the immediate consequences, and all but a few of the characteristics of these, were irrelevant to the rightness or wrongness of the action. To define a type of action, such as "lying", we must take a few outstanding features of the act or of its immediate consequences. In any concrete instance of lying the act will have many remote consequences which the agent can foresee ; and all its consequences, immediate and remote, will have many characteristics beside the one which makes it a lie by definition. Any Intuitionist who claims to be able to see that every lie as such must be wrong is claiming to see that all the remoter consequences of a lie, and all the other characteristics of the consequences except those involved in the definition of the act as a " lie ", are irrelevant to the wrongness of the act.

It is now easy to see what is the connexion between the epistemological division of ethical theories into Intuitionist and Empirical and the ontological division of them into Deontological and Teleological. (*a*) As we have seen, on a Teleological theory, both singular judgments of the form : " This act is right (or wrong) " and universal judgments of the form : " All acts of a certain kind are right (or wrong) " essentially involve judgments about all the consequences of the act or class of acts so far as these can be foreseen at all. Such judgments are of course purely empirical, like all judgments which involve particular causal laws. So a teleological theory is, to this extent, necessarily an empirical or inductive theory. (*b*) Nevertheless, every Teleological theory does involve at least one *a priori* judgment. For it will always involve some judgment of the form : " Anything that had a certain non-ethical characteristic (*e.g.*, pleasantness) would necessarily be intrinsically good." Such judgments have nothing to do with causation. They claim to express a necessary connexion between a certain non-ethical characteristic and the ethical characteristic of goodness. The only kind of induction on which they are based is what Mr Johnson calls " intuitive induction ", such as we use in coming to see that shape and size are necessarily connected, and not what he calls " problematic induction," such as we use in making the probable generalisation that all cloven-footed animals chew the cud. (*c*) Any Deontological theory which claims to make universal judgments of the form : " All acts of such and such a kind are right (or wrong) " does claim to make *a priori* judgments in a sense in which teleological theories deny that they can be made. For it defines the kind of action under consideration by *one or a few* characteristics of its *immediate* consequences ; and it claims to see that these *suffice* to make all such actions right (or wrong), and that the more remote consequences and the other characteristics of the consequences will always be irrelevant to the rightness (or wrongness) of the action. It is plain that, if such judgments can be made at all, they must be *a priori*. They may be compared with the judgment that, if the sides of a triangle be equal, this *suffices* to make it equiangular, and that the size, position, colour, etc., of the triangle are irrelevant. A Deontologist of this kind is called by Sidgwick either a *dogmatic* or a *philosophic* Intuitionist. The distinction between these two subdivisions corresponds to the distinction which we have drawn between *pluralistic* and *monistic* Deontologists. For a Dogmatic Intuitionist is one who holds that there are many independent intuitively certain judgments asserting that such and such kinds of action are necessarily right (or wrong). And a Philosophic Intuitionist is one who holds that all the more concrete judgments of this kind can be subsumed under one or a few supreme moral principles which are intuitively certain. It is worth while to remark at this point that, although it is theoretically possible for a teleological theory to be pluralistic (since it may hold that there are several independent characteristics, each of which would suffice to make a thing intrinsically good), and although it is theoretically possible for a deontological theory to be monistic, yet in fact teleological theories have tended to be monistic and deontological theories to be pluralistic. No one has produced a plausible monistic deontological theory ; whilst universalistic hedonism is a fairly plausible form of monistic teleological theory. And this fact has often made people prefer teleological theories, since monism in such matters is more satisfactory to the intellect than pluralism.

(d) As I have said, a Deontologist might hold that it was necessary to consider all the foreseen consequences of an action before one could decide whether it was right or wrong. If such a Deontologist made universal judgments about the rightness or wrongness of certain types of action he would have to confine them to statements about general tendencies, just as the Teleologist has to do. He could not say : " Every lie is as such necessarily wrong," though, in the case of any particular lie, he might be able to say that *this* lie is certainly right or certainly wrong. He could, no doubt, make the generalisation that *any* lie told in exactly similar circumstances with exactly similar foreseen consequences would necessarily be right, if *this* lie be right, or wrong, if *this* lie be wrong. But such generalisations are hardly worth making. This kind of Deontologist seems to be what Sidgwick means by an *Æsthetic* Intuitionist.

(1, 2) This is perhaps as much as we need say on the general topic of Intuitionism. We can now pass to Sidgwick's criticism of the morality of common-sense. Into the details of this I shall not enter. The essence of the matter is this. Sidgwick holds that common-sense does claim to be able to see by inspection that certain types of action are necessarily right (or wrong) without regard to the goodness or badness of their consequences. And, although it does not ignore intended consequences, since it defines many types of action by reference to some of the characteristics of some of their intended consequences, yet it holds that *certain* characteristics of the *immediate* consequences *suffice* to make such actions right (or wrong). Common - sense then is dogmatically intuitive, though this does not necessarily imply that it does not use other and incompatible criteria of right and wrong. This seems to me to be true.

The upshot of his very elaborate discussion of common-sense morality is as follows. If there be genuine moral axioms they must fulfil the following conditions. Their terms must be clear and distinct ; the propositions themselves must continue to seem self-evident no matter how carefully they be examined, and no matter with what difficulties we may confront them ; and they must be mutually consistent. Moreover, it is important that there should be a clear consensus of opinion in their favour. If something seems self-evident to me and does not seem so to someone else who, so far as I can see, is as competent as I and is really contemplating the same situation as I, I am reduced to a state of hesitation. There are two special dangers about alleged ethical axioms. In the first place, we are liable to confuse strong impulses with genuine intellectual insight, and to judge as wrong what we impulsively dislike. Secondly, rules which really rest on custom and the opinion of the society in which we have been brought up may gain the appearance of moral axioms. A grown man seems to himself to know intuitively what politeness or honour or fashion forbids. Yet such codes certainly have been imposed on him from without, and are largely lacking in rational justification. It is quite certain that common-sense morality contains a great deal of material of this kind. Now a careful discussion of the alleged axioms of common-sense morality shows that they do not answer to the required conditions. Agreement exists only so long as we keep to vague generalities and simple cases. As soon as we go into detail doubts and difficulties arise, both as to the meaning of the terms and as to the range of application of the principles. The central part of each duty seems clear, but it is surrounded with a margin of uncertainty. And, when the duties which it has laid down as absolute and unexceptionable conflict, common-sense either suggests no principle of reconciliation, or one so complex and qualified as to be no longer self-evident, or else it falls back on some teleological principle such as Utilitarianism.

I think that anyone who reads the relevant chapters in Sidgwick will agree that the extreme form of Intuitionism which he ascribes to common-sense cannot be maintained. And he is no doubt right in thinking that common-sense wants to hold something like this, and retreats from it only at the point of the bayonet. Sidgwick's conclusion is that we are forced to a mainly teleological view, eked out by a few very abstract intuitions about right and wrong modes of distributing good and evil. This does not seem to me to be certain ; and I propose as briefly as possible, and therefore somewhat dogmatically, to state a form of Intuitionism which is not open to Sidgwick's objections and is not flagrantly in conflict with reflective common-sense.

(a) Whenever a man is called upon either to act or to abstain from action he is in presence of a highly complex situation, composed of pre-existing persons, institutions, and things, in various relations to each other and to himself. Let us call this the "initial phase". Whether he acts or abstains from action this phase will be succeeded by others. The initial phase, together with its subsequent developments, may be called a "total course of events". If the agent abstains from action there will be what I will call an "unmodified course of events". If he acts he will introduce an additional cause-factor into the initial phase, and this will make the subsequent phases, and therefore the total course of events, different from what they would otherwise have been. We then have a "modified course of events". According to what action he performs we shall have a correspondingly different modified course of events. Now of course each phase will itself be highly complex. If we denote the unmodified course by $F_1 F_2$ . . . F_n, then any phase such as F_r will consist of factors which we might symbolise by f_{r1}, f_{r2}, . . . f_{rm}. Suppose that, instead of abstaining from action, the man does a certain act x. The initial phase will then consist of all the factors in F_1 together with the additional factor x, which of course will not simply be added to the rest but will stand in perfectly definite relations to them. The subsequent phases will be modified in a characteristic way by the addition of this cause-factor to the initial phase and will become $F_2^x F_3^x$ . . . F_n^x.

(b) Now it seems to me that we have to distinguish two

quite different ethical features of the action x, viz., its fittingness or unfittingness to the total course of events as modified by it, and its utility or disutility. I will now try to explain what I mean by these two notions. Fittingness or unfittingness is a direct ethical relation between an action or emotion and the total course of events in which it takes place. As this course of events consists of a number of successive phases, it is possible that a certain action may be fitting to some of the phases and unfitting to others. In particular it might be " immediately fitting ", i.e., it might be appropriate to the initial phase F_1, but it might be unfitting to some or all of the later modified phases F_2^x, etc. Again, since each phase is itself complex, the action might be fitting to certain factors of a certain phase but unfitting to other factors of that phase. It is quite easy to give examples. If I am asked a certain question and answer it in a certain way I may be answering that question truly but my answer may lead to subsequent false inferences. It might then be said that this answer was fitting to the initial phase, but was unfitting to subsequent phases in the course of events as modified by it. It would then become a question whether a true answer, or a lie, or silence was the most fitting action on the whole, given the initial phase. The second complication may be illustrated as follows. I may be an elector to an office, and one of the candidates may have done me a service. To prefer him to a better qualified candidate would fit one aspect of the situation, since it would be rewarding a benefactor ; but it would be unfitting to other factors in the situation, since it would be an act of bad faith to the institution which was employing me as an elector and an act of injustice to the other candidates. The statement that " x is more fitting to be done in the situation F_1 than y is " means that x is more fitting to the whole course of events $F_1F_2^x$ . . . F_n^x than y is to the whole course of events $F_1F_2^y$ . . . F_n^y. The fittingness of an act to a whole course of events will be a function of its fittingness or unfittingness to each phase in the series, and its fittingness to any phase in the series will be a function of its fittingness or unfittingness to each factor or aspect of that phase. By analogy with mechanics we may talk of the " resultant fittingness " and the various " component fittingnesses ". But, unfortunately, there is no simple general rule, like the parallelogram of forces, by which the resultant fittingness can be calculated from the various component fittingnesses.

(c) Having now tried to explain what I mean by the " fittingness " of an action, I will next consider its " utility ". We have now to leave out of account the relations of fittingness or unfittingness between an action and the modified course of events which it initiates, and to consider simply the intrinsic goodness or badness of such a course of events. This will be determined by the qualities of the component events and their relations to each other. The statement that " x is more useful to be done than y in the situation F_1 " means that, apart from all reference to fittingness and unfittingness, the course of events $F_1F_2^x$ . . . F_n^x is on the whole intrinsically better than the course of events $F_1F_2^y$ . . . F_n^y. The intrinsic goodness of a whole course of events is a function of the intrinsic goodness or badness of its successive phases, and the intrinsic goodness or badness of any phase is a function of the intrinsic goodness or badness of its various factors or aspects. If Hedonism were true our calculations would be simplified, because no characteristic but pleasure or pain would have to be considered in our estimate. But the notion of utility is wider than this, and it would still have application even if the Hedonistic view of what constitutes intrinsic goodness were found to be inadequate or false. We have to take account of the consequences of an act both in considering its fittingness and in considering its utility in a given initial situation. For the act has not to fit merely the *initial* phase or the total course of events which *would* have occurred if the initial phase had been allowed to develop without inter-ference from the agent. It has to fit the total course of events which *will* occur if the initial phase is modified by it as an additional cause-factor. And of course it is still more obvious that utility in a given situation involves a reference to consequences. For it just is the causal characteristic of producing a course of events which have such qualities or such relations among themselves as to be intrinsically good.

(*d*) Now it seems to me that the rightness or wrongness of an action in a given initial situation is a function of its fittingness in that situation and its utility in that situation. The pure Deontologist would deny that its utility or dis-utility was relevant to its rightness or wrongness. The pure Teleologist would deny that there is such a relation as direct fittingness or unfittingness, and would make its rightness or wrongness depend entirely on its utility or disutility. Both these extremes seem to me to be wrong, and to be in flagrant conflict with common sense. As against the pure Teleologist I would say that we all do recognise relations of fittingness and unfittingness. And, as against the pure Deontologist, I would say that we do think it reasonable to weigh utility against fittingness; and that a sane person judges it right, though regrettable, to do an act which is unfitting if this be the only means open to him of avoiding a course of events which, from their qualities and their mutual relations, would be intrinsically very evil. " It hath been the wisdom of the *Church of England*, ever since the first compiling of her Publick Liturgy, to keep the mean between the two extreams, of too much stiffness in refusing, and of too much easiness in admitting any variation from it." And I intend to follow the excellent example of my national Church.

(*e*) If I am right, the kind of Intuitionist with whom Sidgwick contends in his discussion of the morality of common-sense makes two fundamental mistakes. In the first place, he *identifies* rightness with fittingness, and fails to see that utility is also a factor in determining rightness. Secondly, he takes far too simple-minded a view of fittingness. He thinks that the fittingness of an action is completely determined by its relations to the initial situation or the phase that immediately succeeds it. And he forgets that even these phases may be very complex, and that the fittingness of the action to each factor must be considered.

It seems quite clear that the Intuitionist will have to moderate his claims very greatly. He will be confined to statements about *tendencies* to be right and *tendencies* to be wrong. He can say that a lie has a very strong tendency to be wrong, and that it will be wrong unless telling the truth would have very great disutility or unless the situation be of a certain special kind in which it is a matter of honour to shield a third person. And it is very doubtful whether any general rules can be given for balancing one kind of fittingness against another or for balancing fittingness on the whole against utility on the whole. When it comes to estimating resultant fittingness from component fittingnesses and unfittingnesses, and to estimating total rightness from total fittingness and total utility, we are soon reduced to something analogous to those perceptual judgments on very complex situations which we have constantly to make in playing games of skill. No doubt this is an unsatisfactory conclusion, and at first sight it compares ill with the sweet simplicity of Utilitarianism. But, if it is so, it is so. And perhaps we may say that Utilitarianism is at once too simple in theory and too difficult in practice to satisfy either the philosopher or the plain man for very long.

It remains to say something about the few highly abstract principles which Sidgwick does regard as intuitively certain. They are the following. (i) If an action would be right when done by A and wrong when done by B in precisely the same circumstances, there must be some qualitative dissimilarity between A and B which accounts for this. The mere fact that B is numerically other than A is irrelevant. (ii) If an action would be right when done by A to B and would be wrong when done in precisely similar circumstances by A to C, there must be some qualitative dissimilarity between B and C to account for this. The mere fact that B is numerically other than C is irrelevant. (iii) Any general rule ought to be applied impartially to all persons who come within the scope of the rule.

I will comment on these three principles before I mention the others which Sidgwick accepts. The first two, though not absolutely verbal, are extraordinarily trivial. Any pair of individuals always do differ qualitatively from each other in innumerable ways. Some of these qualitative differences are, and some are not, ethically relevant. And qualitative dissimilarities which are ethically relevant to certain types of action will be ethically irrelevant to others. If A admires red hair and B does not, this may make it right for A and wrong for B to propose marriage to the red-haired C ; and it may make it right for A to propose to C but wrong for him to propose to the otherwise similar but yellow-haired D. But if A had to rescue either C or D from drowning, and could not rescue both, the difference in the colour of their hair would not be an adequate ground for saving one and letting the other drown. What we want are some self-evident principles as to precisely what kinds of qualitative differences are relevant and what are irrelevant grounds for two people to act differently in similar circumstances or for the same person to act differently in similar circumstances towards two people. Sidgwick's principles are rather like the famous *Principle of Indifference* in Probability. Two alternatives are equally probable if there be no relevant dissimilarities between them ; but what kinds of dissimilarity are relevant and what are not ? If I had the chance of saving the life of one, but not of both, of two persons, would the fact that one was my mother and that the other was my second cousin be a relevant ground for saving the former ? As regards the third principle it is difficult to see that it states an absolutely unexceptionable duty. Certainly, if I have to administer a rule inflicting a penalty on all members of a certain defined class, it will be both unfitting and contrary to utility if I inflict the penalty on some members of the class and not on others. And I shall be inexcusable if I break it in favour of someone who does not differ relevantly from those on whom I inflict the penalty. But this is merely a particular case of the second rule. Suppose, however, that I see that there is a relevant difference between certain members of the class contemplated by the rule and others, am I never to break the rule in their favour ? May not the unfittingness of ignoring these relevant differences in some cases outweigh the unfittingness and the disutility of making exceptions to the rule which it is my duty to administer ? Such conflicts plainly can arise where a man has to administer an obviously unjust and inadequate rule ; and, when they reach a certain degree of acuteness, it is very hard to be sure about the duty of the officer. We might be inclined to say that it was *his duty* to break the rule, but that his *employers* would have a *right* to punish him for doing so.

I pass now to Sidgwick's three remaining principles. (iv) Mere difference in the date in one's life in which any good is to be enjoyed makes no difference to its value. This, as he points out, is quite compatible with its being reasonable to prefer a nearer to a remoter good on the grounds of the greater likelihood of getting it, of greater keenness of appreciation in youth, and so on. The only doubt that I feel about this principle is concerned with order in time. Most people would be inclined to think that a life which began unhappily and ended happily was to be preferred to one, containing the same balance of happiness, which began happily and ended unhappily. It is difficult to be sure whether they really think that mere order is relevant, as their language would suggest. For there are the secondary pleasures and pains of anticipation and memory to be considered. The anticipation of happiness is always pleasant, and is perhaps more so if one is now unhappy. The anticipation of unhappiness is always unpleasant, and is perhaps more so if one is now happy. The memory of past happiness tends to be painful if one is now unhappy ; whilst the memory of past unhappiness is on the whole not unpleasant if one is now happy. Now the primary happiness of the earlier half of the one life may be reduced by the secondary unhappiness of anticipating the primary unhappiness of its later half; and the primary unhappiness of its later half will certainly be increased by the secondary pain of remembering the lost primary happiness of the first half. In the case of the other life the primary unhappiness of the first half may be reduced by the secondary pleasure of anticipating the primary happiness of the second half; and the primary happiness of the second half will not be reduced, and may be increased, by the memory of the primary unhappiness of the first half. So perhaps the truth of the matter is simply this. Of two lives which contain the same amounts of *primary* happiness and unhappiness, occurring in opposite order in time, the life in which the primary unhappiness precedes the primary happiness will contain more *secondary* happiness and less *secondary* unhappiness than that in which the primary happiness precedes the primary unhappiness. If this be the whole truth, the case under discussion is no real exception to Sidgwick's principle. But I do not feel completely certain that it is the whole truth, and to that extent I feel a faint doubt about the principle.

The two remaining principles are of extreme importance in connexion with the controversy between Egoistic and Non-egoistic types of ethical theory. They are as follows. (v) The good of any one individual is of no more importance, from the point of view of the Universe, than the equal good of any other. And (vi) it is my duty to aim at good generally, so far as I can bring it about, and not merely at a particular part of it. From these two principles he deduces what he calls the *Principle of Rational Benevolence*, viz., that I ought to try to produce good states in any other individual as much as in myself, except in so far as I am less certain of being able to produce them in him, or less certain that such states in him would be good, or can see that more good would be sacrificed in me than would be produced in him.

It will be best to defer the discussion of these two principles and of Sidgwick's inference from them till we deal with the question of Egoism. In the meanwhile I think we can say that, on their negative side, Sidgwick's principles are principles of *indifference* or *impartiality*. They tell us that certain kinds of difference, viz., the numerical difference between one individual and another, and the difference in temporal position between one event in a man's life and another, are *not* ethically relevant grounds for a difference of action or treatment or valuation. On their positive side they assert that a difference in action or treatment or valuation always *does* need justification, and that it must be justified by some kind of dissimilarity of quality or relation.

(2) *Hedonism.* We can now pass to the type of theory called " Hedonism ", which is a form of teleological theory. As I have said, the discussion is best subdivided into (2, 1) *Hedonism in General;* (2, 2) *Egoistic Hedonism;* and (2, 3) *Universalistic Hedonism* or *Utilitarianism.*

(2, 1) We divided this into (2, 11) *The Ethical Problem,* and (2, 12) *The Factual Problem.* I will now say something about each of these in turn.

(2, 11) Since Hedonism, in its most rigid form, would be a purely teleological theory, a complete discussion of it would have to begin by considering whether any purely teleological theory of ethics could possibly be adequate. This question we have already discussed in connexion with Intuitionism, and we need say nothing further about it. In any case Sidgwick, though a Hedonist, is not a pure teleologist, since his six ethical intuitions are deontological propositions. The ethical question that remains is this. Is it the case that nothing is intrinsically good or bad except experiences, that no characteristic of an experience has any bearing on its intrinsic value except its pleasantness or painfulness, and that the measure of its intrinsic value is the nett balance of pleasantness over painfulness which characterises it? Sidgwick discusses this question in *Book III, Chap. XIV*.

It seems to me important to begin by trying to get a clear idea of what we mean by " a pleasure " and " a pain " ; for, on this point psychologists, to my mind, are very confused. The old tripartite division subdivides all mental events into Cognitions, Conations, and Feelings. And it seems to identify " Feelings " with pleasures and pains. Now this seems to me to be a radically unsatisfactory and unscientific division. I would first divide mental events into those which are and those which are not directed to objects. If there be any members of the second class, and I think it is plausible to maintain that there are, I confine the name " Feelings " to them. In the first class would certainly come Cognitions, Conations, and Emotions. You cannot cognise without cognising something, or will without willing something, or have an emotion without having it towards something. As regards those mental events which are called " Sensations," it seems to me that some, *e.g.*, visual and auditory sensations, are plainly Cognitions, and therefore fall into the first class. With regard to others it is difficult in practice to decide whether they ought to go into the first or the second class, though it is certain that any one of them must in fact go into one class or the other. There are some "Sensations", *e.g.*, those which we get from

processes in our bodies, which are often called " Feelings ",
and which it seems highly plausible, though not absolutely
necessary, to put in the second class. Now I am very much
inclined to agree with M'Taggart that really all members of
the first class are Cognitions. It is plain that Emotion and
Conation presuppose cognition, and that it is cognition
which provides them with their objects. Now it seems
plausible to suggest that, *e.g.*, to fear something just *is* to
cognise that thing and to have this cognition " toned " or
qualified in a certain characteristic way. In fact to fear an
object is to cognise it " fearfully " ; to desire an object is
to cognise it " desiringly " ; and so on. Of course these
qualitative differences among cognitions carry with them
all kinds of *causal* differences. If I cognise an object fearfully my subsequent mental states and bodily actions will
tend to be characteristically different from what they would
be if I cognised it desiringly. If this be so, the fundamental
division of mental events is into Cognitions and Feelings.
And a cognition is called an " Emotion " if it has any one
of the innumerable specific kinds of emotional quality ; it
is called a " Conation " if it has the " desire-aversion "
quality ; and so on. It seems plain that these qualities are
not mutually exclusive, like determinates under the same
determinable. The very same cognition may have several
different emotional qualities and also the conative quality.
It will then count both as a conation and as a mixed emotion.

We are now in a position to deal with pleasures and
pains. It seems to me that there is a quality, which we
cannot define but are perfectly well acquainted with, which
may be called " Hedonic Tone ". It has the two determinate
forms of Pleasantness and Unpleasantness. And, so far as
I can see, it can belong *both* to Feelings and to those

Cognitions which are also Emotions or Conations. Whether it can belong to Cognitions which have neither an emotional nor a conative quality, if such there be, is more doubtful. " A pleasure " then is simply any mental event which has the pleasant form of hedonic tone, and " a pain " is simply any kind of mental event which has the unpleasant form of hedonic tone. There is not a special *kind* of mental events, called " pleasures and pains " ; and to think that there is is as if one should solemnly divide human beings into men, women, and blondes. It is of course true that the commonest, and some of the most intense, pleasures and pains are feelings, in my sense of the word. But remorse, which is memory of certain events, having a certain emotional tone, is plainly a pain as much as toothache. And hope, which is expectation of certain events, having a certain emotional tone, is plainly as much a pleasure as the sensation of smell which we get from a rose or a violet.

Now any mental event which has hedonic quality will always have other qualities as well, and its specific hedonic quality will often be causally determined by its specific non-hedonic qualities. Thus the painfulness of remorse and the pleasantness of hope are determined respectively by the specific kinds of emotional quality which these two cognitions have. And this is even more obvious in the case of bodily feelings. Headaches and toothaches are both pains, for they both have unpleasant hedonic tone. But each has its own specific sensible quality of " headachiness " and " toothachiness", beside further modifications, such as "stabbingness", " throbbingness ", etc., which may be common to both. And the painfulness of these feelings seems to be causally determined by their non-hedonic sensible qualities. At this point I cannot refrain from throwing out an interesting question which I must not pursue further. Is the connexion between such and such non-hedonic qualities and such and such a form of hedonic quality *merely* causal and logically *contingent*, or is it intrinsically necessary ? Is it, *e.g.*, logically possible that there should have been minds which had experiences exactly like our experiences of acute toothache in all their *sensible* qualities, but in whom these sensations were *pleasantly* toned ? The reader may find it amusing to speculate on this question for himself.

We can now deal with the question of pleasures and pains of different quality, which Mill raised, but which he and his critics have so lamentably failed to state clearly. We must first divide the characteristics of any experience into Pure Qualities and Relational Properties. We must then further subdivide the Pure Qualities into Hedonic and Non-hedonic, and the Relational Properties into Causal and Non-causal. Take, *e.g.*, remorse. Its hedonic quality is unpleasantness. It has, beside, that characteristic emotional quality in virtue of which we call it " remorse ". It has the non-causal relational property of being a cognition of one's own past misdeeds. And it may have the causal property of tending to make us avoid in future such actions as we are now regretting. Now it is perfectly plain that there are " differences of quality " among pleasures and pains in the sense that two experiences which were exactly alike in hedonic quality might differ in non-hedonic quality (as a headache and a toothache do), or in non-causal relational property, or in causal property. The pure Hedonist holds that differences of non-hedonic quality and non-causal relational property make no difference to the intrinsic value of an experience. Nothing is relevant to the value of the experience except its hedonic quality and a certain one

of its causal properties, viz., what Bentham called its
" fecundity ". Fecundity is the causal property of tending
to produce other experiences which are pleasant or painful.
Mill presumably held that, although no experience would
have any intrinsic value, positive or negative, unless it were
pleasant or painful, yet of two experiences which had
precisely the same hedonic quality and precisely the same
fecundity one might be better than the other in virtue of
some difference in non-hedonic quality, or in non-causal
relational property, or in some causal property other than
fecundity. This view appears to be perfectly consistent
logically, whether it be in fact true or not.

There is, however, another and more subtle sense in
which it is conceivable that pleasures or pains might " differ
in quality ". It is commonly assumed that hedonic tone is
a determinable quality having two and only two determinate
forms under it, viz., pleasantness and unpleasantness, though
of course each can be present in various degrees of intensity.
This may very well be true ; but there is another possibility
which is at least worth mentioning. Is it not possible that
there may be several different determinate forms of pleasantness and unpleasantness, just as there are several different
shades of redness and several different shades of blueness ?
If this were admitted, it might be held that nothing is
relevant to the goodness or badness of an experience except
its hedonic quality and its fecundity, and yet that two
experiences which had exactly the same degree of pleasantness and the same fecundity might differ in value because
they had this pleasantness in different determinate forms.
It is just conceivable that Mill may have meant this. He
was so confused that he probably did not himself know
precisely what he meant ; very likely he was thinking in

a vague way of both these entirely different senses of
" qualities of pleasure ", without ever clearly distinguishing
them. A person who took the present view might be called
a " pure hedonist " but not a " purely quantitative hedonist ".

As regards the characteristics which make an experience
intrinsically good or bad. Sidgwick is definitely a pure
quantitative hedonist. He seems not to have envisaged the
possibility which I have described as pure, but not purely
quantitative, hedonism. And his discussion is to some
extent confused by the assumption that pleasures and pains
are a specific *kind* of experience, instead of being *any* kind
of experience which happens to have pleasantness or
painfulness.

I do not propose to go into the details of Sidgwick's
argument. In the end, as he is well aware, each man must
decide such questions for himself by direct inspection. All
that the philosopher can do is to make sure that no relevant
facts have been ignored, that no logical fallacies are committed, and that the issue is not confused by verbal
ambiguities. I will therefore put the matter as briefly and
clearly as I can in my own way. The contention which we
have to examine is that no relational property of an
experience, and no quality of it except its hedonic quality,
has any bearing on its intrinsic goodness or badness. If
this were so, it would follow that no causal characteristic
of it can have any bearing on its goodness or badness as a
means except its fecundity, *i.e.*, its tendency to produce
pleasant or painful experiences. I shall first try to convince
the reader that this is not in fact true. And I shall then try
to point out the kind of fallacy which is, I think, committed
by those persons who profess to show that it is true.

(i) Since this is a general proposition, it can be refuted

if we can produce a single convincing contrary instance.
Now consider the state of mind which is called "malice".
Suppose that I perceive or think of the undeserved misfortunes of another man with pleasure. Is it not perfectly
plain that this is an intrinsically bad state of mind, not
merely *in spite of*, but *because of*, its pleasantness? Is it
not plain that any cognition which has the relational
property of being a cognition of another's undeserved misfortunes and the hedonic quality of pleasantness will be
worse in proportion as the pleasantness is more intense?
No doubt malice is a state of mind which on the whole
tends to increase human misery. But surely it is clear that
we do not regard it as evil, simply as a means. Even if we
were quite sure that all malice would be impotent, it seems
clear to me that we should condemn it as intrinsically bad.

This example, if it be accepted, not only refutes the
general contention of the pure hedonist, but also brings out
an important positive fact. Malice is not intrinsically bad
simply because it is pleasant ; many pleasant states are
intrinsically good. And it is not intrinsically bad simply
because it has the relational property of being a cognition
of another's undeserved happiness ; the sorrowful cognition
of such an object would not be intrinsically bad. The
intrinsic badness of malice depends on the *combination*
of being pleasant with having this particular kind of object.
We must therefore be prepared for the possibility that
there is no single simple characteristic which is necessary
and sufficient to make an experience intrinsically good or
bad. It may be that intrinsic goodness or badness always
depends on the combination of certain characteristics in the
same experience. Any experience which combined the
characteristics c_1 and c_2 might be intrinsically good ; any

that combined c_2 and c_3 might be intrinsically bad ; whilst experiences which combined c_3 and c_1 might be neutral.

(ii) Let us now consider what seems to me to be the fallacy in the arguments of pure hedonists. We must begin by remarking that it is logically impossible that an experience should have no characteristic except hedonic quality. It is as clear that no experience could be *merely* pleasant or painful as that nothing could be black or white without also having some shape and some size. Consequently the hedonist can neither produce nor conceive an instance of an experience which was just pleasant or painful and nothing more ; and so he cannot judge by direct inspection that hedonic quality is necessary and sufficient to determine intrinsic value. He is therefore reduced to reflecting on instances in which hedonic quality is combined with non-hedonic characteristics. Now the utmost that he can do is this. He can take in turn each of the non-hedonic characteristics of experiences which could with any plausibility be thought to affect their intrinsic value. These can occur, or be conceived to occur, without hedonic quality, or with various degrees of pleasantness and various degrees of painfulness. He will claim to establish by inspection propositions of the following kind with regard to each of these non-hedonic characteristics. (*a*) When this characteristic is present and hedonic quality is absent the experience has no intrinsic value. (*b*) When this characteristic is present and hedonic quality is also present the experience has intrinsic value. (*c*) The determinate kind of value (goodness or badness) varies with the determinate kind of hedonic quality (pleasantness or unpleasantness), and its degree varies with the degree of the hedonic quality. Variations in the determinate form or in the degree of this non-hedonic characteristic make no difference to the determinate form or the degree of value of the experience.

I do not think that any hedonist could possibly claim more than to establish these propositions in turn about each non-hedonic characteristic of an experience which seemed worth considering. I have tried to show by a contrary instance that the third of them, at any rate, is not true. But suppose, for the sake of argument that they were all true, what could legitimately be inferred? You could legitimately infer that hedonic quality is *necessary* to give intrinsic value to an experience. You could legitimately infer that none of these other characteristics is necessary to give intrinsic value to an experience; *i.e.*, that, if you take *any one* of them, an experience could be intrinsically good or bad without possessing *that one*. But it would not be legitimate to infer that any experience could have intrinsic value if it had *none* of these characteristics. For it might be that, although an experience which had hedonic quality could have intrinsic value without c_1 being present, and could have it without c_2 being present, . . . and could have it without c_n being present, yet it could not have intrinsic value unless *one or other* of the non-hedonic characteristics $c_1, c_2, . . . c_n$ were present in addition to the hedonic quality. To take a parallel case; there is no area which a thing must have in order to be round, but it cannot be round without having some area or other. Thus, even if all the premises which the most optimistic hedonist could demand were granted to him, he would have no right to conclude that the hedonic quality of an experience is *sufficient* as well as *necessary* to give it intrinsic value. Even if the *variations* in intrinsic value were dependent on variations in hedonic quality and totally independent of variations in any non-hedonic characteristic, it might still be the case that intrinsic value would not be *present at all* unless there were some non-hedonic characteristic in addition to the hedonic quality. To take a parallel case ; the variations in the time of swing of a pendulum are independent of variations in the mass of the pendulum-bob. But it would not swing at all if the bob had no mass.

All arguments for pure quantitative hedonism, including Sidgwick's, with which I am acquainted overlook these elementary logical points. I conclude then that the arguments for this doctrine are certainly fallacious, and that the doctrine itself is almost certainly false.

Here, if I were wise, I should leave the matter. But I cannot resist the temptation of starting one more hare before I turn to another topic. We have so far talked of pleasantness and painfulness as two determinate forms of a certain determinable *quality* (hedonic tone) which may belong to any kind of experience. We have noted that it is *a priori* impossible that any experience should have *only* hedonic quality ; it must always have some non-hedonic quality (such as toothachiness, throbbingness, etc.), and this will determine its hedonic quality. Now this suggests the following possibility. Is it not possible that what we have called " hedonic *quality* " is really a *relational property* and not a quality at all ? Is it not possible that the statement : " This experience of mine is pleasant " just means : " I like this experience for its non-hedonic qualities " ? I may dislike the experience as a whole, because it will have causal and non-causal relational properties in addition to its non-hedonic qualities. I like the experience of malice for its emotional quality ; but I cannot confine my attention to this. I have to consider also its relational property of having for its object the undeserved misfortunes of another ; and my dislike for the combination of this emotional quality with this relational property overbalances my liking for the experience regarded simply as having the emotional quality. On this view we should no longer divide the qualities of an experience into hedonic and non-hedonic. All its qualities would be non-hedonic. But, if its qualities were such that I liked it *for them* it would be pleasant, and if its qualities were such that I disliked it *for them* it would be painful. And it would remain pleasant in the first case even though I disliked it *on the whole,* and painful in the second case even though I liked it *on the whole.* I think it is worth while to throw out this suggestion ; but I do not wish to attach much weight to it. My argument against pure quantitative hedonism is independent of its truth or falsity. I am inclined to think that Sidgwick is taking a somewhat similar view in the very difficult discussion in *Book II, Chap. II, Sect. 2,* and in *Book III, Chap. XIV, Sect. 4.*

(2, 12) We can now pass to what I have called the *Factual Problem* of Hedonism. This is simply the question whether approximately accurate estimates can be made of the relative balance of pleasure and pain in alternative future possible states of affairs. This is discussed in *Book II, Chaps. III* to *VI* inclusive. Naturally every difficulty which there is in estimating the relative hedonic value of alternative future states of oneself is intensified when one tries to make such estimates about the states of other men, as Utilitarianism needs to do. I have only one comment to make. The admitted difficulties of forming such estimates are often alleged as a conclusive objection to Hedonism in general and to Utilitarianism in particular. This is no doubt legitimate as an *argumentum ad hominem* against any

Hedonist who gives himself airs and maintains that it would be easy to know what our duty is if Hedonism were true. But the important fact for those of us who have no particular ethical axe to grind is this. Hedonism has to be rejected, not because it is too complicated, but because it is far too simple. On any ethical theory which attempts to do justice to all the facts, estimates will have to be made in comparison with which those demanded by Hedonism would be child's play. In the first place, in judging the rightness of an action we shall have to balance its fittingness to the total course of events which it will modify against the intrinsic goodness and badness of these modified events. Secondly, as we have seen, the estimation of this total fittingness involves an elaborate balancing and composition of partial fittingnesses and unfittingnesses. Lastly, we have now seen reason to think that the intrinsic goodness or badness of any state of affairs will depend on many different factors, of which hedonic quality is only one. Living in such a glass-house, we shall be most unwise to cast stones at Utilitarianism on the ground of the impossible complexity of the estimates which it demands of us.

This completes what I have to say about (2, 1) *Hedonism in General*. I do not think that it would be profitable to comment separately on (2, 2) *Egoistic Hedonism* and (2, 3) *Universalistic Hedonism.* The only point that I wish to make is that there would seem to be no need for an egoistic teleological theory to be hedonistic. Green's theory of Self-realisation as the ultimate end to be aimed at is plainly a form of Egoism, and equally plainly not a form of Hedonism. Sidgwick's view appears to be (cf. *Book I, Chap. VII*) that all other forms of Egoism are so vague as to be hardly worth discussing. On investigation they prove either not to be egoistic or to be hedonistic. This may in fact be historically correct, but it does not seem clear that there could not be a perfectly definite form of non-hedonistic Egoism. However this may be, the important point which remains to be discussed is the controversy of Ethical Egoism with Non-egoistic theories of ethics. This comes under the heading

(G) THE RELATIONS BETWEEN THE THREE METHODS. We have already considered the relation of Intuitionism to teleological types of ethical theory, and so we may confine ourselves to the question mentioned above. Let us begin by restricting the discussion to the case of happiness, and afterwards remove this restriction and consider the case of goodness in general. There is no doubt as to what we mean by " my happiness " and " your happiness " ; but, even if Hedonism be accepted, there may be a difficulty in saying what is meant by " my good " and " your good " and " *the* good ".

The first point to notice is that the contrary opposite of Egoistic Hedonism is not Universalistic, but Altruistic, Hedonism. It will be worth while to state each of the three doctrines clearly at this point. Egoistic Hedonism says : " You ought to sacrifice *any* amount of happiness in others if you will thereby increase your own total happiness *to the slightest degree* more than you could by any other course of action open to you." Altruistic Hedonism says : " You ought to sacrifice *any* amount of happiness in yourself if you will thereby increase the total happiness of others *to the slightest degree* more than you could by any other course of action open to you." Universalistic Hedonism says : " If a certain sacrifice of your own happiness will so much increase that of others that the *total nett amount* of happiness is increased, you ought to make this sacrifice ; and if a certain sacrifice of the happiness of others will so much increase your own happiness that the *total nett amount* is increased, you ought to sacrifice this amount of the happiness of others." The Pure Egoist holds that it is his duty to ignore the happiness of others, except as it may affect his own. The Pure Altruist holds that it is his duty to ignore his own happiness, except as it may affect the happiness of others. The Universalistic Hedonist holds that it is his duty to consider simply the nett amount of happiness, and to ignore the circumstance of whether it is situated in himself or in others.

Before going into details I will make certain obvious comments. (i) It seems to me quite clear that common-sense would reject Pure Egoism as a grossly immoral doctrine. (ii) When Altruism is clearly stated common-sense would hardly accept it even as an unattainable ideal. It hardly condemns the doctrine as immoral ; but it would use the milder expressions " Quixotic " or " Fanatical " about it. (iii) Universalistic Hedonism seems neither immoral nor Quixotic, and yet I doubt whether common-sense would feel perfectly comfortable about it. Some actions which would be right if Universalistic Hedonism be true would seem to common-sense to be rather coldly selfish, whilst others would seem to be rather Quixotically altruistic. We must allow for the fact that common-sense *is* rather confused ; and for the further fact that it may be desirable to praise as an ideal what we should condemn as an actuality, provided we know that most people are likely to go wrong by keeping too far from this ideal. This, I think, adequately explains the rather embarrassed attitude which common-sense takes towards Altruism. It knows that most people tend to err on the egoistic side, and not on the altruistic. It cannot very severely condemn occasional excesses in the altruistic direction without seeming to condone frequent lapses in the egoistic direction.   Yet, when Altruism is clearly formulated as a general principle, it plainly does not commend itself to the common-sense of enlightened and virtuous persons.   (iv) All three ethical theories presuppose that neither *psychological* Egoism nor *psychological* Altruism is true.   They assume that we can and do desire as ends both our own happiness and the happiness of others ; if they did not, the " ought " in them would be meaningless. Ethical Egoism holds that we ought not to let our desire for the happiness of others lead us into actions which would be detrimental to our own happiness ; Ethical Altruism holds that we ought not to let our desire for our own happiness lead us into actions which would be detrimental to the happiness of others ; and Universalistic Ethical Hedonism holds that we ought not to let either desire lead us into actions which would be detrimental to the nett total happiness.   (v) Egoism would have one great practical and theoretical advantage over both Altruism and Universalism.   It, and it only, avoids the necessity of considering a " sum " or " aggregate " of happiness, which is not the happiness of any*one*, but is somehow made up of the happiness of several different people.   The Universalist has to consider the aggregate happiness of every one, including himself ; the Altruist has to consider the aggregate happiness of every one except himself ; but the Egoist has to consider only his own happiness.   This saves the Egoist from very great difficulties, both practical and theoretical.

Let us now consider whether Egoism is a possible ethical theory.   The fundamental difference between the Egoist and the Universalist may be put as follows. The Universalist says : " If a state of consciousness having a certain quality (*e.g.*, pleasantness) would, for that reason, be intrinsically good, then its occurrence *in any mind* is a fitting object of desire *to any mind*." The Egoist says : " If a state of consciousness having a certain quality (*e.g.*, pleasantness) would, for that reason, be intrinsically good, then its occurrence in any mind is a fitting object of desire *to that mind* and to that mind *only*.

The first point to notice is that the Egoist's doctrine, when thus stated, cannot be accused of any arbitrariness or partiality. He does not claim anything for *his* Ego which he is not prepared to allow to any other Ego. *E.g.*, if he is a Hedonist, he admits that equally pleasant states of mind are equally good things, no matter whose states of mind they may be. But he holds that each of us is properly concerned, not with *all* good things, but only with a certain restricted class of good things, viz., those which are states of his own mind. Within the class of things which it is fitting for A to desire as ends it is fitting for him to proportion his desires to the goodness of the things desired. But it is unfitting for A to desire as an end anything that falls outside this class, no matter how good it may be, or how much better it may be than anything that falls within the class. And exactly the same is true, *mutatis mutandis*, of B.

I cannot see that there is any internal inconsistency in Egoism, when stated in this form. It may be remarked that it is possible to state a view which would be intermediate between pure Egoism and pure Universalism. It might be suggested that it is fitting for A to desire to *some* degree the existence of *any* intrinsically good state of mind ;

but that, of equally good states of mind, one in himself and another in someone else, it is fitting for him to desire the existence of the former more intensely than that of the latter. Pure Egoism, as I have said, seems to be flagrantly contrary to common-sense morality ; but I am not sure that the compromise which I have just proposed is not more in accord with the judgments of common-sense than is Pure Universalism.

Before leaving the subject it is important to notice that the above defence of the logical consistency of ethical Egoism would be incompatible with a purely teleological view of ethics. The consistent Egoistic Hedonist holds that pleasure and nothing else is good, and that an equally pleasant state is equally good no matter where it occurs. He knows quite well that, in many cases, if he sacrificed some of his own pleasure, others would gain far more pleasure than he has lost. Yet he holds that any such action would be wrong. Such a view would be quite impossible if he held the teleological theory that " right " and " conducive to intrinsically good results " are mutually equivalent. It can be made consistent only on the extreme deontological view that such an action would be unfitting, and that its unfittingness suffices to make it wrong on the whole no matter how intrinsically good its consequences might be.

If we refer back to the two principles from which Sidgwick deduces his *Principle of Rational Benevolence*, we shall see that the Egoist might accept the first but would have to reject the second. He could admit that " the good of any one individual is of no more importance, from the point of view of the Universe, than the equal good of any other." He would merely remark that, after all, he is not the Universe, and therefore it is not obvious that he ought to take the Universe's point of view. And he might add that, unless the Universe be supposed to be a person, which was certainly not Sidgwick's opinion, all talk about its "point of view" must be metaphorical, and the precise meaning of the metaphor is not easy to grasp. He would have to deny that "it is my duty to aim at good generally, so far as I can bring it about, and not merely at a particular part of it," which is the second of the two premises from which Sidgwick deduces his *Principle of Rational Benevolence.* According to the Egoist it is not his duty to aim at "good generally", *i.e.*, regardless of where it may occur; it is his duty to confine his attention to aiming at those good states of mind which will be states of his own mind. Now Sidgwick's difficulty was that *both* the principle that I ought to be *equally* concerned about equally good states of mind, no matter where they may occur, *and* the principle that I ought to be *more* concerned about a good state in my own mind than about an equally good state in any other mind, seemed to him self-evident when he inspected each separately. And yet they are plainly inconsistent with each other, so that, in one case at least an ethical principle which is in fact false must be appearing to be necessarily true. All that I can say in the matter is that Pure Egoism, *i.e.*, the doctrine that I ought not to desire to any degree as an end the occurrence of good states of mind in anyone but myself, seems plainly false; whilst Universalism does not seem plainly true. It does seem to me conceivable, though not self-evident, that I ought to desire *more strongly* the occurrence of a good state of mind in myself than the occurrence of an equally good state of mind in anyone else; whilst it seems self-evident that I ought to desire *to some degree* its occurrence anywhere. Sidgwick seems to have ignored the fact that, in considering the rightness or wrongness of a desire for a certain object, we have to consider, not only whether it is or is not appropriate to desire this object at all, but also what degree of desire it is appropriate to feel for this object if it be appropriate to desire it at all. It is fitting to desire the pleasures of the table, and it is fitting to desire the beatific vision ; but it is not fitting to desire the former as intensely as the latter.

I will now leave Egoism, and make a few remarks on Universalism in general and Universalistic Hedonism in particular. Let us begin by considering what can be meant by the total nett happiness (a) of an individual, and (b) of a collection of individuals. We might compare pleasantness with the sensible quality of whiteness, and unpleasantness with the sensible quality of blackness. Now any shade that is not purely white or purely black may be called " grey ". The greys can be arranged in an order from pure black, as one limit, to pure white, as the other limit. This series can be divided into three parts, viz. : (i) the greys that are more like pure black than pure white ; (ii) those which are more like pure white than pure black ; and (iii) that which is as like black as white. These might be called respectively " the blackish-greys ", " the whitish-greys ", and " the neutral grey ". To say that a certain man is on the whole happy at a certain moment may be compared to saying that a certain area is pure white or whitish-grey at a certain time. The same analogy would hold, *mutatis mutandis*, for the statement that he was on the whole unhappy or in a neutral condition at a certain moment. Suppose there were $n-1$ just distinguishable black-greys, and $n-1$ just distinguishable white-greys, then we might

assign ordinal numbers to each member of the series from
pure black to pure white inclusive, as follows :—

$$-n, -n+1, \ldots -1, 0, 1, \ldots n-1, n.$$

Exactly the same could be done with the pleasure-pain
series. Next we must notice that the same shade of grey
could be present in various different intensities, and the
same seems to be true of any given pleasure-pain quality.
If there is a series of just distinguishable intensities from
zero upwards, we could assign ordinal numbers to the
members of this series. These would all be positive, as
follows :—

$$0, 1, \ldots m, \ldots$$

Now an area might have a certain shade of grey of a
certain intensity for a certain time and then change in
intensity or shade. We could divide its history into successive
slices so short that the intensity and shade of greyness were
sensibly constant throughout any such period. The same
would be true, *mutatis mutandis*, of a mind and its history.
Suppose that the whole history of the area can be divided
up into l such successive slices of duration $t_1, t_2, \ldots t_l$
respectively. Throughout a typical one t_r of these, let it
have a greyness whose ordinal number is n_r and whose
intensity has the ordinal number m_r. Take the product
$m_r n_r t_r$. This will be positive if n_r be positive, negative if
n_r be negative, and zero if n_r be zero ; *i.e.*, if the area be
whitish-grey throughout the period t_r this product will be
positive, if it be blackish-grey the product will be negative,
and if it be neutral grey the product will be zero. All this
can be applied, *mutatis mutandis*, to the history of a mind.
In this case m_r will represent the intensity, and n_r the

position of the pleasure-pain quality in its scale, of the phase of experience which occupies the short period t_r in the history of this mind. We now take the algebraical sum of all such products as $m_r n_r t_r$; *i.e.*, the sum

$$m_1 n_1 t_1 + m_2 n_2 t_2 + \ldots \; m_r n_r t_r + \ldots \; m_1 n_1 t_1,$$

which might conveniently be written as

$$\sum_{r=1}^{r=1} m_r n_r t_r.$$

Now this sum of products might be either positive, zero, or negative. If it be positive we should say that the area had been " on the whole white " throughout its history ; if it were negative we should say that the area had been " on the whole black " throughout its history. In the case of a mind we should say that it had been " on the whole happy " if the sum were positive, and " on the whole unhappy " if the sum were negative. And, the greater the numerical value of the sum, the " more happy " or the " more unhappy ", according to whether it be positive or negative, do we say that this life has on the whole been.

So far we have confined ourselves to a single grey area or a single mind. In such cases the addition of the products does correspond to something that actually takes place, viz., the adjunction of successive phases to each other in the history of the area or of the mind. But the Utilitarian cannot confine himself to a single mind ; he has to consider what he calls " the total happiness of a collection of minds ". Now this is an extremely odd notion. It is plain that a collection cannot literally be happy or unhappy. The oddity is clearly illustrated if we continue to use the analogy of greyness. Suppose that a number of different areas, which are not adjoined to each other, all go through

successive phases of greyness. What could we possibly
mean by " the total whiteness of this collection of areas " ?
What the Utilitarian in fact does is this. He first makes
a sum of products, in the way described, for the whole
history of each mind ; he then adds all these sums together.
He thus forms a double sum which might be denoted by

$$\sum_{S=1}^{S=N} h_S$$

where h_S is the sum of products for a typical mind M_S, and
there are N minds, M_1, M_2, . . . M_S, . . . M_N, to be considered. If this double sum is positive he says that this
collection of minds " has a positive balance of happiness ",
and the greater its numerical value the greater is the balance
of happiness which he ascribes to the collection.

It will at least enable us to avoid verbal difficulties if
we adopt a suggestion of M'Taggart's and talk of the total
happiness *in* a collection rather than the total happiness *of*
a collection. We shall say then that this double sum
represents the total balance of happiness *in* the collection
of minds M_1 . . . M_N. Even so it is extremely difficult to
see that the *arithmetical* addition of one *number* h_S to another
represents any kind of adjunction *in rerum naturâ*. However
this may be, the command which the Pure Utilitarian gives
us is to maximise this double sum so far as we can. This,
he tells us, is the whole duty of man.

Now I have three comments to make. (i) Among the
things which we can to some extent influence by our actions
is the number of minds which shall exist, or, to be more
cautious, which shall be embodied at a given time. It would
be possible to increase the total amount of happiness in a
community by increasing the numbers of that community

even though one thereby reduced the total happiness of each member of it. If Utilitarianism be true it would be one's duty to try to increase the numbers of a community, even though one reduced the average total happiness of the members, so long as the total happiness in the community would be in the least increased. It seems perfectly plain to me that this kind of action, so far from being a duty, would quite certainly be wrong.

(ii) Given a fixed collection of minds, the existence of a given amount of happiness in this collection would be compatible with many different ways of distributing it among the individual members. The collection composed of A and B might have in it a certain amount of happiness, and this sum might be made up either through A and B being both moderately happy, or through A being rather happy and B rather miserable, or by A being intensely happy and B intensely miserable. Now a purely teleological Utilitarian would have to hold that an action of mine would be right provided it increased the total happiness in the community as much as any other action open to me at the time would do, and that the way in which I distributed this extra dose of happiness among the members of the community was a matter of complete indifference. I do not know that this form of Utilitarianism has been held by anyone ; it is certainly not the form which Bentham or Sidgwick held. Both consider it self-evident that it can never be right *arbitrarily, i.e.,* without being able to assign some ground other than the numerical difference of A and B, to treat A more or less favourably than B in the distribution of happiness. This, however, does not carry us far. We want to know what differences between A and B are, and what are not, proper grounds for giving one more

and the other less of a certain extra dose of happiness.
It seems to me that, for a pure Utilitarian, one and only
one consideration would be relevant. If and only if giving
a larger share of this extra dose of happiness to A than
to B would tend to increase the total happiness in the
community in future more than giving an equal share to
A and B would do, it is right to give A a larger share than B.
A, *e.g.*, might be the kind of man who would work harder
and produce more consumable goods if he were made
happier, whilst B might not. This kind of difference, and
this only, would be relevant. In fact the only legitimate
ground for preferring one distribution to another should be
the greater fecundity of that distribution. Now, an extremely
unequal distribution might have much greater fecundity
than a more equal one ; and this is the justification which
has commonly been given for social arrangements in which
most people are rather poor and a few people are very rich.
Yet it seems clear that, although this greater fecundity *is*
relevant, it is not the *only* relevant factor. A very unequal
distribution does seem to be *ipso facto* somewhat objection-
able, though it may be right to put up with this evil for
the sake of the advantage of greater fecundity. Nor is
this all. It might be that a distribution which gave more
happiness to A than to B, *and* a distribution which gave
more to B than to A, would each have more fecundity than
one which gave them an equal share. If so, the Utilitarian
presumably ought to reject the equal distribution and
accept *one* of the unequal distributions. But on what
principles is he to decide between two unequal distributions,
of equal fecundity, one of which favours A at the expense
of B whilst the other favours B at the expense of A ?
Either his choice is a matter of complete indifference, or

some other factor beside fecundity must be ethically relevant.

(iii) The third point which I have to make is this. We have said that you cannot literally talk of the happiness *of* a community, but only of the happiness *in* it. This, however, does not seem to me to be true of goodness. It seems to me that you can quite literally talk of the goodness or badness *of* a community, as well as of the goodness or badness *in* it. No doubt the former depends on the latter. If there were no goodness in a community the community would not be good. The goodness of a community depends in part on the distribution of the goodness which is in it among its members ; and of two communities, both of which have the same amount of goodness in them, one may be better than the other because in it this amount of goodness is more fittingly distributed. This would be true even if the only goodness in a community were happiness, as the Hedonist holds. The fact is that any collection of minds worth calling a " community ", is a highly complex spiritual substance with a character of its own. It is not a mind, though it is composed of interrelated minds ; and it is not an organism, though the analogy of organisms may at times be useful. No doubt many expressions which we commonly use both of individuals and communities are used metaphorically in the latter application. When I say : " What Bloomsbury thinks to-day, King's College, Cambridge, thinks to-morrow," I am no doubt using " thinks " in a metaphorical and definable sense ; whilst I am using it in its literal and indefinable sense if I say : " What Mr. Keynes thinks to-day Mr. Lloyd George thinks he thinks to-morrow." But I see no reason to believe that this is so with the terms " good " and " bad ". There are indeed good qualities which can belong to individuals and not to communities, and there are other good qualities which can belong to communities and not to individuals ; but, so far as I can see, " good " means precisely the same in both applications.

It remains only to say something about Sidgwick's suggestion that it might be reasonable to postulate the existence of a powerful and benevolent God who will make up to us those sacrifices of our own happiness which we make here and now at the dictate of the *Principle of Rational Benevolence.* It is surely quite plain that no such postulate would free ethics from the theoretical inconsistency which Sidgwick finds in it. There are two principles which are logically inconsistent with each other, and, on reflexion each seems to Sidgwick equally self-evident. No God, however powerful and however benevolent, can alter the fact that these two principles are logically incompatible and that therefore something which seemed self-evident to Sidgwick must in fact have been false. The postulate that, in the long run, I shall lose nothing by acting in accordance with the *Principle of Rational Benevolence* would, no doubt, provide me with an additional motive for acting in accordance with it when, apart from this postulate, the apparently equally self-evident principle of Egoism would dictate a different course of action. Thus, the only function of the postulate would be to make it a matter of practical indifference whether I acted in accordance with one or other of two principles, one of which must be false and both of which seem true. This would be a comfort ; but it is difficult to suppose that this is an adequate ground for making the postulate.

Sidgwick seems to think that the making of such a postulate might be admitted to be reasonable if it be admitted that it is reasonable to make postulates on similar grounds in other departments of experience, *e.g.*, in natural science. Now a postulate is a proposition having the following characteristics. (i) It is neither intuitively nor demonstratively necessary and neither intuitively nor demonstratively impossible ; (ii) it can neither be proved nor disproved by experience and problematic induction ; and (iii) to act as if it were true will have better consequences than to act as if it were false or doubtful. These " better consequences " may be either (*a*) increase of knowledge and theoretical coherence, or (*b*) increase of happiness, virtue, practical efficiency, and so on. In the first case we talk of a *theoretical*, and, in the second, of a *practical*, postulate. Now compare and contrast Sidgwick's postulate of a benevolent and powerful God, who will make up to us the happiness which we have sacrificed in acting benevolently, with the scientific postulate that, if two apparently similar things behave differently in apparently similar situations, there must be some difference in the things or the situations which will bring the difference in behaviour under a general law. It is plain that, if we act on the scientific postulate we shall look for such differences ; whilst, if we act as if the postulate were false or doubtful, we shall very soon give up looking for them. Now, if we look for them, we may find them and thus increase our knowledge ; whilst, if we do not look for them, we certainly shall not find them. The justification for making the scientific postulate is thus plain. We have already seen that Sidgwick's postulate cannot be justified as a means of increasing our knowledge or introducing more coherence into our beliefs. It leaves the theoretical incoherence where it was, except that it adds the difficulty of why the benevolent and powerful being should allow a false moral principle to seem as necessarily true as a true one. If it is to be justified at all, it must be justified as a practical postulate. Since science does not make practical postulates, the analogy of science is not here directly relevant. Sidgwick's postulate must be justified, if at all, by the fact that to act as if it were true will increase our practical efficiency and our comfort. The conscientious man who finds the Principles of Egoism and of Rational Benevolence equally self-evident will be saved from the discomfort and hesitation which would arise when the two principles seemed to dictate different courses of action, provided he makes this postulate. But I am very much afraid that he would be saved from discomfort and hesitation *only* if he had *other grounds* for believing in the existence of a benevolent and powerful being, such as Sidgwick postulates, or if he could forget that he was merely postulating the existence of this being. You would not get much comfort from postulating the existence of God so long as you remembered that you were postulating it only in order to give yourself comfort. But of course it is psychologically possible to forget such inconvenient facts with a little practice, and then the postulate might increase the comfort and efficiency of a conscientious man whose ethical intuitions conflicted in the special way in which Sidgwick's did.

But, even so, one perplexity would remain. A conscientious man would wish to act, not only *in accordance with* a right principle, but *from* a right principle. Now it results from the postulate that he will be acting in accordance with a right principle whether he acts from Egoism or Benevolence ; for the postulate ensures that any action which is in accordance with either will be in accordance with both. But, if the agent acts on principle at all, he must be acting either on the egoistic or the benevolent principle. In one case he will be acting from a right principle and in the other from a wrong principle ; but, postulate or no postulate, he will never be able to know which is the right and which is the wrong one.

CHAPTER VII

Conclusion : Sketch of the Main Problems of Ethics

I HAVE now fulfilled to the best of my ability my under-taking to expound and criticize the ethical theories of Spinoza, Butler, Hume, Kant, and Sidgwick. I propose to end my book by giving a sketch of what seem to me to be the main problems of ethics, illustrated by reference to the writers whose works we have been studying.

(1) ANALYSIS OF ETHICAL CHARACTERISTICS. I propose to give the name " ethical characteristics " to whatever characteristics are denoted by the words " good ", " bad ", " right ", " wrong ", " ought ", and " duty ", and by any other words which are plainly mere synonyms for some word in this list. Now the first and most fundamental problem of pure ethics is whether these characteristics are unique and peculiar, in the sense that they cannot be analysed *without remainder* in terms of non-ethical charac-teristics. Even if this were so, it would not follow that all of them were unanalysable and consequently indefinable. It might still be possible to analyse and define some of them in terms of one or more of the others either with or without non-ethical characteristics.

Those theories which hold that ethical characteristics *can* be analysed without remainder into non-ethical ones may be called (1, 1) *Naturalistic Theories ;* those which hold that they cannot may be called (1, 2) *Non-Naturalistic Theories.* Hume and Spinoza definitely hold naturalistic

views. Sidgwick is definitely non-naturalistic about " right "
and " ought ". His discussion about " good " is so complicated that it is difficult to be sure whether he comes to
a naturalistic or a non-naturalistic conclusion. But the
impression which I get is that, after offering a very complicated naturalistic analysis in terms of desire, he finally
admits that it is not adequate. With many writers it is
extremely hard to be certain whether they are naturalists
or not. It is very common to find that the following two
propositions are not clearly distinguished from each other,
viz. : (a) " The ethical characteristic E *synthetically entails
and is entailed by* the non-ethical characteristics N_1, N_2, . . ." ;
and (b) " The ethical characteristic E is *analysable without
remainder into* the conjunction of the non-ethical characteristics N_1, N_2, . . ." Many moralists are liable to think
that they believe (b) when they really only believe, or only
have produced reasons for believing (a). Non-naturalistic
theories can, and generally do, accept some propositions of
the first kind. *E.g.*, Sidgwick holds that all happiness is
good and that nothing is good but happiness. But he denies
that to be good can be analysed into containing a positive
balance of happiness. Butler's distinction between the
psychological power and the moral authority of conscience
make it fairly clear that he was not a naturalist. Kant
has been accused of naturalism by Moore in his *Principia
Ethica*, but it is not at all clear to me that the accusation
is well-founded. No doubt Kant says that what I, as an
empirical self, *ought* to do is what I, as a purely rational
noumenal self, *necessarily would* do. But it is not clear that
he means this to be an analysis of the term " ought ". Mill
presumably meant to be a naturalistic hedonist. But it is
difficult to be sure in the case of such an extremely confused

writer that he really was one. We will now say something about the subdivisions of Naturalistic ethical theories.

(1, 1) *Naturalistic Theories.* These have taken many different forms, according to what non-ethical characteristics have been supposed to constitute the complete analysis of ethical characteristics. So far as I know, the most important have been the following. (1, 11) *Theological Naturalism.* An example would be Paley's view that " right " means " commanded by God ". (1, 12) *Biological, Sociological, or Evolutionary Naturalism.* It is hardly worth while to attempt to separate these, as those who have held any of them have tended to hold the rest in various proportions. Typical examples are the following. " To be virtuous means to perform the specific activities of the species to which you belong efficiently " (Spinoza). " Better conduct means conduct that comes later in the course of evolution, and is more complex than earlier conduct of the same kind " (Herbert Spencer). " Right action means action which tends to promote the stability and increase the complexity of human society " (many Sociologists). (1, 13) *Psychological Naturalism.* This attempts to define ethical characteristics in terms of certain psychical characteristics such as pleasantness, approval, and so on. Hume's theory is a typical example of it. It is much the most important and plausible form of Naturalism ; and the other types, when pressed with objections, often tend to fall back on it. We will therefore consider the various forms which Psychological Naturalism might take.

In the first place it might take the form of (1, 131) *Private,* or (1, 132) *Public* Psychological Naturalism. If, *e.g.*, a man holds that a " right " action means an action which evokes in *him* a certain kind of emotion when *he*

contemplates it, he is a Private Psychological Naturalist.
If he holds that a " right " action means one which evokes
a certain kind of emotion in all or most men, or in all or
most Englishmen, or in all or most Etonians, he is a Public
Psychological Naturalist. It is most important not to
confuse the distinction between Naturalistic and Non-
Naturalistic theories with the distinction between Subjective
and Non-Subjective theories. A subjective theory is one
which would make all ethical judgments to consist of statements by the speaker about his own mental attitude towards
an object at the time of speaking. On this view there is
nothing in ethics to discuss, and it would be mere rudeness
to question any ethical judgment that anyone might choose
to make. Now it is evident that the non-psychological
forms of Naturalism are not in the least subjective in this
sense. The psychological form *may* be subjective, for it
may be private ; but it *need* not be, for it may be public.
The question whether all or most men or all or most Etonians
do feel a certain emotion when they contemplate a certain
action is open to discussion and statistical investigation.
We have seen that Hume's form of Psychological Naturalism
is public. Later on we shall see that there is another
distinction, viz., that between *Relational* and *Non-Relational*
Theories which is highly relevant to the present point.

Now a Psychological Naturalist might develop his theory
in two ways which are *prima facie* quite different. Of course
he might use one of these two types of analysis for one
ethical characteristic, *e.g.*, goodness, and the other for
another ethical characteristic, *e.g.*, rightness. Let us take
the concept of intrinsic goodness. A Psychological Naturalist
might hold that to be " intrinsically good " means (*a*) to
have a certain psychical *quality*, *e.g.*, pleasantness, or (*b*) to

be the object of a certain mental *attitude, e.g.,* approval. Naturalistic Hedonism is an example of the first type of theory, whilst Hume's doctrine is an example of the second. We might call these two types of theory respectively *Mental Quality Theories* and *Mental Attitude Theories.* On the Mental Quality type of theory the publicity of an ethical characteristic would mean that a certain kind of object produced in all or most observers mental states with a certain kind of quality, *e.g.,* pleasantness. On the Mental Attitude type of theory it would mean that a certain kind of object evokes towards it a certain kind of emotion in all or most observers, *e.g.,* approval. If the suggestion which I threw out in discussing Hedonism in connexion with Sidgwick be true, Hedonism itself will be a form of Mental Attitude theory. For the suggestion was that pleasantness and painfulness are not really qualities of experiences but relational properties of them. It was suggested that " the experience X is pleasant to me " means " I like the experience X for its non-hedonic qualities." On this view the Naturalistic Hedonist asserts that " X is intrinsically good " means that X is an experience which the person who has it likes for its non-hedonic qualities. And publicity, on such a view, would consist in the fact that experiences of certain kinds are liked for their non-hedonic qualities by all or most men who have them.

Now both kinds of Public Psychological Naturalism could be divided up on two different principles. (*a*) They might be subdivided according to the nature of the group of experients used in the definition. The most important division here would be according to whether the mental state was supposed to be caused, or the mental attitude evoked, (i) in all or most human beings, or (ii) in a certain sub-group of the human race, *e.g.*, the members of a certain society. The first type of theory defines ethical concepts in terms of specific properties of the human mind as such. The second does not. Hume's theory is an example of the former. It would be fair to say that the former type of theory makes morality " natural " (in the sense in which liking sugar is natural), whilst the second makes it more " artificial " (in the sense in which disapproving the combination of a frock-coat and brown boots is artificial). (*b*) Psychological Naturalism might also be subdivided according to the mental quality or the mental attitude which is used in defining ethical characteristics. Thus the quality might be pleasantness, as the Hedonists hold, or it might be quantity and complexity of experience ; and the attitude might be approval or disapproval, as Hume held, or a sublimated form of fear or egoism.

There is another important principle of subdivision among theories of the Psychologically Naturalistic type. Are ethical terms to be defined by reference to the *actual* experiences of *actual* men or groups of men, or to the *hypothetical* experiences which it is supposed that certain *idealised* men or groups of men would have ? Very often the Naturalist starts with the first type of theory, and afterwards, when pressed with objections, falls back on the second. He begins, *e.g.*, to talk of the emotions which would be felt by an idealised " impartial observer ", whilst admitting that no actual observer is completely impartial. We will call the two types of theory respectively *Factual* and *Ideal* Naturalism. Now Ideal Naturalism is not necessarily inconsistent, for the ideal man or group may be defined in purely non-ethical terms, like the perfect gas and the frictionless fluid. But the Ideal Naturalist is on a very slippery slope, and he scarcely ever manages to avoid inconsistency. In defining his ideal he nearly always un-wittingly introduces some characteristic which is in fact ethical, and thus fails to do what, as a Naturalist, he claims to do, viz., to define ethical characteristics in completely non-ethical terms.

This completes the classification of possible types of Naturalistic Theory. We come now to a very important division of theories about the analysis of ethical concepts, which crosses the division of such theories into Naturalistic and Non-Naturalistic. This is the distinction between *Relational* and *Non-Relational* theories. With regard to any ethical characteristic it may be asked whether it is a pure quality, like *red* ; or a pure relation, like *between* ; or a relational property, like *loved-by-Jones*. Of course some ethical characteristics might be of one kind and some of another. *E.g.*, it might be held that *good* is a pure quality, whilst *right* is a relation between an action or intention or emotion and an agent, on the one hand, and a situation, on the other. Some people have held, again, that the fundamental ethical notion is, not good and bad, but better and worse. And others have held that " good " means what it would be right for every one to desire.

There is a close connexion between the distinctions of Naturalistic and Non-Naturalistic and Relational and Non-Relational respectively. It seems to be this. (*a*) Non-Naturalistic theories are compatible with either a relationist or a non-relationist view of ethical characteristics, or with any combination of the two. (*b*) Any form of Naturalistic theory which defines ethical characteristics in terms of the mental attitude which a certain man, or a certain class of men, or the whole human race, takes towards certain actions or intentions is plainly relational. For it makes all ethical characteristics into relational properties, like *loved-by-Jones* or *disliked-by-most-Etonians*. Exactly the same remarks apply to the Theological form of Naturalism. (*c*) The only doubtful case would seem to be the form of Psychological Naturalism, such as Naturalistic Hedonism, which defines ethical characteristics by mental *qualities*, such as pleasantness. It might seem at first sight that this form of Naturalism was non-relational. But, in the first place, as we have seen, it is possible that " pleasant " really means " liked by an experient for its non-hedonic qualities ". And, quite apart from this possibility, there is a distinction which must be drawn. If this type of theory defines " good " as *producing* in all or in certain classes of human minds mental states having a certain quality, it is obviously as relational as any other form of Naturalistic theory. But, if it defines " good " as *having* a certain mental quality, then it is not relational. *E.g.*, if a Naturalistic Hedonist defined " good " as productive of pleasant experiences, his theory would be relational even though pleasantness were a pure quality. But, if he defined " good " as pleasant, in the sense in which only an experience can be pleasant, his theory would be non-relational provided that pleasantness is a pure quality.

(2) EPISTEMOLOGICAL QUESTIONS. The questions which we have discussed so far are purely logical and ontological. They refer simply to the problem : " What is the right analysis of ethical characteristics ? " and not at all to the problem : " How do we come to have ideas of ethical characteristics and to believe propositions which involve them, and what mental faculties are involved in doing so ? "

We pass now to these epistemological questions. The problem has generally been put in the form : " What part, if any, is played by Reason ; and what part, if any, is played by emotion, feeling, and sentiment, in the formation of ethical concepts and the making of ethical judgments ? "

I have already pointed out, in connexion with Hume and Sidgwick, that Reason must not be identified with the power of reasoning. It includes three cognitive powers, viz., (a) the power of forming a priori concepts, i.e., concepts of characteristics which are not sensibly manifested in any instance and are not composed of characteristics which have separately been sensibly manifested in various instances ; (b) the power of recognising that a conjunction of attributes is an instance of a necessary connexion between these attributes, i.e., the power of Intuitive Induction, as Mr. Johnson calls it ; and (c) the power of inferring conclusions from premises.

Now no theory of ethics denies that Reason, in the sense of the power of reasoning or inferring, plays a part in the formation of ethical judgments. Take, e.g., even an extreme form of Private Psychological Naturalism. On this view every ethical judgment takes the form : " Whenever I contemplate such an object as X I feel the emotion Y towards it." Now it is clear that reasoning might be needed in making an ethical judgment, even of this kind, in two ways. (i) In order to determine what exactly is the nature of the object which I am contemplating. The total object may be an action done in a certain situation and likely to have certain consequences. And I may need to use reasoning in order to determine exactly what the situation is and what the consequences are likely to be. (ii) In order to generalise my present judgment by Problematic Induction. I may argue that I shall probably feel the same kind of emotion to similar objects on future occasions. And, on this view of ethics, this means that I infer that all similar objects will probably be good (or bad) in future in the only sense in which the theory allows me to say that this object is good (or bad) now.

This, I think, is the only sense in which any Naturalistic theory can admit that Reason is concerned in ethics. As we have seen, this is definitely asserted by Hume. Now I shall call a theory which does not admit that Reason plays any part in ethics except that of reason*ing* (2, 1) a *Non-Rationalistic Theory*. We see then that all Naturalistic theories are Non-Rationalistic theories.

(2, 2) A *Rationalistic Theory* would be one that admits that Reason plays some part in ethics beside that of mere reasoning. And it is necessarily a Non-Naturalistic theory. Now the concepts of ethics, even though they were *sui generis*, might conceivably be empirical, like *red* and *between*. Or they might be *a priori*, as I am inclined to think that *cause* and *substance* are. Then again the universal judgments of ethics might be empirical generalisations, like " all grass is green ", or intuitively or demonstratively necessary propositions, like " anything that has shape must have size " or " the square-root of 2 cannot be a rational number ". It is important to remember that there can be empirical judgments which involve *a priori* concepts, *e.g.*, " friction *causes* heat " ; and that there can be *a priori* judgments which involve empirical concepts, *e.g.*, " there cannot be *shape* without *size* ". Consequently there are four possible views for a Non-Naturalistic theory to take in this matter, viz., that ethics involves (*a*) both *a priori* concepts and *a priori* judgments, or (*b*) *a priori* concepts but no *a priori* judgments, or (*c*) *a priori* judgments but no *a priori* concepts, or (*d*) neither *a priori* concepts nor *a priori* judgments.

We see then that it is logically possible for a Non-Naturalistic theory to be Non-Rationalistic, viz., in case (*d*). But I must confess that I do not know of any instance of such a theory. We see further that there are three possible forms of Rationalistic theory, viz., (2, 21) *Two-sided Rationalism* ; (2, 22) *Rationalism of Concepts with Empiricism of Judgments* ; and (2, 23) *Rationalism of Judgments with Empiricism of Concepts.* Of the writers whom we have discussed it is plain that Sidgwick is a Two-sided Rationalist. He holds that the concept of *right* or *ought* is *a priori*, and he holds that we can see that what is pleasant and it only is necessarily good. Moreover, he holds that we can intuite certain necessary propositions about rightness, viz., the various abstract principles about impartiality and distribution which we have considered in the chapter on his ethics. I think it is pretty plain that Kant was also a Two-sided Rationalist. I do not know of instances of the more moderate kinds of Rationalism in ethics, but persons better read than I in the history of the subject might be able to think of some.

So much then for the part played by Reason in ethical cognition. Let us now consider the various views which might be taken about the part played by Emotion or Feeling in ethical cognition. Let us begin with Naturalistic theories. (*a*) Emotion and feeling play no important cognitive part in any but the psychological form of Naturalism. At most the other forms of Naturalism might hold that pleasant feeling or approving emotion are on the whole more or less trustworthy signs of the presence of the non-psychological characteristics by which these theories define ethical terms. Thus Spinoza would hold that pleasure is a trustworthy sign, provided it be *Hilaritas* and not mere *Titillatio*, that one is performing efficiently some action characteristic of one's species, and therefore that one was doing a good action or was in a good state. (*b*) In Psychological Naturalism feeling or emotion is an essential part of the *content* of ethical judgments. For, on this theory, when I say that so-and-so is good or right what I am asserting is that some person or group of persons does or would experience a certain feeling or emotion in contemplating this object.

Let us now take Non-Naturalistic theories. Here the emotion or feeling is never part of the *content* of an ethical judgment, in the sense that we are asserting that such and such an emotion or feeling would be experienced by such and such people. But it might be the case that the presence of certain kinds of emotion or feeling is a necessary condition for recognising the presence of ethical characteristics, and thus indirectly a necessary condition for making ethical judgments. The occurrence of sensations, *e.g.*, is a necessary condition of our getting the notions of colours and shapes, and therefore is a necessary condition for making judgments such as " this is red " and " that is round ". Yet these judgments are not simply assertions about our sensations. Similarly, it might be that we could not have got the notions of *right*, *good*, etc., and therefore could not make such judgments as " this is right " or " that is good ", unless we had felt certain emotions in certain situations. And yet these judgments might not be merely assertions about our emotions and feelings.

On the Non-Naturalistic type of theory how do we become aware of ethical characteristics, and how do we arrive at universal ethical judgments ? If ethical concepts be empirical, like the concepts of " red " and " between ", we must have been presented with instances which manifest them to us ; and we must either abstract them from these instances or construct them from concepts so abstracted. Now it is obvious that these characteristics are not manifested to us by any of our senses. One does not literally see or feel or taste the rightness of right actions or the goodness of good motives. So we should have to postulate some peculiar kind of experience, analogous to sensation, yet different from any of the ordinary sensations. This, I suppose is what the moralists who talked about a " Moral Sense " had, or ought to have had, in mind ; though I am afraid they used their terms very loosely. Now it would be natural to try to identify the " sensations " of this so-called " Moral Sense " with certain emotions which we undoubtedly do have, which we call " Feelings of Approbation and Disapprobation ". So I think that the most plausible form of the *Moral Sense Theory* would be that ethical concepts are empirical, and that we derive them by abstraction from instances which are presented to us by means of the emotions of Approbation and Disapprobation, in somewhat the same way as that in which we derive our concepts of colours from instances of them presented to us by means of visual sensations. Such a theory, when clearly stated, certainly does not seem very plausible. And this may be a good ground for holding that, if ethical characteristics be *sui generis*, as Non-Naturalistic theories maintain, then the concepts of them must be *a priori* and not empirical.

If our concepts of ethical characteristics be not empirical, they are not abstracted, or constructed from what has been abstracted, in this way. There will then be no need to postulate a Moral Sense. But we may still suppose that Reason needs certain specific kinds of experience to furnish the *occasions* on which it recognises these characteristics. This would be analogous to the way in which, on the view that the concept of causation is *a priori*, Reason recognises the causal relation on the occasion of experiences of regular sequence, although we do not abstract the notion of causation from such experiences. Now it would be plausible, on this view, to suggest that the emotions of Approbation and Disapprobation furnish the necessary occasions on which Reason recognises ethical characteristics, such as *goodness* and *rightness*. This theory would be a form of *Ethical Intuitionism*. It might be called the *Milder Form of Intuitionism about Ethical Concepts*. Some moralists, however, seem to have held that ethical characteristics are recognised by Reason without any special kind of emotional experience being needed to furnish it with the occasion to form these concepts. It seems to me probable that Kant took this view. It is a logically possible theory, but all analogy seems to be against it. I will call it the *Extreme Form of Intuitionism about Ethical Concepts*.

So much for the different possible views about the formation of ethical concepts. Let us now consider the ways in which we might be supposed to arrive at universal ethical judgments. Such judgments are of two kinds, which I will call *Pure* and *Mixed*. A pure ethical judgment asserts a universal connexion between two ethical characteristics. An example would be : " It is one's *duty* to try to produce the *best* result that is open to one." A mixed ethical judgment asserts a universal connexion between an ethical and a non-ethical characteristic. An example would

be : " Any experience which is *pleasant* is *intrinsically good*."
I propose to confine my attention for the present to mixed
ethical judgments.

If such judgments be empirical they must be generalisations reached by problematic induction. We observe, *e.g.*,
a number of pleasant experiences and find that they are all
intrinsically good. And we meet with no cases of pleasant
experiences which are not intrinsically good. Then we
generalise in the usual way, and conclude that probably all
experiences which are pleasant are intrinsically good. In
this case of course our judgments, for all we know, may be
false even in the actual world, and certainly might have
been false in other possible worlds.

If, on the other hand, such judgments be *a priori* the
most plausible supposition is that they are reached by
intuitive induction. We observe, *e.g.*, a number of instances
of lying, and notice that they are all wrong. We then
reflect, and see or think we see, a necessary connexion
between the non-ethical characteristic of being an intention-
ally misleading statement and the ethical characteristic of
being wrong. If this be so, the judgment would necessarily
be true, not merely of the actual world, but of all possible
worlds. I will call this view the *Milder Form of Intuitionism
about Ethical Universal Judgments.* But some moralists
seem to have taken a much more extreme view. They
have held that we start with the knowledge of certain
universal ethical propositions before meeting with instances
of them. We do not first meet with this, that, and the other
instance of lying ; notice that each is wrong ; and then
come to see that lying as such is necessarily wrong. We
start with a knowledge of the general proposition that
lying as such is wrong ; and then, meeting with a case of

lying, we argue : " This is an instance of lying, and is therefore wrong." Such a view, again, is logically possible, but all analogy is against it. I will call this type of theory the *Extreme Form of Intuitionism about Ethical Universal Judgments*.

It is important to notice a certain consequence of the distinctions which we have been drawing, because it is not generally recognised. Any ethical theory which professes to state universal connexions between certain ethical and certain non-ethical characteristics can take three different forms, which are often confused with each other. Suppose we take Hedonism as an example. The proposition connecting goodness with pleasantness may be supposed to be (i) analytic, or (ii) synthetic. And, if it be supposed to be synthetic, it may be supposed to be either (*a*) necessary, or (*b*) contingent. Thus three quite different forms of Hedonism are logically possible, viz., (1) *Naturalistic Hedonism*, which would assert that to be " intrinsically good " *means* to contain a balance of pleasure ; and (2) *Non-Naturalistic Hedonism*, dividing into (2, 1) *A Priori Hedonism*, which would assert that anything that was intrinsically good would *necessarily* contain a balance of pleasure, and conversely, and (2, 2) *Empirical Hedonism*, which would assert that everything in the actual world which is intrinsically good *does in fact* contain a balance of pleasure, and conversely. Obviously a precisely similar trichotomy could be made, no matter what was the non-ethical characteristic which is supposed always to accompany and be accompanied by the given ethical characteristic.

Although it is thus logically possible to combine an empirical view of the fundamental universal propositions of ethics with a non-naturalistic and rationalistic view of the fundamental ethical concepts, I do not think that this alternative has the slightest plausibility. It seems to me that, if Naturalism be false, then it is almost certain both that the fundamental concepts and the fundamental judgments of ethics are *a priori*. This of course is Sidgwick's view. No doubt some people would accept this hypothetical proposition and use it as an argument in favour of Naturalism.

This completes what I have to say about the epistemological problems which can be raised in connexion with ethics.

(3) QUESTIONS ABOUT VOLITION AND MOTIVES. A good deal of purely psychological discussion on this subject has always been undertaken by moralists. Theories about motives may first be divided into (3, 1) *Egoistic* and (3, 2) *Non-Egoistic*. Psychological Egoism is the doctrine that nothing can move a man to action or decision except his own present experiences and his expectations of his own future experiences. Egoistic theories may be divided into (3, 11) *Hedonistic* and (3, 12) *Non-Hedonistic*. The former assert that one's only springs of action are one's present pleasures and pains or the expectation of one's future pleasures and pains. This is the theory which we have discussed in connexion with Sidgwick under the name of *Psychological Hedonism*. As we have seen, Butler, Hume, and Sidgwick agree in rejecting Psychological Egoism and therefore Psychological Hedonism. Spinoza was a Psychological Egoist. Kant appears to have thought that all desires other than the desire to act in accordance with the moral law could be reduced to the desire for one's own happiness. I should say that T. H. Green was a Psychological Egoist of the non-hedonistic type ; *i.e.*, he appears to hold that the only prospect that could move me is the

prospect of some future state of myself, but he does not hold that this state must be conceived as pleasant or painful in order to attract or repel me.

There has been a great controversy as to whether " Reason " can ever furnish a motive for action. Hume, *e.g.*, makes a point of denying that it can, whilst Butler and Kant and Sidgwick take the opposite view. The problem is very badly stated. In the first place there are the ambiguities in the word " Reason " which we have pointed out in dealing with the function of Reason in ethical cognition. Then again moralists have been liable to confuse the two quite different questions of Reason as a faculty used in moral cognition and Reason as supplying a motive to moral action. They seem often to have thought that an affirmative or negative answer to one of these questions entailed an affirmative or negative answer respectively to the other. The real question is this : " Does the recognition by Reason that a certain proposed course of action is right or wrong by itself stir a desire for doing or avoiding it ? " Is there in human and other rational beings, among their other conative tendencies, also the tendency to seek what is believed to be right, as such, and to avoid what is believed to be wrong, as such ? Or must the contemplation of the proposed course of action always stir some other conative tendency if it is to excite desire or aversion ? The answer seems to be that there almost certainly is this peculiar conative tendency in human beings. But this fact has to be established simply by introspective analysis. It cannot be inferred from the fact that Reason is needed for the cognitive function of forming the ideas of ethical characteristics and of making universal ethical judgments. There is one actual example of a philosopher who admitted that some of the principles of morality are intuitively certain propositions recognised by Reason, and yet held that we should have no motive for acting in accordance with them when such action would conflict with our happiness in this world unless we believed that God had attached sufficient rewards and punishments to obedience and disobedience to make obedience worth our while. This philosopher was Locke, who thus combined a non-naturalistic and rationalistic view about the nature of ethical character-istics and about ethical cognition with Psychological Hedonism about human volition and action.

At this point there are seven questions that can be raised. (*a*) Is there such a desire as the desire to do what is believed to be right, as such, at all? (*b*) If so, is it ever *sufficient* by itself to determine our actions, or does it always need the *support* of some other motive, such as desire to be thought well of by others? (*c*) Does it ever suffice to determine our actions in *opposition to* all other motives that are acting at the time? (*d*) Is there any sense, and, if so what is it, in which we can say that this desire *always could have* overcome all opposing motives, even though in fact it did not do so? It is here that the metaphysical problem of Determinism and Indeterminism begins to be relevant to ethics. (*e*) Is it essential for the validity of moral judgments that (*d*) should be answered in the affirma-tive? And, if it be relevant to the validity of some, but not all, kinds of moral judgment, which are those to which it is relevant? (*f*) Are *all* actions done with this motive right? And (*g*) are *only* actions done with this motive right? The last four questions play an essential part in Kant's ethics, and in Sidgwick's discussion of the ethical importance of the controversy between Determinism and Indeterminism.

(4) QUESTIONS ABOUT EMOTIONS AND SENTIMENTS. At this point the question of emotion and feeling in ethics enters again. We have already considered what part, if any, they play in ethical cognition. But in most actions emotion is a middle term between cognition and conation. We contemplate some possibility; and if, and only if, our cognition of it is emotionally toned, we feel desire or aversion for this possibility. The question then is this. Is there any specific emotion connected with the cognition of right and wrong in human beings? And, if so, is it essential that this emotion should be felt if the recognition of right or wrong is to stir desire or aversion? Some moralists have held that there is such a specific emotion. Kant, with his *Achtung*, is a case in point. Others have denied it. And, even if it be admitted to exist, it might be held either (*a*) that it is an idle accompaniment of the cognition of right or wrong, and that we should desire the former, as such, and feel aversion to the latter, as such, even though this specific emotion were not felt; or (*b*) that, without the intermediary of the emotion, the cognition of right or wrong would not stir the conative tendency to seek the former and to shun the latter. Kant appears definitely to have taken the former of these alternatives.

(5) HOW FAR CAN ETHICS BE REDUCED TO A SYSTEM? We will suppose henceforth, for the sake of argument, that Naturalism is rejected, and that it is admitted that there are ethical characteristics which cannot be analysed without remainder into non-ethical terms. The following questions can then be raised:

(5, 1) How, if at all, are the various ethical characteristics connected with each other? It is evident that they fall into two very different classes. On the one hand we have notions like " right ", " ought ", " duty ", etc. We may call these *Concepts of Obligation*. On the other hand we have concepts like " goodness ", " merit ", etc. These may be called *Concepts of Value*. Now obviously the first thing to do is to clear up these concepts as far as possible ; to point out any ambiguities in the uses of the words ; and to consider whether there be any analogies in non-ethical matters to these concepts. Thus, *e.g.*, we might point out that " ought " is used in a partly different sense when we say that we ought or ought not to *act* in a certain way in a certain situation, and when we say that certain kinds of emotion ought or ought not to be *felt* in certain situations. The first sense of " ought " implies " could " ; the second does not. I have gone into this question in connexion with Sidgwick. Then again we should have to point out the difference between " good-as-means " and " good-as-end ", and so on. Also we should have to consider the analogy or lack of analogy between, *e.g.*, moral and logical obligation, *i.e.*, the kind of obligation which is expressed when we say : " If you accept so-and-so you ought not to reject so-and-so which is logically entailed by it." And we should have to consider the analogy or lack of analogy between, *e.g.*, moral and æsthetic value.

Now, when this process of clearing up ambiguities and considering analogies has been completed, we can begin to consider the connexion or lack of connexion between the two types of ethical characteristic. The first possibility (5, 11) is that Moral Obligation and Moral Value have no special connexion with each other. This has hardly ever been held. If we reject it we have (5, 12) theories which hold that there is some special connexion between the two.

Now such theories might take the following forms. (5, 121) The concepts of obligation are fundamental and the concepts of value are definable in terms of them. Thus it might be held that the notion of *fittingness* is fundamental, and that " X is intrinsically good " means that it is fitting for every rational being to desire X. Such theories might be called *Deontological*. (5, 122) The concepts of value are fundamental, and the concepts of obligation are definable in terms of them. Such theories may be called *Teleological*. *E.g.*, it might be held that " X is a right action " means that X is likely to produce at least as good consequences as any action open to the agent at the time. Utilitarianism, in some of its forms, would be an example of this. But Sidgwick, though a Utilitarian, definitely rejects the view that " right " *means* " conducive to good ". (5, 123) Neither concept might be definable in terms of the other, but there might be synthetic and necessary connexions between them. Many people who would deny that the proposition " I ought to do X " *means* that X will probably have the best consequences of all actions open to me at the time, would yet hold it to be self-evident that I ought to do the action which will probably have the best consequences of those open to me at the time.

Of course, whichever of these alternatives we might take, there would be a number of possible varieties of that alternative. *E.g.*, granted that the rightness of an action is connected in *some* way with the goodness of its consequences, we should have to ask whether it depends (*a*) on the actual goodness of the actual consequences, or (*b*) on the actual goodness of the probable consequences, or (*c*) on the probable goodness of the actual consequences, or (*d*) on the probable goodness of the probable consequences. And, however we might answer these questions, there would be another fundamental question to be raised, viz., whether the rightness of actions which would produce an equal amount of good could be different according to whether this good would exist only in the agent, or only in others, or in both the agent and others. Thus the alternatives of *Ethical Egoism*, *Ethical Altruism*, and *Ethical Universalism* would have to be considered at this point. And, in addition it would be necessary to consider the suggestion which I threw out in discussing the relations between the various Methods in Sidgwick. The suggestion, it may be remembered, was that, whilst it is fitting for me to desire the occurrence of intrinsically good states, no matter where they may occur, yet of two equally good states, one in me and one in another mind, it may be fitting for me to desire the occurrence of one with greater intensity than that of the other.

(5, 2) Having considered the relations between concepts of value and concepts of obligation, we now can take each in turn and inquire how much systematic unity there is in each department separately. We begin (5, 21) by raising this question about intrinsic goodness. Is there any non-ethical characteristic which is (*a*) common, but not peculiar, or (*b*) peculiar, but not common, or (*c*) common and peculiar to all things that are intrinsically good ? Let us consider the characteristic of pleasantness for example. It might be held (*a*) that anything that is intrinsically good is pleasant, but that some bad or indifferent things are also pleasant. Or (*b*) that anything that is pleasant is intrinsically good, but that some unpleasant or indifferent things are also intrinsically good. Or (*c*) that all that is intrinsically good is pleasant and all that is pleasant is intrinsically good. The last is presumably the minimum which a man must hold in order to count as an Ethical Hedonist. It will be noted that Ethical Hedonism implies that the characteristic of being an experience is common, but not peculiar, to all things that are intrinsically good. For everything that is pleasant is an experience, though not all experiences are pleasant. It is evident that any theory which holds that there is a non-ethical characteristic which is both common and peculiar to all things that are intrinsically good introduces a much greater unity into this department of ethics than a theory which denies this. Theories like Ethical Hedonism may be called *Monistic Theories of Value*. Theories which hold that there is no non-ethical characteristic common and peculiar to things that are intrinsically good may be called *Pluralistic Theories of Value*.

(5, 22) It is clear that very much the same questions can be raised, and that very much the same alternatives are logically possible, about the universal propositions of Ethics which involve the notions of rightness or duty. Suppose that there are a number of such propositions, such as " Lying is always wrong ", " Gratitude is always due to benefactors ", and so on. Then the question can be raised : " Are these all logically independent, so that each has to be intuited by a separate act of Rational Intuition ? Or is it possible to bring them all under one or a small number of fundamental ethical principles, and to regard each of them as simply stating the application of the primary principle or principles to certain classes of situation. Or again is there some self-evident second-order principle which states some feature common and peculiar to all true propositions of the form : " So and so is right (or wrong) ? " The first view seems to have been held by certain extreme supporters of the infallibility of conscience. The second is held by Utilitarians. They would say that the fundamental principle which is self-evident is that we ought to try to maximise human happiness. More specific principles, such as " Lying is wrong ", are derivative from this and the factual proposition that, when all its consequences are taken into account, lying does tend to diminish human happiness. The third view is characteristic of Kant. He thinks he can see that *any* principle of conduct which ought to be accepted and acted upon must have a certain formal characteristic, and that *only* such principles will have this formal characteristic. We may distinguish theories of the second and third kinds from those of the first kind as *Monistic Theories of Obligation*.

I have now given what appears to me to be a fairly adequate sketch of the main problems of Ethics, and of the various kinds of theory which are logically possible about each of them. I may, not unfairly, be asked before ending the book to state my own views on the subject. So far as I have any I will now state them very briefly and dogmatically.

(1) No form of Ethical Naturalism seems to me to be in the least plausible except the psychological form, and I am not acquainted with any definition of ethical concepts in purely psychological terms which seems to me to be satisfactory. I therefore think it very likely, though not absolutely certain, that Ethical Naturalism is false, and that ethical characteristics are *sui generis*. (2) If such terms as *right, ought, good*, etc., be *sui generis*, I think it almost certain that the concepts of them are *a priori* and not empirical. But I should suppose that Reason would not form concepts of these characteristics unless experience provided it with suitable occasions. And I think that these

occasions may very well be the feeling of emotions of approval and disapproval in certain situations. (3) It seems to me that there are necessary propositions connecting ethical with non-ethical characteristics, and that they can be seen to be necessary by inspection. I believe, *e.g.*, that in any possible world painfulness would *pro tanto* make an experience bad, though the experience might have other qualities and relational properties which made it on the whole good. On the other hand, I do not say that any particular kind of experience, such as toothache, which all human beings find painful, would even tend to be bad in all possible worlds. For it appears to be quite possible that there might be minds who found sensations with this sensible quality exquisitely pleasant. I think that there are also self-evident propositions of the form : " Such and such a type of intention or emotion would necessarily be fitting (or unfitting) to such and such a kind of situation." In any possible world it would be fitting to feel gratitude towards one's benefactors and unfitting to feel pleasure at the undeserved suffering of another. But it does not follow that any propositions about *total rightness* are self-evident. For an action may fit some factors and some phases in a developing situation and be unfitting to others ; and its rightness will also depend partly on the intrinsic goodness and badness of its consequences. Here again I do not doubt that Reason needs to meet with concrete instances of fitting or unfitting intentions and emotions before it can rise, by Intuitive Induction, to the insight that *any* such intention or emotion would necessarily be fitting (or unfitting) in *any* such situation. (4) When I introspect and analyse my experiences as carefully as I can I seem to find among my other conative tendencies a standing desire to do what I believe to be right, as such, and to avoid what I believe to be wrong, as such. Sometimes it overcomes other desires and sometimes it is overcome by them. But, even if it were always overcome, I should still recognise its presence, making right-doing a little easier and pleasanter, and wrong-doing a little harder and less pleasant, than they would otherwise be. (5) I do not, however, find it easy to believe that, even when this desire was *in fact* so weak as to be overcome by others, it *could* have been present in such strength as to have overcome the others, although everything else in the universe up to this time had been exactly as it in fact was. For this seems to conflict with certain fundamental metaphysical propositions which I cannot help thinking to be necessary. (6) I am almost certain that "right" and "ought" cannot be defined in terms of "good". But I am not sure that "X is good" could not be defined as meaning that X is such that it would be a fitting object of desire to any mind which had an adequate idea of its non-ethical characteristics. (7) I think that, in the case of a community of interrelated minds, we must distinguish between the total goodness in the community and the total goodness of the community. The latter depends partly on the former, partly on the way in which the former is distributed among the members of the community, and partly on certain relations between the members. What we ought to try to maximise is the total goodness *of* the whole community of minds, and it is conceivable that we may sometimes have to put up with less total goodness *in* the community, than might otherwise exist, in order to accomplish this. (8) I do not think that there is any one non-ethical characteristic which is common and peculiar to everything that is intrinsically good. Nor do I think that all the self-evident principles of ethics can be brought under any one supreme principle. All attempts to do this seem quite plainly to over-simplify the actual situation.

This danger of over-simplification is the note which I should wish most to stress in bringing my book to an end. One lesson at least has been taught us so forcibly by our historical and critical studies in the theory of Ethics that we ought never to forget it in future. This is the extreme complexity of the whole subject of human desire, emotion, and action ; and the paradoxical position of man, half animal and half angel, completely at home in none of the mansions of his Father's house, too refined to be comfortable in the stables and too coarse to be at ease in the drawing-room. So long as we bear this lesson in mind we can contemplate with a smile or a sigh the waxing and waning of each cheap and easy solution which is propounded for our admiration as the last word of " science ". We know beforehand that it will be inadequate ; and that it will try to disguise its inadequacy by ignoring some of the facts, by distorting others, and by that curious inability to distinguish between ingenious fancies and demonstrated truths which seems to be the besetting weakness of the man of purely scientific training when he steps outside his laboratory. And we can amuse ourselves, if our tastes lie in that direction, by noticing which well-worn fallacy or old familiar inadequacy is characteristic of the latest gospel, and whether it is well or ill disguised in its new dress.

It might be retorted that we have gone to the other extreme and made the fact of right action inexplicable. Quite simple people, there is no reason to doubt, often act rightly in quite complicated situations. How could they possibly do so if the problem is so involved as we have made it out to be ? The answer to this objection is to compare right action with playing a ball rightly at tennis or cricket, and to compare the theory of right action to the mechanical and hydrodynamical theory of the action of the racket or bat and the flight of the ball. The good player responds, without explicit analysis or calculation, to a highly complex situation by actions which an observer possessed of superhuman powers of analysis and calculation would deduce as the solution of his equations. We can no more learn to act rightly by appealing to the ethical theory of right action than we can play golf well by appealing to the mathematical theory of the flight of the golf-ball. The interest of ethics is thus almost wholly theoretical, as is the interest of the mathematical theory of golf or of billiards. And yet it may have a certain slight practical application. It may lead us to look out for certain systematic faults which we should not otherwise have suspected ; and, once we are on the look out for them, we may learn to correct them. But in the main the old saying is true : *Non in dialectica complacuit Deo salvum facere populum suum.* Not that this is any objection to dialectic. For salvation is not everything ; and to try to understand in outline what one solves *ambulando* in detail is quite good fun for those people who like that sort of thing.

INDEX OF PROPER NAMES

Honeyman, Charles ; Sidgwick unjustly compared with, 12.

HUME, DAVID ; his clearness of style, 2 ; his life and works, 7-9 ; his theology, 11 ; his relation to Butler, 53 ; his ethical theory, 84-115 ; compared with Kant, 116 ; ignored Categorical Imperatives, 123 ; his theory of ethical judgments, 177, 178 ; his theory of moral action, 179, 274 ; was an Ethical Naturalist, 257 ; was a Public Psychological Naturalist, 260 ; held the Mental Attitude form of Psychological Naturalism, 262 ; rejected Psychological Egoism, 273.

Ibn Ezra ; his influence on Spinoza, 3.

Jellyby, Mrs. ; 31.
Johnson, Dr. S. ; on Hume's death, 9.
Johnson, Mr. W. E. ; on Intuitive Induction, 214, 265.

KANT, IMMANUEL ; on the teaching of ethics, xxiii ; his obscurity, 2 ; his life and works, 9-11 ; close connexion between his ethics and his theology, 14 ; compared with Butler, 53, 83 ; on moral action, 179, 274 ; was a Monistic Deontologist, 207, 281 ; not an Ethical Naturalist, 258 ; was a Two-Sided Ethical Rationalist, 267 ; his relation to Psychological Hedonism, 273 ; on moral freedom, 275 ; on the emotion of *Achtung*, 276.
Karl Ludwig of the Palatinate, Prince ; invites Spinoza to be a Professor at Heidelberg, 4.
Kepler ; 122.
Keynes, Mr. J. M. ; his influence on Mr. Lloyd George, 252.
King's College, Cambridge ; influence of Bloomsbury upon, 252.

Laurence, Saint ; 12.
Locke, John ; his form of Psychological Hedonism, 188 ; his theological ethics, 275.

McTaggart, J. McT. E. ; on " value *in* " and " value *of* ", 134, 249 ; a pupil of Sidgwick, 143 ; held that human minds never begin to exist, 200 ; accepted determinism of mental events, 201 ; his theory of emotion, 229.
Maimonides, Moses ; his influence on Spinoza, 3.
Maurice, F. D. ; 13.
Mill, J. S. ; his ambiguous use of " desirable ", 174 ; claims to deduce Universalistic Ethical Hedonism from Egoistic Psychological Hedonism, 183-184 ; confuses " doing what one pleases " with " doing what one finds pleasant ", 186 ; his explanation of disinterested love of virtue, 189 ; his theory of qualities of pleasure, 231-233 ; was perhaps a Naturalistic Ethical Hedonist, 258.
Milton, John ; 194.
Molière ; 194.
Moore, Prof. G. E. ; a pupil of Sidgwick, 143 ; accuses Kant of Ethical Naturalism, 258.

Nero ; his relations with Agrippina, 111.
Newnham College, Cambridge; Sidgwick's interest in, 13.
Newton, Sir I. ; 143.

Paley, William ; his Theological Naturalism, 259.
Paul, Saint ; less widely appreciated than Mr. Charles Chaplin, 173.
Pietists ; their early influence on Kant, 9.
Plato ; compared with Butler, 57.

Rousseau, J. J. ; his treatment of Hume, 8.
Russell, Hon. B. A. W. ; his adverse opinion of Kant, 10 ; his inordinate respect for Psycho-analysts, 24.

St. Clair, Gen. ; Hume's connexion with, 7.